CW00530196

ONE HANDED COOKS

One Handed Cooks is a baby, toddler and family food website that features a wide range of simple, healthy and clever recipes to help parents make food a source of enjoyment and nourishment for their children. Written with an Accredited Practising Dietitian (APD) as part of the team, it also offers friendly and realistic nutrition information, as well as tips on managing fussy eating behaviours. In 2014, the *One Handed Cooks* magazine was released nationally and it has since become an Australian leader in the area of baby, toddler and family food. Join the friendly and engaging One Handed Cooks community on social media and say 'Hello'.

onehandedcooks.com.au

ALLIE GAUNT

Formerly a professional nanny and advertising copywriter, Allie created the hugely successful One Handed Cooks blog in 2012. When her first child, Harry, started solids she found herself preparing food with a baby on one hip and was keen to connect with other parents and share her positive experiences. Allie is passionate about feeding children nutritious, homemade food and making mealtimes happy, and she has inspired families around the world to make positive, healthy changes for their children.

JESSICA BEATON

Jessica is an Accredited Practising Dietitian with a passion for inspiring families to enjoy happy mealtimes and a healthy love of food. She is a keen cook and combines her personal journey as a mum with 15 years of evidence-based training and experience as a dietitian to simplify the science and educate parents in a friendly and practical way. Since joining One Handed Cooks in 2013, Jessica has undergone training in 'Picky Eaters vs Problem Feeders: The Sequential Oral Sensory (SOS) Approach to Feeding' and 'Making SENSE of Mealtimes'.

SARAH BUCKLE

Sarah is a dedicated primary-school teacher with a passion for baking. She is the photographer and food stylist for One Handed Cooks, capturing the enjoyment of childhood and cherished food moments while showcasing simple, wholesome food to perfection.

The content in this book is written in consultation with an Accredited Practising Dietitian, however it must be used as a general guide and not as the only source of information on children's food and/or nutrition. This book is not intended to dictate what constitutes reasonable, appropriate or best care for your child, nor is it intended to be used as a substitute for the independent judgement of a physician or other qualified healthcare professional. Always discuss any concerns or questions about the health and wellbeing of your child with a qualified healthcare professional.

For Harry & Amelia,
George & Hamish

ONE HANDED COOKS

How to raise a healthy, happy eater – from baby to school age

Allie Gaunt, Jessica Beaton
and Sarah Buckle

VIKING
an imprint of
PENGUIN BOOKS

Introduction 1

TEACH YOUR CHILDREN HOW TO EAT 7

OFFER VARIETY FROM THE START 47

ACCEPT THE MESS 79

LET PHASES COME AND GO 99

STAY IN CONTROL 119

EAT MEALS AT THE TABLE 141

SCHEDULE MEALTIMES AND SNACKS 163

MAKE FOOD ENJOYABLE 183

INCLUDE 'SOMETIMES' FOODS 203

BE A GOOD ROLE MODEL 221

BASICS 235

Acknowledgements 242

Bibliography 242

Index 244

INTRODUCTION

Raising a child who has a healthy, positive relationship with food – who enjoys mealtimes, is adventurous and enjoys a wide variety of foods, and who understands basic nutrition – is every parent's dream, and we're here to help you make it a reality. We believe the key is to instil positive food associations and healthy eating behaviours from your child's very first mouthful by cooking nutritious food using a variety of ingredients, making mealtimes a source of pleasure and limiting highly refined and processed foods.

While nutrition guidelines provide detailed information about *what* and *when* to feed children, they offer little information about *how* to feed them, and we believe this is just as important. Elements such as correct posture, spoon technique, role modelling suitable behaviour and encouraging the exploration of food all play a vital role in a child's journey with food. In addition, the way a parent responds to any challenges and anxieties around mealtimes can affect their child's attitude towards food. Although it's never too late for children to improve their eating behaviours, raising a child to be a good eater from the start will help them reach their full potential much sooner.

WHY HOMEMADE IS BEST

Whether it's for your baby, toddler or whole family, shifting back to a natural way of eating with primarily homemade foods has benefits that far outweigh the convenience of pre-packaged items. While we are fortunate to have an abundance of good-quality commercial foods available, they often contain excess salt, unnecessary filler ingredients, artificial colours and flavours, and other preservatives, so they are best reserved for times of need.

Babies who are predominantly fed commercial purees when they start solids quickly become accustomed to their flavour and smooth texture. These purees often include a high percentage of fruit (even when they have a savoury flavour), a low percentage of meat or other foods containing protein, and they rarely vary in texture. Feeding your baby commercial purees may be more convenient, but it can lead to refusal of homemade purees or finger foods, which naturally vary in texture depending on the ingredients used. It is also harder to offer a wide variety of flavours that will prepare children for family meals when your child will only accept commercial baby food.

NUTRITION BASICS

The simplest way to maintain a nutritionally balanced diet for optimal growth, development and wellbeing is to ensure all the core food groups are being represented in suitable quantities. The six core groups are as follows:

Vegetables

These are an excellent source of important vitamins and minerals, as well as health-promoting fibre, antioxidants and natural plant chemicals called phytochemicals, which give fruit and vegetables their vibrant colours. Enjoying a wide range of plant-based foods, particularly vegetables, is a vital element in a balanced diet.

Introduce your baby to a wide variety of vegetables before their first birthday – pureed and mashed, roasted and steamed, grated and chopped. Let them explore them without any pressure to eat, and keep up the variety as they grow older.

It is recommended toddlers enjoy around two and a half serves of vegetables daily: one serve equals a cup of salad vegetables; half a cup of cooked vegetables, legumes or sweetcorn; half a medium potato or sweet potato; or a tomato. This is achievable by offering a small amount of vegetables at each meal and snack time, and adding grated, chopped or pureed vegetables to dishes like bolognese, pies, pastas, risottos, fritters, fishcakes and patties, nuggets and muffins. By the time your children are at primary school they should be eating five serves of veggies a day.

Grains and cereals

Grains and cereals, including bread, rice, pasta, noodles, oats, couscous and quinoa, provide carbohydrates and fibre, along with many other nutrients that are required for energy production, such as B vitamins and folate. Carbohydrate-rich foods provide the brain and body with the energy required for growth, development, playing, learning and remembering.

Where possible, choose wholegrain or wholemeal breads, cereals and pasta. There is no need to start your child on white varieties unless they have difficulties digesting (or tolerating) larger amounts of fibre. Older children are more likely to accept wholegrain products if they are exposed to them early on.

The recommendation for older babies is to consume two serves of grains and cereals per day, while children aged four to eight generally need four serves a day. One serve equals a slice of bread or bread roll, or half a cup of cooked rice, pasta, noodles, porridge, muesli or quinoa.

Fruit

The ultimate convenience food, fruit is a wonderfully nutritious accompaniment for a main meal and makes a healthy snack option. It is a good source of fibre to help aid digestion, it can help boost iron absorption, and it is packed full of important vitamins, minerals, antioxidants and phytochemicals.

Fresh fruit is best, so limit dried fruits and avoid fruit juice and fruit drinks (see Foods to Avoid, opposite). Be mindful of how much fruit your child consumes, especially if they love it, to ensure they are not having too much and therefore missing out on other food groups.

A baby only needs a small amount of fruit each day, such as 1–2 tablespoons of fruit puree or half a piece of fruit. Toddlers can meet their fruit requirements with one serve of fruit spread over the whole day, such as an apple, banana, pear, two small apricots, a kiwifruit, a cup of diced fruit or 30 g dried fruit (occasionally). Older children and adults require two serves of fruit a day for good health.

Lean meat, poultry, fish, eggs, tofu, legumes, nuts and seeds

These foods are good sources of protein, iron and zinc, which are essential for young children. They also provide vitamin B12, iodine, selenium, healthy fats and many other vitamins and minerals needed for children's growth, development and the immune system.

Red meat should be introduced to your baby from around 6 months of age, as it is particularly rich in iron and zinc. Offering a small amount of high-protein foods to your baby every day, including red meat around three times a week, will help them maintain adequate stores of these essential nutrients.

Toddlers only need one serve of these foods every day, so even if they aren't eating much meat they are probably still meeting their dietary requirements. One serve is the equivalent of 65 g cooked meat (90–100 g raw), 80 g cooked poultry (100 g raw), 100 g cooked fish (115 g raw), 2 eggs, a cup of cooked legumes, 130 g tofu or 30 g nuts, seeds or nut/seed butters. Kids aged four to eight need around one and a half serves a day, while older children need two and a half serves per day.

Vegetarian babies: Dairy foods, eggs, tofu, legumes, nuts and seeds are all sources of high-quality protein that would otherwise be provided by meat, chicken or fish. Be sure to offer adequate amounts of vegetarian iron-rich foods as well, such as iron-fortified cereals, eggs, legumes and green leafy vegetables. Including a food that is high in vitamin C will help maximise the absorption of iron from plant-based foods.

Dairy and dairy alternatives

Milk, cheese and yoghurt are an important source of calcium, which is needed for the development of strong bones, healthy teeth and muscle function. They are also a source of other important nutrients, including protein, zinc, riboflavin, vitamin A and vitamin B12.

Breastmilk or formula should be your baby's main drink until they are 12 months old, but cheese, unsweetened yoghurt and a little cow's milk with cereal or in cooking can be introduced from around 6 months. Full-fat dairy products are recommended until 2 years of age, as children need the energy from the fat they provide.

Children under 4 years of age require one and a half serves of dairy foods per day and children aged four to eight require two serves per day. One serve equals 1 cup (250 ml) cow's milk or calcium-fortified dairy alternative, 2 slices (40 g) cheese or ¾ cup (200 g yoghurt). Consuming more than 600 ml of milk per day can reduce a child's appetite for mealtimes, contributing to fussy eating behaviours and iron deficiency, so be mindful of how much milk your toddler is drinking, particularly if they also enjoy cheese and yoghurt.

Fats and oils

Fats are important in our daily diet, especially for babies and toddlers, as they provide energy and ensure we can absorb fat-soluble nutrients, such as vitamins A, D, E and K. They also provide us with essential omega-3 fatty acids that are required for optimal brain development and eye health, as well as hormone function, heart health and general wellbeing.

Offer your child mostly unrefined monounsaturated and polyunsaturated fats from plant sources, such as extra virgin olive oil, avocados and nut and seed oils. Limit saturated fats (except from sources like lean meat and dairy foods) and avoid trans fats, which are found in deep-fried foods and commercial baked goods. On food labels, trans fats are listed as hydrogenated or partially hydrogenated vegetable oils.

WHEN TO SEEK HELP

Children will rarely eat the same amount of food each day, as their growth needs and activity levels vary. Some children have seemingly insatiable appetites, while others eat small amounts yet still achieve typical growth and development. However, most should be enjoying a variety of foods from all the food groups and, on average, their portion sizes should meet their daily recommended intake. If your child is refusing food, see pages 100–101 for information on possible causes and how to deal with them.

If you have any concerns regarding the growth, development, health and wellbeing of your child or the nutritional adequacy of their diet, seek the advice of a relevant healthcare professional. Doctors, child and family health nurses, paediatricians, Accredited Practising Dietitians (APDs), speech pathologists, occupational therapists, physiotherapists and child psychologists are all qualified to assist in improving the quality of children's diets and/or eating behaviours. In some cases, treatment may involve more than one of these professionals. If your family doctor or child and health nurse believe that areas of your child's health need addressing, they will alert you to their concerns.

FOODS TO AVOID

The following foods should not be offered to babies for various health and nutrition reasons:

Honey: avoid until 12 months of age due to the risk of infant botulism

Cow's and goat's milk: should not be your child's main drink before 12 months of age, as they have a high renal solute load, which places unwanted strain on the kidneys. They are also poor sources of iron and can contribute to iron-deficiency anaemia

Soy, rice milk, oat, almond milk: should not be your child's main drink before 2 years of age (unless recommended by a health professional) as they are nutritionally incomplete

Skim and low-fat dairy: avoid until 2 years of age, as the energy and fat provided by full-fat dairy is an important source of energy for growing babies and toddlers

Fruit juice and sweetened drinks: avoid these until 12 months of age or as long as possible, because they reduce the appetite for whole fruits, more nutritious foods and milk, and can cause tooth decay

Whole nuts, seeds, raw carrot, celery sticks and chunks of apple: avoid until 3 years of age due to the risk of choking

Raw or undercooked eggs: avoid until 2 years of age due to the risk of salmonella poisoning

Salt and high salt foods: avoid until 12 months of age or as long as possible, because too much salt/sodium can place strain on your baby's developing kidneys and create a preference for salty foods

Tea, coffee and caffeinated drinks: avoid for as long as possible, as too much caffeine can overstimulate the nervous system and it reduces the absorption of calcium

Artificial sweeteners: avoid for as long as possible due to the unknown safety and side effects of these products.

FOOD ALLERGIES AND INTOLERANCES

Around one in 20 children and one in 100 adults suffer from food allergies. The risk of developing this type of allergy is greatest during a child's first year of life because of their immature digestive system. Cow's milk, eggs, shellfish, fish, peanuts, tree nuts, sesame, soybeans and wheat are the most common food allergies for young children. Fortunately, they often disappear by the time the child reaches school age, however allergies to peanuts, tree nuts, seeds and seafood tend to be lifelong.

A food allergy is the result of an overreaction by the immune system to a food after it is consumed, inhaled or, in severe cases, touched. Symptoms are immediate and include hives, itchiness, redness, eczema, bowel problems, tummy pain, vomiting or diarrhoea, swelling of the tongue and coughing or wheezing. In the most severe cases, an allergic reaction can result in anaphylaxis, a life-threatening reaction that usually occurs 20 minutes to 2 hours after exposure to the allergen. Signs and symptoms of an anaphylactic reaction may include swelling of the face, throat and/or tongue; difficulty breathing; skin redness and hives; abdominal discomfort; vomiting; and drowsiness. Immediate treatment and medical attention is essential.

Food intolerances are caused by a chemical reaction in the body. There are many different types and groups of foods that commonly cause food intolerances. Sometimes the culprits are natural chemicals, such as salicylates, amines, glutamate and monosodium glutamate (MSG), that are found in a wide range of foods including fruits, vegetables, herbs, nuts, spices, tea and coffee. Artificial additives, including preservatives such as sulphites in dried fruit and colours like tartrazine, may also be a trigger. Yeast, wheat, gluten and milk can cause problems, too. Symptoms of food intolerances are wide-ranging, often general in nature and vary from person to person. Common reactions include headaches or migraines, skin rashes, bloating and diarrhoea, sweating, mouth ulcers, sinus trouble, allergy-like reactions, general irritability and restlessness.

If you suspect your child has a food allergy or intolerance, do not try to treat it yourself. Professional diagnosis and treatment from a medical practitioner or Accredited Practising Dietitian (APD) specialising in food allergy and intolerance is essential. They will advise you on suitable alternatives and dietary advice to ensure your child's nutritional needs are met.

INTRODUCING ALLERGENIC FOODS

The current advice on starting solids is not to delay the introduction of highly allergenic foods, even if there is a family history of food allergy. Other than introducing iron-rich foods early on, there are also no recommendations on the order in which foods should be introduced or the number of new foods that can be introduced at a time.

Introducing highly allergenic foods at around 6 months, rather than 12 months as was advised previously, may actually reduce the likelihood of your baby developing a food allergy. Continuing to breastfeed while introducing solids may also protect against the development of food allergies.

If you are worried about introducing a common allergen, delay the introduction of any other new food for two to three days, both before and after, to make it easy to identify any reactions. Keep an eye out for reactions the first few times your baby eats a possible allergen, as they may not occur until the second or third time the food is consumed. If you are particularly concerned, seek the advice of an appropriate health professional.

DAIRY SUBSTITUTES

Calcium-fortified dairy-free milks usually provide less fat and protein than cow's milk so are not suitable alternatives for children aged under two unless recommended by a health professional. (Babies under 12 months require breastmilk or formula.) Dark-green leafy vegetables, tinned sardines, tinned salmon (including the bones), almonds, sesame seeds and dried fruits are also sources of calcium.

Avocado: use instead of butter, in sandwiches and when baking loaves and savoury muffins.

Coconut oil: use as a light frying oil or to replace butter when baking. Choose extra virgin or virgin coconut oil.

Dairy-free milks: soy, rice, oat and almond milk can all be used to replace cow's milk in cooking, but they are not suitable as the main drink for children under two.

Extra virgin olive oil: use as a light frying oil, to replace butter when baking or to drizzle over bread or toast.

Macadamia oil: use as a light frying oil, to replace butter when baking or in salad dressings.

Nut creams: almonds and cashews can be processed into a smooth cream that can be used to thicken soups or to spread over the top of baked goods.
Pure coconut milk/cream: use in Asian recipes and cakes, custards and desserts.
Silken tofu: blend and sweeten for a 'creamy' topping or use as an alternative to ricotta.

EGG SUBSTITUTES

Eggs are high in protein and vitamin B12, so offer a variety of protein-rich foods instead, such as meat, poultry, fish, dairy, nuts and seeds (many of these also provide vitamin B12). Eggs provide vitamins A and D, too, which are also found in cheese and oily fish, such as salmon, tuna, sardines and herrings. Dairy foods supply vitamin A as well. Commercial 'egg replacers' are available for cooking, or use the following substitutes (each equals 1 egg).
Agar agar: combine 1 tablespoon agar agar with 1 tablespoon water. Use in sweet dishes and baked goods.
Apple sauce (unsweetened) or puree: use ¼ cup (75 g) apple sauce or puree. Use in sweet dishes and baked goods.
'Chia egg': combine 1 tablespoon chia seeds with ⅓ cup (80 ml) water. Set aside for 5 minutes to soak, then stir and continue to soak for a further 5 minutes or until the mixture has a gel-like consistency.
'Linseed egg': combine 1 tablespoon ground linseed (flaxseed) with ⅓ cup (60 ml) water. Set aside for 1 minute to soak, then stir until thick and creamy.
Nut butter: use 3 tablespoons pure smooth peanut or almond butter. Use in sweet dishes and baked goods.
Banana: mash ½ ripe banana. Use in sweet dishes and baked goods.

NUT SUBSTITUTES

For vegetarian children who may otherwise get protein from nuts, look to eggs, dairy foods, tofu and legumes including chickpeas, red kidney beans, lentils and cannellini beans instead. When buying food, read labels carefully as traces of nuts can be present in many foods. Most health food shops have pure ingredients that have not been manufactured with contamination. Buying in bulk online is cost-effective when you find a product you love.
Seeds: can be used in many recipes as a substitute for nuts. Pepitas (pumpkin seed kernels) and sunflower seeds work particularly well and can be ground into a meal or crushed.
Coconut: shredded or desiccated coconut can be a good substitute for nuts when cooking sweet snacks.
Unblended sesame oil: use instead of nut oils to flavour savoury and Asian meals.

GLUTEN AND WHEAT SUBSTITUTES

Offer gluten-free, fibre-rich carbohydrate sources, such as vegetables, quinoa, brown rice, millet, sorghum, legumes, lentils, nuts and seeds to ensure your child consumes enough fibre and to contribute to their folate and iron intake. (Red meat, poultry, fish and eggs are also good sources of iron.) If the allergy is to wheat, not gluten, products containing rye and barley can be eaten.
Gluten-free flour: replace plain flour with arrowroot/tapioca, rice flour, soya flour, quinoa flour, buckwheat flour or potato starch. Commercial gluten-free flour mixes are available in supermarkets and are suitable for baking.
Grains: use quinoa, quinoa flakes, millet, rice, corn/polenta or buckwheat. Quinoa flakes can used to replace oats in cooking. (Oats are not considered to be gluten- or wheat-free in Australia.)
Nut meal: use to replace plain flour in some biscuits or cakes (the texture may be heavier and more moist).
Thickeners: use cornflour (not wheaten), arrowroot or rice flour to thicken sauces or coat meat/fish before cooking.

FISH AND SEAFOOD SUBSTITUTES

Compensate for the omission of seafood with lean (red) meats, which are high in protein and zinc, and also provide vitamin B12 and omega-3 fatty acids. Omega-3 enriched products, such as eggs, milk, yoghurt, bread and orange juice, are also sources of omega-3 fatty acids.

KEY TO RECIPE SYMBOLS

We use the following symbols for our recipes:

(F) Freezable	(DF) Dairy-free
(GF) Gluten-free	(EF) Egg-free
(WF) Wheat-free	(V) Vegetarian

Note that the ingredient substitutions provided for allergies and intolerances in recipes are suggestions only.

CHAPTER 1

TEACH YOUR CHILDREN HOW TO EAT

From the signs that indicate your baby is ready to start solids, to good eating posture and the ideal spoon technique, this chapter will get you off to the best possible start on your child's journey with food. Make their diet varied and interesting from the beginning with our simple and tasty mixed purees, textured meals and early finger foods.

The first time you give your baby solid food can be rather daunting, for both of you. You want them to enjoy it and thrive; they want to tip it over their head and squish it in their fingers! We're here to help you make it a positive experience and create happy memories, as this will determine their relationship with food for years to come. It typically takes a child two to three years to learn how to eat properly, so don't expect overnight results. There's a standard progression from smooth purees to textured and finger foods, which gives them time to develop the oral motor skills they need to swallow, bite and chew.

STARTING SOLIDS

When it comes to food, the biggest concern for many parents is what to offer their baby and when. Traditionally, babies were started on iron-fortified infant rice cereals, slowly progressing to pureed fruits and vegetables, then meats and eventually more allergenic foods. Research now indicates there is no reason to delay any particular foods (findings even suggest that doing so may increase the risk of allergy and intolerance), so the process is much more relaxed. The 2012 Infant Feeding Guidelines by the National Health and Medical Research Council (NHMRC) recommend commencing solids at around 6 months. The Australasian Society of Clinical Immunology & Allergy (ASCIA) Infant Feeding Advice suggests 'from 4 to 6 months of age, when your child is ready, consider introducing a new food every 2 to 3 days according to what your family usually eats. There are no allergenic foods that need to be avoided.' By the age of 12 months your child should be enjoying a wide variety of foods.

IS MY BABY READY?

Introducing solids too early can cause tummy discomfort, including constipation; the development of allergies and intolerances; reduced intake of breastmilk or formula, which can affect your milk supply or result in mastitis; negative associations with eating; and less acceptance of a variety of foods, flavours and textures. You know your baby best, so watch for the following signs that they're ready.

Here's what to look for:

- The tongue-thrust reflex has gone – they will push or 'thrust' their tongue out when you touch a spoon to it
- They are interested in what you are eating and try to reach out for it
- They start to put objects in their mouth
- They can sit upright, with support if necessary
- Their weight may begin to plateau and they are less satisfied with milk alone.

GOOD EATING POSTURE

Correct positioning and posture are essential elements for a young child's ability to eat and their comfort at mealtimes. They're particularly important from a safety perspective, as they encourage good body and head alignment, which directs food from the mouth into the oesophagus and away from the airway, preventing choking and aspiration of food and fluid into the airways. The hips, knees and feet should be positioned at 90 degrees with weight evenly distributed, and the chair seat and your child's back should be at 90 degrees to support and maintain an upright position. A foot rest is essential and, if necessary, use towels, cushions and wedges to support good posture and positioning.

THE IDEAL SPOON TECHNIQUE

Children love choice and control, so follow these steps to ensure you're creating a positive association with the spoon right from the start.

1. Put your baby in their highchair, appropriately positioned, when they are calm and alert. Sit opposite them with their food
2. Scoop up a small amount of food, being careful not to overload the spoon, and present it just in front of their lips. Your baby will lean in and eat, or turn away or push the spoon away with their hands
3. If your baby refuses to eat, don't force them, as this only creates stress and anxiety, and may result in spoon refusal (see page 100)
4. Remember that the spoon is for feeding and not cleaning. Scraping food from around their mouth is uncomfortable for most babies and they may start to feel anxious at the sight of the spoon
5. At the end of the meal and when they are out of the highchair, gently wipe their face, hands, eyes and hair with a clean, damp cloth.

Your baby may take the spoon out of your hand and try to self-feed or may want their own spoon to hold while you feed them. Follow their cues and be adaptable.

HOW MUCH TO FEED THEM?

Babies differ in their nutrient requirements and energy needs, and can eat a different amount each day depending on their growth and stage of development. The only real way to know if they're hungry or satisfied is by tuning in and learning to recognise their individual cues.

Common signs of hunger include:

- They show excitement when food is presented
- They continue to open their mouth and lean towards the food or bring finger foods to their mouth.

Common signs of fullness include:

- They turn their head away and/or no longer open their mouth for food
- They have lost interest in the food and are easily distracted
- They reject food that is familiar to them and that you know they like
- They become irritable in their highchair.

OFFER A VARIETY OF FOODS

Babies need a wide range and large quantity of nutrients for optimal growth and development, so give them a varied diet full of nutrient-rich foods.

How to introduce variety:

- Offer single purees as well as mixed. Freeze a range of different purees, then mix and match them each day. This exposes your baby to individual flavours that are savoury and sweet
- As your baby progresses, mix in fresh foods such as yoghurt, ricotta, grated cheese, herbs, nut or seed pastes, or cooked rice, couscous, quinoa or small pasta shapes. This helps ensure a wide variety of taste, nutrients and texture
- Use different cooking and serving methods, such as grilling, baking, roasting, blending, fork mashing, slicing into different shapes (sticks, chunks and slices) and offer age-appropriate raw foods
- Avoid offering the same foods prepared the same way on consecutive days, no matter how much your child likes them, to avoid getting stuck in a rut.

GAGGING VERSUS CHOKING

Understanding the difference between gagging and choking is important to help alleviate any fear you may be feeling about it and prevent unnecessary panic at mealtimes. This will help your child maintain a positive and happy association with eating.

Gagging is normal behaviour for babies learning to eat. It is an important safety reflex that happens when food travels too far back into their mouth. The gag reflex closes off the throat and pushes the tongue to the front of the mouth to prevent choking. When your baby gags, they will still be able to breathe and will likely make a few gagging noises, cough, cry or splutter. Don't push your fingers in their mouth to try to remove the food, as this may cause them to choke. Stay calm and praise them with a smile or little clap once they are settled, then offer a sip of water. If your baby frequently gags and vomits on food and it is beginning to affect how they eat, see your doctor.

Choking is more serious and occurs when the airway is blocked by food (or an object), causing the baby or child to stop breathing. They may make a whistling or 'crowing' noise, or no noise at all because their airway is blocked, and they will look panicked and distressed. Areas on their face, such as their lips or underneath their eyes, may turn blue. It's important to attend an infant First Aid course to learn how to respond if your baby begins to choke.

HARD MUNCHABLES

These are large, thick sticks of food that your baby can hold and put in their mouth to gum, munch and explore. They are not for consumption, so your baby shouldn't be able to bite a piece off. Hard munchables are suitable for babies aged 7 to 9 months who have started solids, have good body and head control, and love putting things in their mouths. Their aim is to help teach babies how to move their tongue from side to side, strengthen their jaw muscles to support chewing motions and desensitise the gag reflex, pushing it towards the back of the mouth. Hard munchables include sticks, roughly the size of a thick permanent marker, of raw carrot, celery, capsicum (pepper), hard dried fruit (mango or whole banana), frozen melon strips or frozen pancake strips. Always supervise your child when they are eating, especially when offering hard munchables due to the potential choking risk if they manage to bite off some of the food.

OUR TOP TIPS FOR STARTING SOLIDS

- Gradually progress from purees to mashed foods with mixed textures
- Introduce finger foods from around 6 to 7 months of age, including hard munchables (see page 9)
- Offer easy-to-eat textures your child enjoys alongside textures they might find more challenging
- Let your baby touch, squish and squash new foods
- Praise positive interactions with more difficult textures
- Talk to your baby, toddler or child about the texture of a food and compare it to one they may eat and enjoy
- Eat harder-to-chew textures with your child, exaggerating tongue or chewing motions to demonstrate how it's done
- Observe your baby at mealtimes and respond appropriately to their cues
- Only offer food when your baby is calm and alert
- Deconstruct mixed-texture meals, such as pastas, casseroles, stir-fries and curries, onto a tasting plate (see pages 120–121) and include a small mixed portion on their plate or in a separate bowl.

FEEDING MILESTONES

Learning how to safely and efficiently chew and swallow food takes practice. Give your baby a wide variety of textures appropriate to their stage of development to ensure they master the oral motor skills that are required.

AGE	ORAL MOTOR DEVELOPMENT	APPROPRIATE FOODS
Up to 4 months	• Suck, suckle and swallow	Breastmilk/formula
By 5–6 months	• Begin to eat small amounts of thin, pureed foods from a spoon • Begin to chew using up-and-down 'munching' motions • Gag reflex is disappearing, but some gagging and coughing is normal	Purees
By 7–8 months	• Eat thicker purees and mashed or textured meals from a spoon • Use their hands to pick up finger foods • Begin to bite and chew using an up-and-down motion • Start to use side-to-side tongue movement to move food around in their mouth • Begin to sip from a cup, but usually cough or spit the liquid out	Mashed and chopped foods, finger foods
By 9–12 months	• Move their jaw and tongue to move food around in their mouth • Can hold a spoon, but may not be able to use it • Become more successful with drinking from a cup, but still spill liquid from their mouth	Mashed and chopped foods, finger foods
By 12–18 months	• Stronger jaw and side-to-side tongue movements to move food towards back molars • Emerging rotary chewing motion • Able to self-feed using a spoon, however it's messy • Able to drink from a cup without losing any liquid	Minced, mashed or chopped family foods including soft, tender pieces of meat
By 2–3 years	• Swallow food and liquids without spilling any from their mouth • Established rotary chewing motion • Able to use a spoon and fork	Family foods

F GF WF DF EF

SIMPLE BEEF PUREE

If you're not sure how to offer red meat as a puree, this recipe is a great place to start. You can mix up the vegetables according to whatever you have on hand. We recommend buying MSA (Meat Standards Australia) graded beef from a quality butcher.

MAKES 2 CUPS (500 G)
PREP TIME 10 minutes
COOKING TIME 40 minutes

3 teaspoons olive oil
200 g chuck steak, cut into 2 cm pieces
½ cup (100 g) diced pumpkin (squash)
1 carrot, diced
2 baby new potatoes, peeled and diced
½–1 clove garlic, crushed
1 small tomato, chopped (optional)

1. Heat 2 teaspoons of the oil in a small heavy-based saucepan over medium–high heat. Add the steak and cook, stirring often, until well browned all over. Transfer to a bowl and set aside.
2. Heat the remaining oil in the saucepan, then add the pumpkin, carrot, potato and garlic and cook, stirring, for 5 minutes.
3. Return the steak to the pan with the tomato and 1½ cups (375 ml) water. Bring to the boil, then reduce the heat to low, cover and simmer for 30 minutes or until the meat is cooked and vegetables are tender.
4. Use a slotted spoon to transfer the meat and vegetables to a blender or food processor. Process, adding a little of the cooking liquid at a time, until you reach your desired consistency.

NUTRITION NOTE Iron-rich foods, such as red meat, are recommended as a first food from around 6 months, when your baby shows signs of being ready for solids.

STORAGE Keep in an airtight container in the fridge for up to 2 days. Alternatively, freeze individual portions in airtight containers for up to 2 months.

F GF WF EF

CHICKEN AND SWEETCORN PUREE

This chicken puree contains pumpkin and corn to cater to your baby's innate preference for sweet foods, and is super-quick and easy to make.

MAKES 1½ CUPS (350 G)
PREP TIME 5 minutes
COOKING TIME 10 minutes

150 g chicken breast or thigh fillets, fat trimmed and cut into 2 cm pieces
150 g pumpkin (squash), finely diced
1 cob of corn, husk and silk removed
1 tablespoon fresh ricotta, to serve

1. Place the chicken and pumpkin in a steamer basket over a saucepan of boiling water and cook, covered, for 5 minutes. Cut the corn kernels from the cob and add to the basket. Cook, covered, for a further 5 minutes or until the chicken is cooked through and the pumpkin is tender.
2. Transfer the chicken and vegetables to a food processor or blender, and process, adding some water a little a time (up to ½ cup/125 ml) until you reach your desired consistency. Stir through the ricotta.

NUTRITION NOTE Making your own purees gives your baby the opportunity to experience the different textures of a range of foods. The smooth silkiness of pumpkin or pear can be compared to the coarser, lumpier texture of corn, broccoli or peas, and so on.

STORAGE Keep in an airtight container in the fridge for up to 2 days or freeze individual portions (without ricotta) in airtight containers for up to 2 months.

ALLERGIES/INTOLERANCES ***Dairy:*** replace the ricotta with mashed avocado.

KIWI-GO YOGHURT

Most babies and toddlers love the smooth consistency of yoghurt. Even when flavoured, its colour is rarely bright enough to upset hypersensitive children. Choose plain yoghurt (Greek-style, pot-set or regular) to avoid introducing any artificial colours, flavours and added refined sugars.

MAKES 1 CUP (250 G)
PREP TIME 5 minutes
COOKING TIME Nil

- 2 kiwifruit, peeled and chopped
- 2 mangoes, peeled, seeded and chopped
- 200 g plain Greek-style yoghurt

1. Place the kiwifruit and mango in a blender or food processor and blend until smooth.
2. Stir 2 tablespoons of the fruit puree through the yoghurt.

NUTRITION NOTE Yoghurt is high in calcium and protein, and is a source of other valuable nutrients and non-nutrients, including probiotics. Probiotics help to maintain a healthy, functioning digestive system and research suggests they are also valuable in strengthening the immune system.

STORAGE Keep the leftover fruit puree in the fridge for up to 3 days or freeze individual portions in airtight containers for up to 3 months. Any leftover Kiwi-go yoghurt can be kept in an airtight container in the fridge for up to 3 days.

ALLERGIES/INTOLERANCES ***Dairy:*** serve the fruit puree as is or mix with a small amount of breastmilk or your baby's usual milk instead of the yoghurt.

F GF WF DF EF V

GREEN VEG AND APPLE PUREE

Green vegetables offer many health-promoting nutrients and natural plant chemicals that are necessary for our babies' growth and wellbeing, so it's really important to form positive associations with all things green when starting solids.

MAKES 2 CUPS (520 G)
PREP TIME 5 minutes
COOKING TIME 15 minutes

- 2 apples, peeled, cored and chopped
- 1 cup (85 g) chopped broccoli florets
- 1 small zucchini (courgette), chopped
- ¼ cup (30 g) frozen peas

1. Place the apple in a large steamer basket over a saucepan of boiling water and cook, covered, for 5 minutes.
2. Add the broccoli and zucchini to the basket and cook for a further 5–7 minutes or until tender. Add the peas and steam for a further 2 minutes or until the peas are cooked through.
3. Transfer the apple and vegetables to a blender or food processor and process, adding some water a little at a time (up to ¾ cup/180 ml), until you reach your desired consistency.

NUTRITION NOTE Serve some steamed broccoli florets or zucchini as finger food alongside to further encourage learning about food, texture and eating.

STORAGE Keep in an airtight container in the fridge for up to 3 days. Alternatively, freeze individual portions in airtight containers for up to 3 months.

FISH, CAULIFLOWER
AND LEEK PUREE
KIWI-GO
YOGHURT
GREEN VEG AND
APPLE PUREE
CARROT, PARSNIP
AND CASHEW PUREE

CARROT, PARSNIP AND CASHEW PUREE

Carrot and parsnip puree was a surprising favourite for all our babies when they started solids. It is extremely versatile and can be mixed with meats, other vegetables, fruits, cheese and even cashews, as we have done here. The cashews are processed to a smooth consistency that adds to the creaminess of this yummy puree.

MAKES 2 CUPS (500 G)
PREP TIME 5 minutes
COOKING TIME 12 minutes

2 carrots, diced
2 parsnips, diced
⅓ cup (50 g) raw unsalted cashews

1. Place the carrot and parsnip in a steamer basket over a saucepan of boiling water and cook, covered, for 10–12 minutes or until tender.
2. Transfer the vegetables to a food processor or blender, add the cashews and process well, adding some water a little at a time (up to ½ cup/125 ml), until you reach your desired consistency and there are no chunks of cashew.

NUTRITION NOTE Research suggests that delaying the introduction of allergenic foods, including tree nuts, when starting solids may actually increase the risk of food allergy and intolerance (see page 4).

TIP Older children and adults might enjoy this as a mash to accompany roast meats.

STORAGE Keep in an airtight container in the fridge for up to 3 days. Alternatively, freeze individual portions in airtight containers for up to 3 months.

ALLERGIES/INTOLERANCES If you aren't ready to try nuts with your baby, simply omit them or try mixing a tablespoon of fresh ricotta or mashed avocado through the puree instead.

FISH, CAULIFLOWER AND LEEK PUREE

Once you have progressed from first tastes, fish is a nutritious addition to your baby's diet. Pairing it with a few simple ingredients that they might already know will assist a smooth transition.

MAKES 1½ CUPS (375 G)
PREP TIME 5 minutes
COOKING TIME 12 minutes

150 g boneless firm white fish fillet (such as flathead, blue-eye trevalla, bream, snapper)
½ small head cauliflower, leaves and stem removed, florets chopped
2.5 cm-length leek, white part only, finely chopped
¼ cup (60 ml) water or milk
1 tablespoon grated cheddar cheese, to serve (optional)

1. Place the fish in a steamer basket over a saucepan of boiling water and cook, covered, for 3–4 minutes, until just cooked through and the flesh flakes easily. Transfer to a bowl and set aside.
2. Place the cauliflower in the steamer basket, scatter over the leek and cook, covered, for 6–8 minutes or until tender. Add to the bowl with the fish.
3. Mash or puree, adding a little of the water or milk at a time, until you reach your desired consistency. Stir through the grated cheese, if using.

NUTRITION NOTE Babies and young children are particularly vulnerable to the effects of mercury, so be sure to choose low-mercury fish for their meals.

STORAGE Keep in an airtight container in the fridge for up to 2 days. Alternatively, freeze individual portions in airtight containers for up to 2 months.

ALLERGIES/INTOLERANCES ***Dairy:*** choose water instead of milk and omit the optional cheese.

PORK PUREE

When your baby is ready for more texture, stir cooked brown rice, quinoa or couscous through this puree.

MAKES 2 CUPS (500 G)
PREP TIME 10 minutes
COOKING TIME 20 minutes

1 tablespoon olive oil
½ small onion, chopped
200 g pork fillet, fat trimmed and cut into cubes
1 small clove garlic, crushed
1 cob of corn, husk and silk removed
½ cup (125 ml) salt-reduced vegetable stock or homemade vegetable stock (see page 240)
½ carrot, chopped
½ zucchini (courgette), chopped
½ small sweet potato, peeled and chopped
¼ cup (30 g) frozen peas
1 small apple, peeled, cored and diced

1. Heat the oil in a heavy-based saucepan over medium heat. Sauté the onion for 3 minutes, then add the pork and garlic and cook, stirring, for 3 minutes.
2. Cut the corn kernels from the cob and add to the pan along with the remaining ingredients. Bring to the boil, then reduce the heat, cover and simmer for 10–15 minutes or until the pork is cooked through and the carrot is tender. Add a little water (up to ¼ cup/60 ml) if the mixture begins to dry out. Use a stick blender or food processor to process the mixture until you reach your desired consistency.

NUTRITION NOTE Lean pork is a healthy choice for babies and toddlers. It's a good source of protein, B vitamins, zinc and omega-3 fatty acids.

STORAGE Keep in an airtight container in the fridge for up to 3 days. Alternatively, freeze individual portions in airtight containers for up to 2 months.

ALLERGIES/INTOLERANCES ***Gluten:*** use gluten-free vegetable stock.

F GF WF DF EF V

RED LENTIL AND VEGGIE PUREE

Lentils are a pantry staple in our kitchens. They are cheap, versatile, quick to cook and an easy way to add texture and protein to baby purees.

MAKES 2 CUPS (500 G)
PREP TIME 10 minutes
COOKING TIME 15 minutes

150 g sweet potato, peeled and cut into 1 cm pieces
1 carrot, chopped
1 apple, peeled, cored and diced
¼ cup (50 g) split red lentils

1. Place the sweet potato, carrot, apple, lentils and 1 cup (250 ml) water in a small heavy-based saucepan over high heat. Bring to the boil, then reduce the heat and simmer, covered, for 15 minutes or until the lentils, vegetables and apple are tender.
2. Use a stick mixer, blender or food processor to process the mixture, adding a little more water if required, until you reach your desired consistency.

NUTRITION NOTE Split red lentils contain slightly less fibre than other lentils and legumes, so they're not as likely to cause gas or discomfort in susceptible children.

STORAGE Keep in an airtight container in the fridge for up to 3 days. Alternatively, freeze individual portions in airtight containers for up to 3 months.

TASTE THE TROPICS PUREE

This deliciously sweet and smooth fruit puree is packed full of vitamin C. It also makes a great natural sweetener when stirred through plain Greek-style yoghurt, rice cereal or porridge.

MAKES 2 CUPS (500 G)
PREP TIME 5 minutes
COOKING TIME 10 minutes

2 ripe pears, peeled, cored and chopped
¼ large papaya, peeled, seeded and diced
1 ripe small mango, peeled, seeded and sliced
1 passionfruit (optional), halved

1. Place ¾ cup (180 ml) water in a small heavy-based saucepan and bring to the boil over high heat. Add the pear and papaya, reduce the heat and simmer, covered, for 10 minutes, stirring occasionally, until the fruit is soft. Remove from the heat and drain in a fine-meshed sieve.
2. Place the pear, papaya and mango in a food processor or blender. Process until silky smooth or until the mixture reaches your desired consistency.
3. Stir through the passionfruit pulp, if using, for flavour and texture.

NUTRITION NOTE If your baby is experiencing constipation, the mango and pear in this puree may help soften their stools and relieve discomfort.

TIP Save the mango seed and place in an airtight container in the fridge for up to 2 days to use as a cool and tasty teether for your baby to enjoy.

STORAGE Keep in an airtight container in the fridge for up to 3 days. Alternatively, freeze individual portions in airtight containers for up to 3 months.

STEWED RHUBARB AND PEAR PUREE

Here, the rhubarb and pear cook down to a slightly textured puree that is delicious on its own, mixed with yoghurt or added to breakfast cereals or porridge.

MAKES 1 CUP (250 G)
PREP TIME 5 minutes
COOKING TIME 10 minutes

3 stalks rhubarb, trimmed and diced
1 large pear, peeled and chopped

1. Place the rhubarb, pear and ½ cup (125 ml) water in a small heavy-based saucepan and bring to the boil over medium heat. Reduce the heat and simmer for 5–10 minutes or until soft. Leave as is or mash to your preferred consistency.
2. Serve warm or cold on its own, mixed with yoghurt or spooned over porridge (see page 150) or quinoa bircher (see page 146).

NUTRITION NOTE The pear adds enough sweetness to combat the tartness of the rhubarb without the need for added sugar.

STORAGE Keep in an airtight container in the fridge for up to 3 days. Alternatively, freeze individual portions in airtight containers for up to 3 months.

STEWED RHUBARB
AND PEAR PUREE
TASTE THE
TROPICS PUREE
RED LENTIL AND
VEGGIE PUREE
PORK PUREE

1ST

WINNER WINNER CHICKEN DINNER

MAKES 2 CUPS (460 G)
PREP TIME 5 minutes
COOKING TIME 18 minutes

- 1 tablespoon olive oil
- 5 cm-length leek, white part only, finely chopped
- 300 g chicken breast fillet, fat trimmed and diced
- 1 sweet potato, peeled and diced
- 1 cup (250 ml) salt-reduced vegetable stock, homemade vegetable stock (see page 240) or water
- 1 cup (120 g) chopped cauliflower florets

There are some flavour combinations that babies just love, and sweet potato, leek and cauliflower is one of them. This recipe is a favourite on the One Handed Cooks website and can be used as a base or modified. Try replacing the chicken with more veggies or other sources of protein, such as pork or legumes. This is a great staple to keep in the freezer.

1. Heat the oil in a heavy-based saucepan over low-medium heat. Add the leek and sauté for 3 minutes or until soft.
2. Increase the heat to medium. Add the chicken and sweet potato, pour over the stock or water and bring to the boil. Reduce the heat and simmer, stirring occasionally, for 5 minutes.
3. Add the cauliflower, cover and cook for a further 8 minutes or until the vegetables are tender and the chicken is cooked through. Transfer to a food processor and process until the mixture reaches your desired consistency.

NUTRITION NOTE Sweet potato is rich in beta-carotene, which is important for vision and the immune system.

TIP Stir through a small handful of grated cheddar cheese before serving.

STORAGE Keep any leftovers in an airtight container in the fridge for up to 3 days. Alternatively, freeze individual portions in airtight containers for up to 2 months.

ALLERGIES/INTOLERANCES ***Gluten:*** use gluten-free stock.

SALMON AND VEGGIE MASH

MAKES 1 CUP (210 G)
PREP TIME 10 minutes
COOKING TIME 30 minutes

- ½ small sweet potato, peeled and cut into 1.5 cm cubes
- 1 teaspoon olive oil
- 100 g boneless salmon fillet, skinned
- ½ cup (40 g) chopped broccoli florets
- 2 tablespoons frozen peas
- 1–2 tablespoons your baby's usual milk
- 2 tablespoons fresh ricotta or grated cheddar cheese

Rich in the essential omega-3 fatty acids needed for healthy brain development and vision, this lovely salmon mash is a wonderful first fish meal for babies. If you are short on time, simply steam the sweet potato over a saucepan of boiling water and pan-fry the salmon. Alternatively, you could use good-quality tinned salmon instead of fresh.

1. Preheat the oven to 180°C (160°C fan-forced) and line a baking tray with baking paper.
2. Toss the sweet potato in the olive oil, spread over the lined tray and bake for 20 minutes. Turn the sweet potato, add the salmon to the tray and bake for a further 8 minutes or until the salmon is cooked and the sweet potato is tender.
3. Meanwhile, cook the broccoli and peas in a steamer basket over a saucepan of boiling water for 2–3 minutes or until bright green and tender.
4. Place the sweet potato, salmon, broccoli, peas and ricotta or cheddar, if using, in a large bowl and mash with the back of a fork or a potato masher, adding a little of the milk at a time until you reach your desired consistency. (Alternatively, process the mixture in a food processor or using a stick blender.)

FUSSY EATING TIP Introducing fresh salmon prepared in different ways early in your baby's food journey will promote enjoyment of this nutritious food and helps prevent it from being refused in the toddler years.

STORAGE Keep in an airtight container in the fridge for up to 2 days. Alternatively, freeze individual portions (without the ricotta or cheese) in airtight containers for up to 2 months.

ALLERGIES/INTOLERANCES ***Dairy:*** use water or dairy-free milk, and omit the ricotta or cheese.

CHICKEN AND MUSHROOM BOLOGNESE

MAKES 2½ CUPS (625 G)
PREP TIME 15 minutes
COOKING TIME 35 minutes

2 teaspoons olive oil
½ onion, finely diced
1 clove garlic, crushed
250 g free-range chicken mince
2 Swiss brown mushrooms, finely chopped
1 zucchini (courgette), coarsely grated
2 sprigs thyme, leaves picked
1 tablespoon no-added-salt tomato paste (puree)
400 g tin no-added-salt chopped tomatoes
cooked small pasta (such as stars, macaroni or risoni), to serve
finely chopped flat-leaf parsley and finely grated parmesan, to serve (optional)
steamed vegetables and fruit, to serve

Our children love tomato-based sauces such as bolognese, so we created this chicken variation to mix things up a little. Making a few small alterations, such as using chicken mince and adding mushrooms and thyme, introduces change in a familiar and comfortable way.

1. Heat the oil in a frying pan over medium heat. Add the onion and garlic and sauté for 2–3 minutes or until softened.
2. Add the chicken mince and cook, breaking it up with a wooden spoon, for 5-7 minutes or until browned. Add the mushrooms and zucchini and cook, stirring often, for a further 2–3 minutes or until softened.
3. Add the thyme, tomato paste, tomatoes and ½ cup (125 ml) water. Bring to the boil, then reduce the heat and simmer for 15–20 minutes or until the sauce has reduced.
4. Place a portion of the sauce in a bowl, mix in some pasta and sprinkle with parsley and parmesan, if using. (If you require a smoother texture, use a food processor or blender to process the sauce to your desired consistency before mixing in the pasta.) Serve with vegetables and fruit alongside.

NUTRITION NOTE Mushrooms add an extra depth of flavour to meals without the need for added salt. They also provide a variety of essential nutrients, such as important B vitamins including folate and B12, copper and selenium, and are abundant in health-promoting antioxidants.

STORAGE Keep in an airtight container in the fridge for up to 2 days. Alternatively, freeze individual portions of bolognese in airtight containers for up to 2 months.

ALLERGIES/INTOLERANCES ***Gluten/wheat:*** serve the sauce with gluten- or wheat-free pasta, quinoa or brown rice. ***Dairy:*** omit the parmesan.

EF

IRRESISTIBLE LAMB PUREE

MAKES 2 CUPS (500 G)
PREP TIME 5 minutes
COOKING TIME 25 minutes

- 2 tablespoons olive oil
- 1 onion, chopped
- 1 stalk celery, trimmed and chopped
- ¾ cup (90 g) chopped cauliflower florets
- 1 waxy potato (such as Dutch cream), peeled and finely diced
- 1 tablespoon chopped chives
- ½ teaspoon dried thyme
- ½ cup (125 ml) salt-reduced vegetable stock or homemade vegetable stock (see page 240)
- 200 g lamb fillet, fat trimmed and diced (or 4 lamb cutlets)

Offer your baby fresh purees made from family meals as often as possible, as they tend to be stronger in natural flavours and more textured than commercial baby food. Experiencing more flavours and textures early in the piece will add immeasurably to your child's enjoyment, acceptance and experience of food.

1. Heat 1 tablespoon of the oil in a small heavy-based saucepan over medium heat. Add the onion and sauté for 3 minutes or until soft. Add the celery and sauté for a further 3 minutes.
2. Add the cauliflower, potato and herbs. Pour over the stock and ½ cup (125 ml) water and bring to the boil. Reduce the heat and simmer for 15–20 minutes or until the potato is tender. Add another ¼ cup (60 ml) of water if the mixture begins to dry out.
3. Meanwhile, heat the remaining 1 tablespoon of oil in a small heavy-based frying pan over medium heat. Add the diced lamb or cutlets, and cook for 3 minutes, then turn and cook for 3 minutes more or until just cooked through. Remove from the heat and set aside to rest.
4. Remove the lamb meat from the bones if using cutlets. Combine the lamb meat and vegetable mixture and use a stick blender or food processor to process until it has an even, textured consistency. Ensure the meat is processed enough so it does not pose a choking risk.

FUSSY EATING TIP If using lamb cutlets, offer the cooked bone to your baby. Teeth or no teeth, they are a great hard munchable (see page 9) for your baby to practise chewing motions on, which will strengthen their oral motor skills.

TIP Stir through cooked brown rice, quinoa or couscous for added texture.

STORAGE Keep any leftovers in an airtight container in the fridge for up to 3 days. Alternatively, freeze individual portions in airtight containers for up to 2 months.

ALLERGIES/INTOLERANCES ***Gluten:*** use gluten-free stock.

BEEF, VEGGIE AND QUINOA MASH

MAKES 4 CUPS (720 G)
PREP TIME 10 minutes
COOKING TIME 20 minutes

½ cup (95 g) quinoa
1 tablespoon olive oil
1 small onion, finely chopped
300 g lean beef steak, diced
½ sweet potato, peeled and diced
2 cups (500 ml) salt-reduced vegetable stock, homemade vegetable stock (see page 240) or water
2 zucchinis (courgettes), chopped
½ cup (60 g) frozen peas
½ cup (80 g) corn kernels, fresh or tinned

This delicious meal is a good source of iron, which is essential for growing babies and toddlers. The recipe makes a sizeable amount so you can freeze leftovers in individual portions, ready to reheat for dinner in a flash.

1. Place the quinoa in a fine-meshed sieve and rinse thoroughly under cold running water. Transfer to a heavy-based saucepan, add 1 cup (250 ml) water and bring to the boil over high heat. Reduce the heat, cover and simmer for 10 minutes. Turn off the heat and set aside, without lifting the lid, for 4 minutes. Fluff the quinoa with a fork and leave to cool.
2. Meanwhile, heat the oil in a large heavy-based saucepan over medium heat. Sauté the onion for 5 minutes or until soft. Add the beef and cook, stirring, until browned all over. Add the sweet potato and stock or water, reduce the heat and simmer, covered, for 8 minutes or until the sweet potato is tender.
3. Add the zucchini, peas and corn and cook for 5 minutes or until the veggies are tender and meat is cooked through. Remove from the heat.
4. Use a stick blender or food processor to process the mixture to your desired consistency. Stir through the cooked quinoa.

NUTRITION NOTE Quinoa is a nutritious first food for babies. It's easy to digest, low in allergens, carbohydrate-rich and high in protein and iron.

TIP Try replacing the quinoa with cooked brown rice, couscous or risoni.

STORAGE Keep in an airtight container in the fridge for up to 2 days. Alternatively, freeze individual portions in airtight containers for up to 2 months.

ALLERGIES/INTOLERANCES ***Gluten:*** use gluten-free stock.

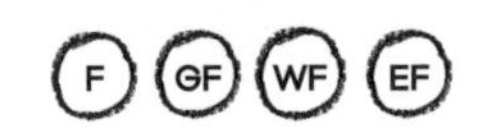

BEEF AND BEAN RICE

MAKES 3½ CUPS (820 G)
PREP TIME 10 minutes
COOKING TIME 30 minutes

½ cup (100 g) brown rice, rinsed
2 teaspoons olive oil
½ onion, finely chopped
½ red capsicum (pepper), seeded and finely chopped
1 clove garlic, crushed
250 g premium lean beef mince
400 g tin no-added-salt chopped tomatoes
½ teaspoon ground cumin
¼ teaspoon sweet paprika
125 g tin red kidney beans, drained and rinsed
plain Greek-style yoghurt, to serve (optional)
diced or mashed avocado, to serve (optional)

Consider this a baby-friendly introduction to chilli con carne, with mild spices and no chilli. The kidney beans add texture, fibre and nutrients, and are also an economical way to bulk up meals – not only for babies, but for the whole family.

1. Place the brown rice in a small heavy-based saucepan with 1 cup (250 ml) water. Bring to the boil, then reduce the heat to low and simmer, covered, for 25 minutes or until it is tender and most of the liquid is absorbed. Turn off the heat and set aside, without lifting the lid, for 5 minutes, then fluff the grains with a fork.
2. Meanwhile, heat the oil in a large frying pan over medium-high heat. Add the onion, capsicum and garlic and sauté for 3–4 minutes or until softened. Add the mince and cook, breaking it up with a wooden spoon, for 5 minutes or until browned.
3. Add the tomato, cumin and paprika and bring to the boil, then reduce the heat and simmer for 15–20 minutes or until the sauce has reduced. Stir in the red kidney beans and simmer until heated through.
4. Stir through the rice and serve topped with a tablespoon of yoghurt and some avocado, if desired.

NUTRITION NOTE Forget white rice – it's better to start off with brown so your baby becomes familiar with the nutty flavour and chewy texture of this nutrient-dense, fibre-rich wholegrain.

TIP Double the recipe to feed the whole family.

STORAGE Keep in an airtight container in the fridge for up to 2 days. Alternatively, do not add the rice, yoghurt and avocado and freeze the beef and bean mixture in individual portions in airtight containers for up to 2 months.

ALLERGIES/INTOLERANCES ***Dairy:*** omit the yoghurt.

SWEET LAMB COUSCOUS

MAKES 2 CUPS (630 G)
PREP TIME 5 minutes
(+ 7 minutes standing)
COOKING TIME 18 minutes

1 tablespoon olive oil
½ onion, finely diced
1 clove garlic, crushed
75 g sweet potato, peeled and diced (about ½ cup)
1 apple, peeled, cored and diced
200 g trimmed lamb, diced
¼ cup (50 g) couscous
coarsely grated apple, to serve

This iron-rich, sweet-tasting meal is a great transition from 'first taste' purees to textured meals. The couscous provides a fine, even texture that young babies usually like.

1. Heat the oil in a small heavy-based saucepan over medium heat. Add the onion and garlic and sauté for 2–3 minutes or until softened. Add the sweet potato, apple and lamb and cook, stirring often, for 5 minutes or until the lamb is browned.
2. Add 1 cup (250 ml) water and bring to the boil. Reduce the heat, cover and simmer for 5–10 minutes or until the lamb is cooked through and the sweet potato and apple are tender.
3. Use a stick mixer, blender or food processor to puree the mixture to your desired consistency. While the puree is still hot, add the couscous and stir to combine, then cover and set aside for 5–7 minutes or until the couscous is tender. Serve topped with grated apple.

NUTRITION NOTE Lamb is rich in iron and zinc, which are important for building a strong immune system to help babies fight infections and reduce the longevity and severity of any symptoms.

STORAGE Keep in an airtight container in the fridge for up to 2 days. Alternatively, freeze individual portions (without the grated apple) in airtight containers for up 2 months.

ALLERGIES/INTOLERANCES ***Gluten/wheat:*** omit the couscous and stir through some cooked quinoa or rice before serving.

LENTIL AND QUINOA DHAL

MAKES 2 CUPS (500 G)
PREP TIME 10 minutes
COOKING TIME 30 minutes

- 2 teaspoons olive oil
- 1 small onion, finely diced
- ½ teaspoon grated fresh ginger
- ½ teaspoon ground cumin
- ¼ teaspoon ground turmeric
- ¼ teaspoon ground coriander
- ½ cup (100 g) split red lentils, rinsed
- ½ cup (95 g) quinoa, rinsed
- 300 g peeled and seeded pumpkin (squash), cut into 2 cm pieces
- 1 carrot, coarsely grated
- 2 tablespoons frozen peas
- 1 tablespoon plain Greek-style yoghurt, to serve (optional)

Introduce your baby to fragrant spices, such as cumin, coriander and turmeric, with this nourishing one-pot wonder. The sweetness and familiarity of pumpkin and carrot will help your baby accept and enjoy this delicious meal.

1. Heat the oil in a heavy-based saucepan over medium heat. Add the onion and sauté for 3–4 minutes or until soft. Add the spices and stir for another minute or until fragrant.
2. Add the lentils, quinoa, pumpkin, carrot and 2 cups (500 ml) water and bring to the boil. Reduce the heat to low-medium, cover and simmer, stirring occasionally, for 20–25 minutes or until the lentils and quinoa are tender. If you prefer a thicker consistency, remove the lid and simmer for a further 5 minutes.
3. Add the peas and cook for 1–2 minutes or until they are tender. Serve as is or with a dollop of yoghurt, if desired.

FUSSY EATING TIP If your baby is reluctant to try this, mix some of the dhal with their favourite vegetable and/or fruit purees, or with a spoonful of plain Greek-style yoghurt.

STORAGE Keep in an airtight container in the fridge for up to 3 days. Alternatively, freeze individual portions (without the yoghurt) in airtight containers for up to 3 months.

ALLERGIES/INTOLERANCES ***Dairy:*** omit the yoghurt and serve with a squeeze of lemon juice.

BANANAVO EGG MASH

MAKES ¾ CUP (180 G)
PREP TIME 5 minutes
COOKING TIME 8 minutes

1 egg
1 small banana, chopped
¼ ripe avocado, peeled and diced

Banana and avocado is a delicious first food combination and a great platform for introducing egg for the first time.

1. Place the egg in a saucepan and cover with cold water. Bring to the boil over high heat, then reduce the heat and simmer for 8 minutes for a creamy hard-boiled egg. Drain and place in a bowl of cold water to cool to room temperature.
2. Peel the egg and mash with the banana and avocado. Serve to your baby as is or spread on toast fingers.

NUTRITION NOTE If you are at all concerned about introducing egg to your baby from an allergy perspective, avoid introducing any other new foods for 3 days before and after the egg, so you can easily identify any reactions.

STORAGE This mash is best enjoyed fresh, but leftovers will keep in an airtight container in the fridge for 24 hours.

ALLERGIES/INTOLERANCES ***Egg:*** simply omit the egg and add a little more avocado instead.

PEACH AND RASPBERRY OATS WITH CHIA AND LSA

MAKES 2 CUPS (450 G)
PREP TIME 5 minutes
COOKING TIME 10 minutes

½ cup (45 g) rolled oats
2 tablespoons quinoa flakes (optional)
1 cup (250 ml) water or your baby's usual milk
1 ripe peach, stone removed and diced
1 ripe pear, peeled, cored and diced
¼ cup (30 g) raspberries, fresh or frozen
chia seeds, to serve (optional)
LSA, to serve (optional)

Many children enjoy porridge for breakfast (or any meal really!) and it's an excellent source of fibre. Sweeten it naturally with fruit and sprinkle over chia seeds and LSA, which is made from ground linseed (flaxseed), sunflower seeds and almonds, for a nutritious boost.

1. Put the oats, quinoa flakes, if using, and water or milk into a small heavy-based saucepan and bring to the boil over medium–high heat. Reduce the heat to low and cook, stirring occasionally, for 6–8 minutes or until smooth and creamy. Remove from the heat and set aside.
2. Meanwhile, bring ½ cup (125 ml) water to the boil in a small heavy-based saucepan over medium heat. Add the peach and pear, reduce the heat to low and simmer, covered, for 6–8 minutes or until soft and tender. Stir through the raspberries and remove from the heat. Transfer to a blender or small food processor and blend to your desired consistency.
3. Combine the fruit puree and porridge. Sprinkle with the chia seeds and LSA, if using, just before serving.

NUTRITION NOTE LSA can be sprinkled over smoothies, porridge or cereals. It offers a good dose of healthy omega-3 fats to promote a healthy heart and brain function, and important minerals such as calcium, zinc and magnesium.

TIP Buy ready-made LSA or make your own by processing equal quantities of linseeds, sunflower seeds and almonds.

STORAGE Any leftovers will keep in an airtight container in the fridge for up to 3 days.

ALLERGIES/INTOLERANCES ***Gluten/wheat:*** use quinoa flakes instead of oats. ***Dairy:*** use water or dairy-free milk. ***Nuts:*** omit the LSA or use ground linseed (flaxseed) instead.

MAPLE PUMPKIN TEMPTERS

Pumpkin is a lovely early food for babies. It is fabulous as a first food mash, but is also irresistible when baked with a little maple and cinnamon and served as a finger food. This recipe works well with sweet potato, too.

MAKES 8
PREP TIME 5 minutes
COOKING TIME 20 minutes

1 teaspoon macadamia or olive oil
1 teaspoon pure maple syrup
¼ (about 230 g) butternut pumpkin (squash), peeled and seeded
pinch of ground cinnamon

1. Preheat the oven to 200°C (180°C fan-forced). Line a baking tray with baking paper.
2. Combine the macadamia or olive oil and maple syrup in a small bowl. Slice the pumpkin into 1 cm × 3 cm batons. Place on the lined tray. Use a pastry brush to brush the maple oil mixture over each finger, then sprinkle with the cinnamon.
3. Bake for 10 minutes, then turn and bake for a further 5–10 minutes, until golden and tender.

FUSSY EATING TIP If possible, avoid serving the same food prepared in the same way over two consecutive days. This will help prevent selective eating and the narrowing down of foods your child will accept.

STORAGE These are best eaten fresh, but can be kept in an airtight container in the fridge for up to 2 days.

BANANA CINNAMON TOAST FINGERS »

Delicate, soft and subtly sweet, these toast fingers are enormously popular. Babies love squishing them between their fingers and when they manage to get some in their mouth they delight in the naturally sweet flavour.

MAKES 4
PREP TIME 5 minutes
COOKING TIME 5 minutes

1 ripe small banana
¼ cup (60 ml) your baby's usual milk
ground cinnamon, to sprinkle
1 teaspoon butter (optional)
1 slice (70 g) thick-cut sourdough bread, crusts removed, sliced into four fingers
hulled strawberries, to serve (or fruit of your choice)

1. Mash the banana with the milk and cinnamon.
2. If using butter, melt it in a frying pan over medium heat (if not, use a non-stick frying pan). Dip the bread fingers in the banana mixture, turning them to coat all sides. Add to the pan and fry for 1–2 minutes each side or until light golden. Carefully transfer to a plate to cool. Serve with strawberries, if desired.

FUSSY EATING TIP First finger foods are often soft and can be rather messy. Remember, it's okay for babies to just play with food, especially if they haven't tried it before. So relax, embrace the mess and join in the fun!

TIP You can use other types of bread, but thick, dense bread gives the best result.

STORAGE These are best served fresh, but can be kept in an airtight container in the fridge for a few hours.

✱ALLERGIES/INTOLERANCES ***Gluten/wheat:*** choose gluten or wheat-free bread. ***Dairy:*** use breastmilk, formula or dairy-free milk.

APPLE AND ALMOND BISCUITS

MAKES 15
PREP TIME 5 minutes
COOKING TIME 15 minutes

1¼ cups (150 g) almond meal
¼ cup (60 g) unsweetened apple puree
1 apple (150 g), peeled, cored and coarsely grated

These lovely, sweet and soft biscuits are winners for many reasons: they take no time to cook, have only three ingredients and no refined sugar, and are packed full of good nutrition for your baby or toddler.

1. Preheat the oven to 170°C (150°C fan-forced) and line a baking tray with baking paper.
2. Place the almond meal, apple puree and grated apple in a large mixing bowl and stir to combine.
3. Roll tablespoonfuls of the mixture into small balls, place on the lined tray and flatten slightly with the palm of your hand. Bake for 12–15 minutes, until light golden. Transfer to a wire rack and cool completely.

NUTRITION NOTE Almonds are high in fibre, contain predominantly healthy monounsaturated fats that promote good health, are an excellent source of vitamin E and provide calcium, iron and zinc.

STORAGE Keep in an airtight container for up to 5 days. Alternatively, freeze individual portions in freezer bags or airtight containers for up to 3 months.

ALLERGIES/INTOLERANCES ***Nuts:*** These are not suitable for babies with allergies to tree nuts. For allergies to almonds only, substitute the almond meal for hazelnut meal.

BABY'S FIRST CARROT CAKE

MAKES 24 MINI CAKES
PREP TIME 5 minutes
COOKING TIME 20 minutes

- ½ cup (125 ml) olive or macadamia oil, plus extra for greasing
- ½ cup (60 g) almond meal
- 1 cup (160 g) wholemeal self-raising flour
- ½ teaspoon ground cinnamon
- 2 eggs
- ¼ cup (60 ml) pure maple syrup
- 1 cup (100 g) coarsely grated carrot
- ½ ripe banana, mashed

Carrot cake is a hit with kids of all ages, and cooking the mixture in a mini muffin tin means you can offer perfect little portions to your baby or toddler. Moist and naturally sweet, they make a lovely treat and we've also used them as the birthday cake for first and second birthday parties with great success.

1. Preheat the oven to 180°C (160°C fan-forced). Grease a 24-hole mini muffin tin (or two 12-hole tins) with extra olive or macadamia oil.
2. Combine the almond meal, flour and cinnamon in a bowl. Whisk the oil, eggs, maple syrup, carrot and banana together in a separate bowl. Add to the dry ingredients and stir with a wooden spoon until just combined.
3. Spoon the mixture into the greased muffin holes. Bake for 20 minutes or until golden and a skewer inserted in the centre of a cake comes out clean. Remove from the oven and transfer to a wire rack to cool.

NUTRITION NOTE Using mini muffin tins is a great way to keep portion sizes under control.

STORAGE Keep in an airtight container for up to 3 days. Alternatively, freeze individual portions in freezer bags or airtight containers for up to 2 months.

ALLERGIES/INTOLERANCES ***Gluten/wheat:*** use gluten- or wheat-free flour. ***Eggs:*** use 2 'chia eggs' (see page 5) or 2 'linseed eggs' (see page 5) instead of the eggs. ***Nuts:*** replace the almond meal with ¼ cup (40 g) self-raising flour.

(V)

EAT-YOUR-GREENS FRITTATA

MAKES 20 PIECES
PREP TIME 15 minutes
COOKING TIME 25 minutes

1 teaspoon olive oil, plus extra for greasing
3 spring onions, trimmed and finely chopped
½ cup (60 g) coarsely grated sweet potato
40 g baby spinach leaves, stems removed
½ cup (40 g) roughly chopped broccoli florets
6 eggs
1 tablespoon plain flour
¼ teaspoon baking powder
½ cup (60 g) grated cheddar cheese

Whiz green vegetables together with eggs and then bake for a delicious frittata that little ones can smush, mush and enjoy.

1. Preheat the oven to 180°C (160°C fan-forced). Grease a shallow 20 cm square cake tin with olive oil and line with baking paper, allowing it to overhang two sides.
2. Heat the oil in a small frying pan over medium heat and sauté the spring onion and sweet potato for 2–3 minutes or until softened. Set aside to cool.
3. Place the baby spinach, broccoli and eggs in a food processor and process until the vegetables are finely chopped. Add the combined flour and baking powder and process until combined.
4. Put the egg mixture, cooked onion and sweet potato, and cheese into a large bowl and stir to combine. Pour into the prepared tin and bake for 18–20 minutes or until set. Remove from the oven and set aside for 5 minutes to cool slightly, then carefully use the overhanging baking paper to lift the frittata out of the tin. Slice into 5 cm × 4 cm pieces and serve.

NUTRITION NOTE In addition to many essential nutrients, green leafy vegetables also provide natural plant chemicals, called phytochemicals, that benefit the immune system, eyesight, bone and heart health.

STORAGE Keep in an airtight container in the fridge for up to 3 days.

ALLERGIES/INTOLERANCES ***Gluten/wheat:*** use gluten-or wheat-free flour. ***Dairy:*** omit the cheese.

(F)

SWEET POTATO AND TUNA CAKES

MAKES 15
PREP TIME 10 minutes
COOKING TIME 25–35 minutes

- ½ sweet potato (about 200 g), peeled and diced
- 2 teaspoons olive oil, plus extra for shallow-frying
- ½ onion, finely diced
- 1 carrot, coarsely grated
- 185 g tin tuna in springwater, drained and flaked
- 1½ cups (105 g) fresh or packaged (150 g) multigrain breadcrumbs
- small handful of baby spinach leaves, finely chopped
- ¼ cup (20 g) finely grated parmesan
- 1 teaspoon finely grated lemon zest
- 3 eggs

Introducing a wide variety of foods early in the piece, when your baby is happy to give almost anything a try, can help prevent food refusal and fussy eating during the 'neophobic' toddler/preschool years. Serve alongside some steamed vegetables or salad for a complete meal.

1. Place the sweet potato in a small saucepan, add enough water to cover and bring to the boil over high heat. Reduce the heat and simmer for 5–10 minutes or until tender. Drain and set aside to cool slightly.
2. Heat the olive oil in a small frying pan over medium heat, add the onion and carrot and sauté for 3–5 minutes or until soft.
3. Place the sweet potato, onion mixture and tuna in a large bowl and lightly mash. Add a third of the breadcrumbs, the spinach, parmesan, lemon zest and 1 lightly whisked egg and mix until well combined.
4. Shape large tablespoonfuls of the mixture into patties. Lightly whisk the remaining eggs in a shallow bowl. Place the remaining breadcrumbs in a separate shallow bowl. Dip each patty into the egg, then coat in the breadcrumbs.
5. Heat about 1 cm of olive oil in a large frying pan over medium–high heat. Fry the patties, in batches to avoid overcrowding the pan, for 2–3 minutes each side or until golden brown and cooked through.

NUTRITION NOTE To keep salt content low, choose quality tinned tuna in springwater or oil.

STORAGE Keep in an airtight container in the fridge for up to 2 days. Uncooked patties can be frozen, wrapped in plastic film, for up to 2 months.

✱ALLERGIES/INTOLERANCES ***Gluten/wheat:*** replace the breadcrumbs with quinoa flakes. ***Dairy:*** omit the parmesan. ***Egg:*** use a 'chia egg' (see page 5) to replace the egg in step 3, then crumb the patties without dipping in egg first.

F

CHICKEN AND APPLE FINGERS

MAKES 10
PREP TIME 10 minutes
COOKING TIME 10 minutes

1 teaspoon rice bran oil
1 carrot, coarsely grated
½ small onion, coarsely grated
1 apple, peeled, cored and coarsely grated
300 g free-range chicken mince
½ teaspoon dried thyme
2 egg yolks
¼ cup (15 g) fresh multigrain breadcrumbs
¼ cup (30 g) grated cheddar cheese

When adding finger foods to your baby's feeding routine, it's important to have them sitting properly before they begin to eat. Proper positioning encourages good head and body alignment, which helps prevent choking, and if they're comfortable they're more likely to enjoy the experience. The ideal sitting position for eating requires the hips, knees and feet to be at a 90 degree angle, with the child's weight evenly distributed.

1. Preheat the oven grill on high and line a baking tray with foil. Brush the foil with the rice bran oil to lightly grease.
2. Place the carrot, onion and apple in a food processor and pulse until finely chopped. Transfer to a large bowl, add the chicken mince and mix until well combined.
3. Add the thyme, egg yolks, breadcrumbs and cheese and mix until well combined. Shape handfuls of the mixture into 8 cm × 2 cm fingers (you should end up with 10 fingers), placing them on the lined tray as you go. Press the top of each finger gently to flatten.
4. Grill the fingers for 5 minutes or until browned, then turn and grill for a further 5 minutes or until browned and cooked through. Remove from the grill and leave to cool. (Alternatively, bake the fingers in a 200°C/180°C fan-forced oven for 10 minutes, then turn and bake for a further 10 minutes or until cooked through.)

NUTRITION NOTE High in protein and carbohydrates, and nutrient rich, this tasty finger food has the right kind of energy needed to fuel growing little bodies.

TIP If making this recipe for a toddler, there's no need to grate the carrot, onion and apple before processing. Grating them first is to ensure there are no large chunks that a baby might find hard to manage.

STORAGE Keep in an airtight container in the fridge for up to 2 days. Alternatively, freeze the uncooked fingers on a lined tray until frozen, then transfer to a freezer bag and freeze for up to 2 months. Thaw before cooking.

ALLERGIES/INTOLERANCES ***Gluten/wheat:*** substitute gluten-free breadcrumbs or quinoa flakes for the breadcrumbs. ***Dairy:*** omit the cheese. ***Egg:*** substitute 2 'chia eggs' (see page 5) or 2 'linseed eggs' (see page 5) for the egg yolks.

PUMPKIN-SPICED QUINOA BALLS

MAKES ABOUT 40
PREP TIME 15 minutes
COOKING TIME 55 minutes

- ½ (about 550 g) butternut pumpkin (squash), seeded and cut into 8 wedges
- 1 tablespoon olive oil
- ½ teaspoon ground cumin
- ½ teaspoon ground coriander
- ½ teaspoon ground nutmeg
- ½ cup (95 g) quinoa
- 1 cup (80 g) finely chopped broccoli florets
- 1 small red onion, finely grated
- steamed vegetables, to serve

This simple finger food is all-natural, with a subtle hint of spice and little pops of texture to excite your baby.

1. Preheat the oven to 180°C (160°C fan-forced) and line 2 baking trays with baking paper.
2. Put the pumpkin into a bowl, add the olive oil and spices and toss to coat. Arrange the pumpkin in a single layer on a lined tray and bake, turning halfway through cooking, for 25 minutes or until soft and caramelised. Remove from the oven and set aside until cool enough to handle.
3. Meanwhile, place the quinoa in a fine-meshed sieve and rinse thoroughly under cold running water. Transfer to a heavy-based saucepan, add 1 cup (250 ml) water and bring to the boil over high heat. Reduce the heat to low, cover and simmer for 10 minutes. Turn off the heat and set aside, without lifting the lid, for 4 minutes. Fluff the quinoa with a fork and leave to cool.
4. Bring a small saucepan of water to the boil. Add the broccoli and cook for 2 minutes or until tender. Drain well.
5. Scoop the pumpkin flesh from the skin and place in a bowl. Squeeze the liquid from the grated onion and use paper towel to pat the onion dry. Add the onion, broccoli and quinoa to the pumpkin and mash together until well combined. Dollop teaspoon-sized balls of mixture onto the remaining lined tray.
6. Bake the balls, turning halfway through cooking, for 30 minutes or until golden brown. Serve with steamed vegetables alongside.

NUTRITION NOTE Spice doesn't always mean 'hot', so don't let the word scare you off when cooking family meals. Incorporating a range of spices into your child's meals will help in the transition to family food and encourage positive eating behaviours.

STORAGE Keep in an airtight container in the fridge for up to 2 days. Alternatively, freeze the uncooked balls, on a lined tray covered with plastic film, until frozen, then transfer to a freezer bag and freeze for up to 2 months.

MINI MEATBALLS

MAKES ABOUT 40
PREP TIME 10 minutes
(+ 30 minutes chilling)
COOKING TIME 25 minutes

½ small sweet potato, peeled and diced
200 g premium lean beef mince
¼ cup (15 g) fresh multigrain breadcrumbs
pinch of dried mixed herbs or 1 teaspoon finely chopped mixed herbs (such as thyme, parsley, oregano; optional)
1 tablespoon no-added-salt tomato paste (puree)

Babies love to try out their emerging independence on food, so anything they can pick up themselves is a surefire winner. These super-soft meatballs make a perfect sensory food for them.

1. Cook the sweet potato in a steamer basket over a saucepan of boiling water for 8–10 minutes or until tender. Remove from the heat, transfer to a large bowl and mash with a fork. Set aside to cool.
2. Add the remaining ingredients to the bowl and mix until thoroughly combined. Cover and place in the fridge for 30 minutes to chill.
3. Preheat the oven to 200°C (180°C fan-forced) and line a large baking tray with baking paper.
4. Shape teaspoons of the mixture into small balls and place on the lined tray. Bake for 15 minutes or until golden brown and cooked through.

NUTRITION NOTE Add more flavours to the meatballs as your baby's tastes develop, such as onion, garlic, more herbs and grated veggies.

TIP For a similar simple ball for your baby, you could use ½ cup (60 g) Basic Bolognese (see page 237) mixed with ½ cup (90 g) mashed sweet potato or thawed baby puree.

STORAGE Keep in an airtight container in the fridge for up to 2 days. Alternatively, freeze the uncooked meatballs on a lined tray until frozen, then transfer to a freezer bag and freeze for up to 2 months.

ALLERGIES/INTOLERANCES ***Gluten/wheat:*** substitute gluten- or wheat-free breadcrumbs or quinoa flakes for the breadcrumbs.

HAZELNUT AND OAT BABY BARS

MAKES 49
PREP TIME 10 minutes
COOKING TIME 45 minutes

1½ cups (135 g) rolled oats
½ cup (80 g) wholemeal plain flour or plain flour
¼ cup (25 g) hazelnut meal
¼ teaspoon ground cinnamon
1 apple (about 150 g) or ripe small pear (about 180 g), peeled, cored and coarsely grated
1 overripe banana (about 200 g), mashed
1 egg
1¼ cups (310 ml) milk

Sweetened with fresh fruit, these little muesli bars for babies are a terrific first finger food. Soft and mushable, they are perfect for little hands and gummy mouths, and a great breakfast option for independent feeders.

1. Preheat the oven to 180°C (160°C fan-forced) and line a 22 cm square cake tin with baking paper, allowing it to overhang two sides.
2. Place the oats, flour, hazelnut meal, cinnamon and apple or pear in a bowl.
3. In a separate bowl, mix together the mashed banana, egg and milk. Add the banana mixture to the dry ingredients and stir to combine.
4. Pour the mixture into the lined tin and bake for 40–45 minutes or until a skewer inserted into the centre of the slice comes out clean. Remove from the oven and allow to cool in the tin for 5 minutes. Use the overhanging paper to lift the slice out of the tin and transfer to a wire rack to cool completely. Cut into 3 cm squares.

NUTRITION NOTE This versatile recipe is easily adaptable for allergies and intolerances, or simply to maximise variety. We've tried adding chia seeds, grated carrot and zucchini (courgette), substituting almond meal for the hazelnut meal and, for older babies, toddlers and preschoolers, adding ¾ cup (120 g) chopped dried fruit.

STORAGE Keep in an airtight container in the fridge for up to 3 days or wrap individual portions in plastic film and freeze for up to 3 months.

✱ALLERGIES/INTOLERANCES ***Gluten/wheat:*** substitute gluten- or wheat-free breadcrumbs or quinoa flakes for the oats, and use gluten- or wheat-free flour. ***Dairy:*** use your preferred dairy-free milk. ***Egg:*** replace the egg with an additional ½ overripe banana, ⅓ cup (100 g) unsweetened apple puree or 1 'chia egg' (see page 5). ***Nuts:*** for allergies to tree nuts, replace the hazelnut meal with plain flour. For allergies to hazelnut, substitute almond meal.

CHAPTER 2

OFFER VARIETY FROM THE START

Becoming familiar with a wide variety of foods as early as possible gives your child the best opportunity to accept and enjoy a nutrient-rich diet that includes all five food groups. They aren't going to like everything you offer straight away – it is completely normal for children to reject food at various times – but don't give up on a food if they become fussy with it. If you consistently create a positive mealtime environment and offer family foods in lots of different ways, eventually your child's diet will expand to include most foods.

Most babies will accept a wide variety of foods, flavours, textures, smells and colours if they're exposed to them early on and are allowed to explore them without any pressure to eat. Ensure their diet is of a good quality overall by giving them foods that are primarily natural, unprocessed and free of artificial colours, flavours and preservatives. The fewer commercial and pre-packaged foods they eat, the better. Fresh, whole foods provide oodles of health-promoting non-nutrients, such as phytochemicals, antioxidants, prebiotics and fibre.

COPING WITH FUSSY BEHAVIOUR

Some babies are fussy about food right from the start, while others will happily accept a wide range of foods until they become a toddler or preschooler. At this age, children often become wary of new and unfamiliar things, and they're also keen to demonstrate their control and independence, so broadening their diet is a challenge. Some of them even begin to refuse foods they previously accepted and exhibit fussy eating behaviours, which is extremely frustrating! The best thing to do is to continue serving their favourite dishes while regularly expanding the menu, rather than allowing it to be restricted.

When it comes to measuring progress during periods of fussy eating, remember you may need to offer a food numerous times before your child will touch it or smell it, let alone put it in their mouth. Instead of pinning your hopes on them eating it every time it's offered, accept their reluctance and praise any small step forward, such as simply tolerating the food being on the same plate as the rest of the meal. Praising and encouraging positive interactions with a food increases the likelihood of your child getting a step closer to eating it.

Our top tips to deal with fussy behaviour:

- Set the scene: make sure your child has five minutes of an activity that calms and relaxes them before each meal. Try playing soothing music, reading a book together or setting up a quiet table activity
- Involve and educate: develop an evolving and continuous dialogue based around the enjoyment of food and nutrition. Shopping, gardening and cooking with kids are powerful persuaders when it comes to eating and trying new foods
- Be a good role model: show your children how to eat new foods by eating with them. Children are more likely to accept new foods if you're enjoying them, too
- Accommodate insecurities and sensitivities: be patient and nurturing with children who are cautious around new foods. Only offer a small amount and serve it alongside a food you know they love
- Be creative: a child may need to be exposed to a new food up to 20 times before they feel familiar with it and accept it. Try presenting it in different ways – they may refuse grated carrot in a sandwich, for instance, but eat it in spaghetti bolognese. Younger children may even like to make shapes or faces out of new foods. If they're relaxed and having fun, they are more likely to touch and interact with it, which encourages familiarity
- Give your child a 'learning plate', which is a smaller plate placed next to their dinner plate. Place the new food on the learning plate, then during the meal you can talk about it and explain why it is good for them. Keeping the new food separate to their meal means they won't feel pressured to eat it, and will happily explore it instead.

THE MEALTIME RITUAL

Creating a 'mealtime ritual' can help ensure eating is a relaxed and enjoyable experience for both you and your child. Devise a ritual that suits your family schedule – it can be as simple or complex as you wish. Here are some examples for different age groups to help you get started.

Baby: When babies know what is coming next they are often more relaxed and open to the experience.

1. Tell your baby it is time to eat
2. Seat them correctly in a highchair (see Good posture for eating on page 8)
3. Bring the meal to your baby. If you are no longer spoon-feeding them, continue to sit with them while they eat anyway, so you can encourage them and praise their efforts
4. When your baby starts to rub their eyes, turn away from the spoon or push the food away, ask if they are finished
5. Some babies find it uncomfortable when their face is wiped clean after a meal. To avoid them developing negative associations with the highchair and face-wiping, take them out of the chair before cleaning them up.

Toddler: Curious and energetic, toddlers often like to test their boundaries, particularly at the dinner table. They may start throwing food, refusing some foods and be less willing to try new foods. A mealtime ritual can help you set the boundaries and keep your cool during any fussy behaviours. Try to serve meals at the same time each day, and at the table without any distractions.

1. If your child responds to musical cues, play some calming music they can associate with mealtimes beforehand and tell them it will soon be time to eat and they need to finish what they're doing
2. Let them know dinner is ready and ask them to come to the kitchen
3. Wash their hands
4. Seat them correctly in a highchair (see Good posture for eating on page 8)
5. Bring the meal to your toddler and begin to spoon-feed them (see page 8) or sit with them while they feed themselves
6. Allow your child to choose what they want to eat, and how much, from the food on offer. This allows them to recognise and respond to hunger and fullness cues
7. Encourage them to say 'please' and 'thank you' to assist with developing table manners
8. Sit with your toddler while they eat, encourage them and praise their efforts without going over the top
9. When they start to rub their eyes, turn away from the spoon, push the food away or begin throwing food, ask if they are finished
10. Remove the meal and take them out of the highchair before wiping their face.

Preschool/school age: Eat together as a family whenever possible so you can role model positive mealtime behaviours. The most effective way for children to learn is by copying adults they trust, so demonstrate good manners and give them your undivided attention. Limit snacks before dinner to ensure they are hungry, and try to serve meals at the same time each day, without any distractions.

1. If your child responds to musical cues, play calming music they can associate with mealtimes beforehand and tell them to finish what they're doing as it will soon be time to eat. If you have given them regular tasks to help prepare for dinner, ask them to do these now
2. Switch off all technology and ask your child to wash their hands and come to the table
3. Serve the food, either by dishing it up on individual plates or taking it all to the table buffet-style and allowing them to put it on their plate themselves
4. Allow your child to choose what they want to eat, and how much, from the food on offer. This allows them to recognise and respond to hunger and fullness cues
5. Talk to them about their day and whatever is going on at the time. While it's good to talk about food and nutrition, don't dwell on this for too long, particularly if they are fussy at mealtimes. Follow their cues and let the conversation flow naturally
6. When everyone has finished their meal, your child can ask to be excused from the table. If they are old enough, they can carry the plates to the kitchen and help wash up or stack the dishwasher.

MEALTIME TIPS AND TRICKS

- Involve the kids in meal preparation and/or setting and clearing the table. Tasks need to be age appropriate, but there are benefits for starting early. Young children may just be in charge of putting serviettes on the table
- Implement a technology switch-off rule at mealtimes. Give children a five-minute warning and keep the time that dinner is served consistent if possible
- Let them choose a few meals each week. Children are more inclined to be excited by, and eat, meals when they have had some input. Make sure one of your meals features a 'new food of the week' to increase variety
- Use any spare time during the day to prep ingredients for dinner, or do some batch cooking on the weekend. A little prepping goes a long way towards alleviating the stress of the 'witching hour', while having a home-cooked meal ready to go in the freezer is helpful if you've been out for most of the day
- If mealtimes are getting a little stale, mix things up with a themed night, such as Mexican, curry or homemade pizza. Include the kids in the meal preparation or ask them to do a drawing to decorate the table.

CHEESY POLENTA CHIPPIES WITH ROAST BEETROOT DIP

MAKES 22 CHIPS AND 1½ CUPS (350 G) DIP
PREP TIME 15 minutes
COOKING TIME 1 hour 20 minutes

2 cups (500 ml) salt-reduced vegetable stock or homemade vegetable stock (see page 240)
1 cup (170 g) polenta
1 cup (120 g) grated parmesan or cheddar cheese
1 tablespoon chopped mixed herbs (such as thyme, parsley, chives, rosemary)
1 tablespoon honey
pinch of salt and pepper (optional)
2 tablespoons olive oil

BEETROOT DIP
1 large (about 250 g) beetroot, trimmed and halved
1 tablespoon olive oil
⅓ cup (50 g) pine nuts
100 g raw unsalted cashews
1 heaped tablespoon fresh ricotta
1 heaped tablespoon plain Greek-style yoghurt

Polenta chips look similar to potato chips, but have much more goodness and are baked, not fried. They are just calling out to be 'dipped' and if that dip is as nutritious as our beetroot one, you are onto a real winner.

1. Bring the stock and 2 cups (500 ml) water to the boil in a heavy-based saucepan over medium–high heat. Reduce the heat to low–medium and gradually add the polenta in a thick, steady stream. Whisk continuously for a couple of minutes or until the mixture is thick and smooth. Stir in the cheese, herbs, honey and salt and pepper, if using. Remove from the heat.
2. Line a 22 cm square baking tin with baking paper, allowing it to overhang two sides. Pour the mixture into the lined tin and smooth the surface. Place in the fridge for at least 20 minutes to set.
3. Meanwhile, to make the beetroot dip, preheat the oven to 180°C (160°C fan-forced). Line a baking tray with baking paper.
4. Place the beetroot halves on the lined tray and drizzle with the olive oil. Bake for 40 minutes, then add the pine nuts and cashews and bake for a further 3 minutes or until the nuts are light golden and a skewer can easily pierce the centre of the beetroot. Remove from the oven and set aside until the beetroot is cool enough to handle. Increase the oven temperature to 200°C (180°C fan forced).
5. Remove the polenta from the fridge and use the overhanging paper to lift it out of the tin. Cut in half, then slice into 2 cm-thick chips. Place on a lined baking tray, drizzle with the oil and then roll each chip in the oil to coat. Bake, turning halfway through cooking, for 30 minutes or until light golden.
6. Meanwhile, wearing gloves to avoid staining, peel the beetroot and roughly chop. Place in a food processor with the pine nuts, cashews, ricotta and yoghurt and process until smooth. Serve alongside the polenta chips.

STORAGE The dip will keep in an airtight container in the fridge for up to 2 days. You can freeze the polenta chips (before baking) for up to 2 months. Wrap the block in plastic film or, if sliced, wrap each chip in plastic film and store in a freezer bag.

*ALLERGIES/INTOLERANCES Omit the honey when preparing the chips for babies under 12 months. ***Gluten:*** use gluten-free stock. ***Dairy:*** omit the cheese, ricotta and yoghurt. ***Nuts***: omit the pine nuts.

NUTRITION NOTE

Herbs are a great way to add flavour to food without the need for added salt, which can be harmful to your child's wellbeing if eaten in excess and even contribute to fussy eating behaviours.

SALMON AND RICOTTA CAKES

MAKES 8
PREP TIME 10 minutes
(+ 10 minutes chilling)
COOKING TIME 16 minutes

200 g tin pink salmon, drained, bones removed and flesh flaked
2 small zucchinis (courgettes), coarsely grated, liquid squeezed out
½ cup (100 g) fresh ricotta
¼ cup (30 g) fresh or frozen peas
1 tablespoon finely chopped dill or flat-leaf parsley
1 teaspoon finely grated lemon zest
2 slices multigrain bread, crusts removed, cut into cubes
1 egg, lightly whisked
freshly ground pepper, to taste
¾ cup (70 g) fresh or ½ cup (50 g) packaged breadcrumbs
¼ cup (60 ml) olive oil or rice bran oil, for frying
seasonal vegetables or side salad, to serve

Introducing herbs to your baby helps broaden the range of flavours they are familiar with. Dill has a strong, distinct flavour, so if it is new to your child, only add a fraction of the suggested amount, then increase the amount each time you make these yummy salmon cakes.

1. Place the salmon, zucchini, ricotta, peas, dill or parsley, lemon zest, bread, egg and a little pepper in a large bowl and mix until well combined.
2. Divide the mixture into 8 equal portions, then shape each portion into a patty. Place the breadcrumbs in a shallow bowl and coat each patty in the crumbs. Place the patties on a tray lined with baking paper and refrigerate for 10 minutes.
3. Heat the oil in a large frying pan over medium heat. Cook the patties, in two batches to avoid overcrowding the pan, for 3–4 minutes each side or until golden. Add a little more oil to the pan if required. Drain on paper towel and serve with vegetables or a salad.

NUTRITION NOTE Tinned pink salmon is rich in omega-3 fatty acids.

STORAGE Keep in an airtight container in the fridge for up to 2 days. Alternatively, freeze individual portions in airtight containers for up to 2 months.

ALLERGIES/INTOLERANCES ***Gluten/wheat:*** Use gluten- or wheat-free bread and breadcrumbs. ***Dairy:*** omit the ricotta or substitute silken tofu. ***Egg:*** substitute a 'chia egg' (see page 5) for the egg.

CHICKEN AND CHIVE SAUSAGES

MAKES 16
PREP TIME 10 minutes
(+ 30 minutes chilling)
COOKING TIME 30 minutes

500 g free-range chicken mince
1 small zucchini (courgette), coarsely grated, liquid squeezed out
¼ cup (15 g) fresh multigrain breadcrumbs
1 egg, lightly whisked
1 teaspoon Dijon mustard
1 tablespoon finely chopped chives
1 litre salt-reduced chicken stock (or half stock, half water)
1 tablespoon rice bran oil
bread rolls, avocado and mixed salad leaves, to serve (optional)

Sausages are a common choice for weekend barbecues and entertaining, as they are simple to cook and generally popular. However, the salt and additive content often found in store-bought sausages relegates them to the 'sometimes' food category (see page 204). It's easy to make your own sausages though, giving you the freedom to pack in a whole lot of goodness so they can be enjoyed more regularly.

1. Place the chicken, zucchini, breadcrumbs, egg, mustard and chives in a bowl and use your hands to thoroughly combine.
2. Divide the mixture into 16 portions and use wet hands to shape each portion into a long, thin sausage. Place on a tray lined with baking paper, cover with plastic film and refrigerate for 30 minutes.
3. Bring the stock to the boil in a large heavy-based saucepan over high heat, then reduce the heat to hold at a simmer. Using a slotted spoon, gently add half the sausages to the simmering stock. Cover and cook for 5–10 minutes or until the sausages are cooked through. Transfer the sausages to paper towel to drain. Repeat to cook the remaining sausages.
4. Heat the oil in a large frying pan over medium heat. Add half the sausages and cook, turning often, until browned all over. Transfer to a plate and set aside while you brown the remaining sausages, adding a little more oil to the pan if required.
5. Serve the sausages in a bread roll with avocado and salad leaves, if desired, or as part of a tasting plate (see pages 120–121).

FUSSY EATING TIP Making your own version of your child's favourite 'sometimes' food means you can control exactly what goes in it.

STORAGE Keep in an airtight container in the fridge for up to 2 days. Alternatively, wrap individual portions of boiled (but not fried) sausages in plastic film and freeze for up to 2 months.

ALLERGIES/INTOLERANCES ***Gluten/wheat:*** use gluten- or wheat-free breadcrumbs and rolls, and gluten-free stock. ***Egg:*** substitute 'egg replacer' or a 'chia egg' (see page 5) for the egg.

ROAST PUMPKIN SOUP WITH AVOCADO DIPPERS

SERVES 4–6
PREP TIME 10 minutes
COOKING TIME 30 minutes

1 butternut pumpkin (squash), peeled, seeded and cut into 5 cm pieces
2 onions, quartered
2 cloves garlic, peeled
¼ teaspoon ground cumin
1 tablespoon olive oil
1½ cups (375 ml) salt-reduced chicken or vegetable stock
¼ cup (60 ml) pouring cream
freshly ground pepper, to taste
4 slices multigrain sourdough bread, toasted
½ ripe avocado, peeled and mashed

Soup is an easy weeknight family meal, but do take the time to roast the pumpkin, onion and garlic as it intensifies their sweetness. Adding a little cumin encourages little ones to accept and become familiar with this popular spice.

1. Preheat the oven to 200°C (180°C fan-forced).
2. Place the pumpkin, onion and garlic in a large roasting pan. Sprinkle with the cumin and drizzle with the olive oil. Toss to coat and roast for 25–30 minutes or until the pumpkin is tender and golden.
3. Transfer everything to a food processor or blender, add the stock and cream and process until smooth, adding a little more stock if a thinner consistency is required. Season with pepper, if desired.
4. Spread the toast with avocado and slice each piece into 3 fingers. Serve alongside the pumpkin soup.

FUSSY EATING TIP Providing nutritious dippers alongside soup gives babies and toddlers, particularly independent self-feeders, an opportunity to interact with, and enjoy, the soup without the need for cutlery.

STORAGE Leftover soup will keep in an airtight container in the fridge for up to 3 days. Alternatively, freeze individual portions in airtight containers for up to 3 months.

ALLERGIES/INTOLERANCES ***Gluten/wheat:*** use gluten- or wheat-free bread, and gluten-free stock. ***Dairy:*** substitute coconut cream for pouring cream.

CHEESY VEGGIE PASTA WITH THYME

SERVES 2–3
PREP TIME 5 minutes
COOKING TIME 8 minutes

1 cup (220 g) dried pasta (such as macaroni, farfalle, risoni)
1 teaspoon extra virgin olive oil
½ small onion, finely chopped
1 tomato, chopped
1 small carrot, coarsely grated
1 small zucchini (courgette), coarsely grated
2 sprigs thyme, leaves only
1 tablespoon pouring cream (optional)
¼ cup (30 g) grated cheddar cheese

This truly is a 'meal-in-minutes', even with a baby on the hip. You can mix up the vegetables according to what you have on hand, and other herbs like basil and parsley would work well instead of the thyme.

1. Cook the pasta in a small saucepan of salted boiling water until al dente, following the instructions on the packet. Drain well.
2. Meanwhile, heat the oil in a small frying pan over medium heat. Add the onion and sauté for 2–3 minutes or until soft.
3. Add the tomato, carrot, zucchini and thyme to the frying pan and cook, stirring, for 4–5 minutes or until softened.
4. Add the cream, if using, and the cheese and stir until the cheese is melted. Toss through the drained pasta and serve.

FUSSY EATING TIP If your baby or toddler is wary of new foods, introduce herbs and spices by adding a small amount to their favourite meals.

STORAGE Leftovers will keep in an airtight container in the fridge for up to 3 days.

ALLERGIES/INTOLERANCES ***Gluten/wheat:*** use gluten- or wheat-free pasta. ***Dairy:*** omit the cream and cheese, and add an additional chopped tomato or 1–2 tablespoons of water or salt-reduced stock.

CHICKEN AND HOKKIEN NOODLE STIR-FRY

SERVES 4–6
PREP TIME 15 minutes
COOKING TIME 10 minutes

400 g fresh hokkien noodles
1 tablespoon peanut oil
500 g chicken thigh fillets, fat trimmed, cut into 2 cm pieces
2 cm piece ginger, thinly sliced or grated
3 spring onions, finely chopped
1 carrot, halved lengthways and thinly diagonally sliced
60 g Swiss brown (or button) mushrooms, sliced
1 cup (85 g) chopped broccoli florets
100 g snow peas, halved lengthways
2 tablespoons salt-reduced soy sauce
1 tablespoon oyster sauce
1 teaspoon caster sugar
¼ teaspoon sesame oil
roughly chopped coriander or Thai basil leaves, to serve (optional)

This stir-fry is a great introduction to family mealtimes for an older baby or toddler. They will like playing with, and eating, the noodles and many of the other elements can be enjoyed as finger food. A relaxed, stress-free mealtime environment is key to encouraging enjoyment of new foods.

1. Place the noodles in a heatproof bowl and cover with boiling water. Soak for 1–2 minutes and break up with a fork. Drain and set aside.
2. Heat half the peanut oil in a large heavy-based frying pan or wok over high heat. Add the chicken and stir-fry for 2–3 minutes or until golden. (Cook the chicken in two batches if necessary to avoid crowding the pan.) Transfer to a plate and set aside.
3. Heat the remaining peanut oil in the pan, then add the ginger, spring onion, carrot and mushrooms and stir-fry for 2 minutes. Add the broccoli and stir-fry for a further 2 minutes. Return the chicken to the pan with the snow peas and noodles and stir-fry for 2–3 minutes or until the noodles are warm and the chicken is cooked through.
4. Stir through the soy and oyster sauces, sugar and sesame oil. Remove from the heat, sprinkle with the coriander or Thai basil, if desired, and serve.

NUTRITION NOTE Many Asian sauces are not suitable for young babies due to their high salt content. When cooking for older babies or toddlers, choose salt-reduced varieties and be mindful of the amount you use.

TIP For a vegetarian dish, use tofu instead of chicken.

STORAGE Keep in an airtight container in the fridge for up to 2 days.

ALLERGIES/INTOLERANCES ***Gluten/wheat/egg:*** replace the hokkien noodles with rice noodles, and use gluten-free soy sauce. ***Nuts:*** use rice bran, light olive or vegetable oil instead of peanut oil. ***Sesame:*** omit the sesame oil.

CHICKEN BURRITOS WITH CUCUMBER SALSA

MAKES 8
PREP TIME 15 minutes
COOKING TIME 10 minutes

500 g chicken breast fillet, fat trimmed, cut into 2 cm pieces
2 tablespoons olive oil
1–2 tablespoons Mexican seasoning mix (see page 238)
8 tortillas (preservative-free varieties or homemade, see page 239), warmed
1 cup (120 g) grated cheddar cheese
roughly chopped coriander leaves (optional), to serve
plain Greek-style yoghurt, to serve (optional)
lime wedges, to serve (optional)

CUCUMBER SALSA

1 Lebanese (short) cucumber, finely diced
½ ripe avocado, peeled and diced
1 punnet (250 g) cherry tomatoes, quartered
1 teaspoon roughly chopped coriander leaves
1 teaspoon fresh lime juice
1 teaspoon caster sugar (optional)
pinch of salt (optional)

Burritos are a wonderful serve-at-the-table meal the whole family can enjoy. Eating together enables parents to role-model healthy eating behaviours and children form positive associations with mealtimes.

1. Place the chicken and 1 tablespoon of the oil in a large bowl. Sprinkle over the seasoning and stir to coat. Cover and place in the fridge for at least 10 minutes to marinate.
2. Meanwhile, to make the cucumber salsa, place all the ingredients in a bowl and gently toss to combine. Set aside.
3. Heat the remaining oil in a large heavy-based frying pan over medium–high heat. Add the chicken and cook for 6–8 minutes or until browned all over and cooked through. Remove from the heat.
4. To serve, top a warm tortilla with some cooked chicken and cheese. Spoon over some cucumber salsa, top with coriander, yoghurt and a squeeze of lime juice, if using. Roll up the burrito and enjoy.

FUSSY EATING TIP For younger children who struggle to eat a burrito without the filling falling out, simply scatter chicken and cheese over a tortilla, roll up tightly and toast in a hot sandwich press for a few minutes to seal. Serve with the cucumber salsa on the side.

STORAGE The cooked chicken and salsa will keep in separate airtight containers in the fridge for up to 2 days.

ALLERGIES/INTOLERANCES ***Gluten/wheat:*** use gluten- or wheat-free tortillas. ***Dairy:*** omit the cheese and yoghurt. ***Vegetarian:*** replace the chicken with pan-fried firm tofu or legumes.

LAMB AND RISONI BAKE

SERVES 6–8
PREP TIME 10 minutes
COOKING TIME 2 hours

- 1.2 kg diced lamb shoulder or leg
- ¼ cup (60 ml) olive oil
- 2 onions, thinly sliced
- juice of 1 lemon
- 2 bay leaves
- 1 clove garlic, crushed
- 2 teaspoons dried oregano
- 1 teaspoon ground cumin
- 1 teaspoon sweet paprika
- 1 litre salt-reduced chicken stock or homemade chicken stock (see page 240)
- 400 g tin no-added-salt chopped tomatoes
- 2 tablespoons no-added-salt tomato paste (puree)
- 2 cups (440 g) risoni
- torn flat-leaf parsley, to serve
- grated parmesan, crumbled feta or plain Greek-style yoghurt, to serve
- steamed vegetables or salad leaves, to serve

This iron-rich family meal is made with tender, slow-cooked lamb. You can puree or finely chop the lamb for young babies.

1. Preheat the oven to 180°C (160°C fan-forced).
2. Place the lamb, olive oil, onion, lemon juice, bay leaves and garlic in a large baking dish. Sprinkle over the oregano, cumin and paprika and toss to combine. Cover with a tight-fitting lid or foil and bake for 40 minutes, stirring occasionally.
3. When the lamb has been cooking for 30 minutes, heat the stock and chopped tomatoes in a saucepan over medium heat until hot. Stir in the tomato paste.
4. Remove the lamb from the oven, pour over the hot stock mixture, cover and bake for a further 1 hour.
5. Remove the lamb from the oven, sprinkle over the risoni and stir to combine, then cover and bake for another 20 minutes or until the pasta is cooked through and most of the liquid has been absorbed. If you prefer a thicker sauce, remove the lid or foil and return to the oven for a further 5–10 minutes or until it reaches your desired consistency.
6. Divide among serving bowls and sprinkle with the parsley and parmesan, crumbled feta or a dollop of yoghurt. Serve alongside steamed vegetables or salad leaves.

NUTRITION NOTE When you're cooking a family meal that young babies or toddlers will also be eating, use no-added-salt or reduced-salt ingredients and avoid adding salt to minimise their intake. You can use a combination of stock and water in this recipe if you wish to decrease the salt further.

STORAGE Keep in an airtight container in the fridge for up to 2 days. Alternatively, freeze individual or family-sized portions in airtight containers for up to 2 months.

ALLERGIES/INTOLERANCES ***Gluten/wheat:*** replace the risoni with arborio rice or quinoa. Cook until the rice or quinoa is tender and the liquid is absorbed – it may take a little longer than the risoni. Use gluten-free stock. ***Dairy:*** omit the grated parmesan, feta or yoghurt.

FUSSY EATING TIP
This simple tempura batter gives fish a light crispy coating, which might encourage acceptance and enjoyment of fish in kids who prefer crunchy textures.

TEMPURA FISH AND SWEET POTATO FRIES

SERVES 4
PREP TIME 15 minutes
COOKING TIME 40 minutes

1 large sweet potato, peeled and cut into 1 cm-thick chips
1 tablespoon olive oil
⅔ cup (100 g) cornflour
salt and pepper, to taste (optional)
½ cup (125 ml) ice-cold soda water
1 cup (250 ml) rice bran oil
400 g skinless, boneless white fish fillets (such as such as flathead, blue-eye trevalla, bream), cut into 1.5 cm-thick strips
mixed salad leaves, to serve

Cooking 'take-away' style meals at home adds some fun to everyday mealtimes and inspires positive sensory experiences for children. Try serving these homemade fish and chips in a paper cone or some brown paper and having your evening meal outdoors. A break in routine might be just the thing to disrupt a pattern of fussy eating behaviour.

1. Preheat the oven to 200°C (180°C fan-forced) and line a large baking tray with baking paper.
2. Place the sweet potato chips in a single layer on another large baking tray. Drizzle with the olive oil, then toss to coat. Bake, turning the chips halfway through cooking, for 35–40 minutes or until tender and golden.
3. Ten minutes before the sweet potato will be ready, place the cornflour in a bowl, season with salt and pepper if cooking for older children and adults, and gradually whisk in the soda water, a little at a time, until you have a smooth batter.
4. Heat the oil in a wok or deep, heavy-based frying pan over medium–high heat. To test whether the oil is hot enough, add a small cube of bread to the oil. If it bubbles and sizzles rapidly, the oil is ready.
5. Pat the fish dry with paper towel. Working in batches to avoid overcrowding, dip the fish in the batter and lower gently into the hot oil. Cook for 2–3 minutes, turning to ensure even cooking, or until the batter is crisp and light golden, and the fish is cooked through. Drain on a wire rack lined with paper towel. You can twice-cook the fish for a crispier batter: return the cooked fish to the hot oil, in batches, for a further 10–20 seconds. Drain on clean paper towel.
6. Serve the tempura fish with the sweet potato fries and salad leaves.

STORAGE This is best enjoyed fresh, but will keep in airtight containers in the fridge (the fish for up to 1 day and the chips for up to 3 days).

SAFETY NOTE Always ensure the safety of your children when cooking with hot oil and frying food.

BEEF, LENTIL AND MUSHROOM PIE

MAKES 1 FAMILY-SIZED PIE
PREP TIME 20 minutes
COOKING TIME 50 minutes

- 1 tablespoon olive oil, plus extra for greasing
- 2 onions, finely chopped
- 300 g premium lean beef mince
- 200 g button mushrooms, thinly sliced
- 400 g tin brown lentils, drained and rinsed
- 1 cup (250 ml) salt-reduced beef stock
- 2 tablespoons no-added-salt tomato paste (puree)
- 1 tablespoon Worcestershire sauce
- 1 tablespoon cornflour
- 1 sheet (25 cm × 25 cm) frozen ready-rolled puff pastry, just thawed
- 1 egg, lightly whisked
- steamed vegetables or salad, to serve
- Sweet potato fries (see page 65), to serve (optional)

Adding vegetables to homemade pie fillings is a great way to boost your child's veggie intake. Try stirring through a cup of grated vegetables, or omit the pastry and top with a vegetable mash instead. If your child is fussy with veggies, you can also make a 'hidden vegetable' sauce (see page 236) to dollop on top.

1. Preheat the oven to 200°C (180°C fan-forced) and grease a round 20 cm pie dish with olive oil.
2. Heat the olive oil in a large heavy-based frying pan over medium heat. Add the onion and sauté for 5 minutes or until soft. Add the beef mince and cook, breaking it up with a wooden spoon, for 5 minutes or until browned. Add the mushroom and lentils and stir to combine.
3. Combine the beef stock, tomato paste, Worcestershire sauce and cornflour in a jug. Pour over the beef mixture, stir to combine and bring to the boil. Reduce the heat and simmer for 10 minutes or until the mixture is thick.
4. Pour the beef filling into the pie dish. Top with the pastry, trim the edges and press down to seal. Cut the pastry trimmings into letters or shapes to decorate the pie if you like. Brush the pastry with the egg and bake for 25–30 minutes or until the pastry is golden brown.
5. Slice the pie into portions and serve with steamed vegetables or a vibrant garden salad and sweet potato fries, if desired.

NUTRITION NOTE Tinned lentils are an economical and nutritious way to bulk up meals. They are high in fibre, a good source of protein and quality carbohydrates, and a vegetarian source of iron.

STORAGE Keep in an airtight container in the fridge for up to 2 days. To freeze the pie, use a disposable pie dish and place the uncooked pie, covered well with plastic film, in the freezer for up to 2 months. Thaw in the fridge overnight, brush the pastry with egg and bake as above.

ALLERGIES/INTOLERANCES ***Gluten/wheat:*** use gluten- or wheat-free pastry, or top the pie with mashed potato or sweet potato instead of pastry. Use gluten-free Worcestershire sauce (or omit it) and stock. ***Egg:*** use egg-free pastry and brush with milk or water before baking.

TIP

To make a mini pie for your toddler, cut out 2 circles of mountain bread, about 2 cm larger than the holes of a regular muffin tin. Layer the circles of bread inside a greased muffin hole to line it. Bake in a 180°C (160°C fan-forced) oven for 5 minutes or until golden. Spoon 1–2 tablespoons of warm beef filling into the bread crust and sprinkle with grated cheese. Bake for 2–5 minutes or until the cheese has melted.

VEGGIE, TOMATO AND QUINOA SOUP

SERVES 6
PREP TIME 15 minutes
COOKING TIME 45 minutes

1 tablespoon olive oil
½ small sweet potato, peeled and diced
1 leek, white part only, finely chopped
1 stalk celery, trimmed and finely diced
1 zucchini (courgette), diced
1 carrot, diced
1 clove garlic, finely chopped
1 litre homemade vegetable stock or chicken stock (see page 240)
400 g tin no-added-salt chopped tomatoes
½ cup (95 g) quinoa, rinsed
2 bay leaves
400 g tin chickpeas, drained and rinsed
½ cup (60 g) frozen peas
small handful of flat-leaf parsley, roughly chopped, plus extra for garnish (optional)
freshly ground pepper, to taste (optional)
grated parmesan, to serve (optional)

This is a super-simple, veggie-packed, family-friendly soup. You can replace the quinoa with chickpeas, cannellini beans, lentils, barley or small pasta, such as risoni, if you like. Simply modify the cooking time as appropriate.

1. Heat the olive oil in a large heavy-based saucepan over medium heat. Add the sweet potato, leek, celery, zucchini, carrot and garlic and cook, stirring, for 10 minutes or until softened, being careful not to let them brown.
2. Add the stock, tomato, quinoa, bay leaves and 1 cup (250 ml) water, increase the heat to high and bring to the boil. Reduce the heat and simmer, partially covered, for 25 minutes or until the quinoa is tender.
3. Add the chickpeas and peas and cook for a further 2–3 minutes or until the peas are tender. Stir through the parsley and season with pepper, if using. Serve sprinkled with extra parsley and grated parmesan, if desired.

NUTRITION NOTE Soups are a nutritious and warming way to maintain a varied, well-balanced and nutrient-rich diet throughout the winter months.

TIPS For young babies, use a slotted spoon to scoop some veggies and quinoa from the soup, add a little water and mash or puree. Toddlers may prefer a thicker soup – use a slotted spoon to scoop out some of the veggies, then add a small amount of the liquid.

STORAGE Keep leftover soup in an airtight container in the fridge for up to 3 days. Alternatively, freeze individual portions in airtight containers for up to 3 months.

ALLERGIES/INTOLERANCES ***Dairy:*** omit the parmesan.

VEGETABLE RATATOUILLE LASAGNE

SERVES 6–8
PREP TIME 15 minutes
COOKING TIME 1 hour 25 minutes

- 1 tablespoon olive oil
- 1 onion, finely chopped
- 1 large clove garlic, finely chopped
- 2 zucchinis (courgettes), diced
- 1 eggplant (aubergine), diced
- 1 small red capsicum (pepper), seeded and diced
- 1 ripe tomato, diced
- 400 g tin no-added-salt chopped tomatoes
- ¼ teaspoon dried oregano
- 3 sprigs thyme, leaves only
- 40 g baby spinach leaves, roughly chopped
- 250 g dried lasagne sheets
- 500 g fresh ricotta
- 2 tablespoons Spinach, broccoli and cashew pesto (see page 236) or Basil pesto (see page 232) (optional)
- 1½ cups (150 g) grated mozzarella or tasty cheese

You won't believe how easy it is to make this delicious vegetable lasagne. Adding a tin of chickpeas, cannellini beans or lentils to the ratatouille mix would also work beautifully and provide additional protein, fibre and iron.

1. Preheat the oven to 180°C (160°C fan-forced).
2. Heat the oil in a large heavy-based saucepan over medium heat. Add the onion and sauté for 4 minutes or until softened, being careful not to let it brown. Add the garlic and sauté for a further minute.
3. Add the zucchini, eggplant and capsicum to the pan and cook, stirring, for 5 minutes or until the vegetables are softened. Add the diced tomato, chopped tomato, ½ cup (125 ml) water, oregano and thyme and simmer, covered, for 15 minutes. Uncover and simmer, stirring occasionally, for a further 15 minutes or until thickened. Stir through the baby spinach.
4. Spread one-fifth (about 1 cup) of the sauce over the base of a 2.5-litre square baking dish. Layer the lasagne sheets on top, then cover with half the remaining sauce. Dot with half the ricotta, then half the pesto, if using, and sprinkle with ½ cup (50 g) grated cheese. Repeat with another layer of lasagne sheets, then the remaining ratatouille mixture, ricotta, pesto, if using, and cheese.
5. Bake for 40–45 minutes or until the lasagne is al dente and the cheese is golden and bubbling.

NUTRITION NOTE Veggies are packed full of vitamins, minerals, fibre and many other antioxidants and natural plant chemicals that promote optimal growth and good health, and help prevent sickness and disease.

STORAGE Keep in an airtight container in the fridge for up to 3 days. Alternatively, freeze individual portions in airtight containers for up to 3 months.

✱ALLERGIES/INTOLERANCES ***Gluten/wheat:*** use gluten- or wheat-free lasagne sheets. ***Dairy:*** serve the ratatouille sauce spooned over cooked pasta (such as spirals). Omit the ricotta, pesto and grated cheese. ***Egg:*** use egg-free lasagne sheets.

STICKY HONEY CHICKEN WITH RICE AND BOK CHOY

SERVES 4
PREP TIME 10 minutes
COOKING TIME 25 minutes

¼ cup (70 g) honey
2 tablespoons salt-reduced soy sauce
1 tablespoon pure maple syrup
1 small clove garlic, finely chopped
500 g chicken thigh fillets, fat trimmed and diced
¼ cup (35 g) cornflour
2 tablespoons rice bran oil
½ small onion, finely chopped
2 baby bok choy, trimmed and leaves separated
sesame seeds and coriander leaves, to serve (optional)
steamed brown rice, to serve

A true crowd-pleaser, this dinner is both delicious and easy to make. Preschoolers and older children will love hearing that sticky honey chicken is on the menu and you shouldn't have any trouble getting them to eat it.

1. Mix the honey, soy sauce, maple syrup and garlic in a small bowl. Set aside.
2. Place the chicken in a bowl, add the cornflour and toss to coat evenly. Heat the rice bran oil in a large heavy-based saucepan over medium-high heat. Cook the chicken, stirring often, for 1–2 minutes or until browned all over (you may need to do this in two batches to avoid overcrowding the pan). Add the onion and cook, stirring, for a further 2 minutes.
3. Pour the soy sauce mixture over the chicken and onion. Bring to the boil over high heat, then reduce the heat to low, cover and cook for 10 minutes, stirring occasionally to prevent the sauce sticking. Remove the lid and cook for a further 10 minutes or until the sauce has thickened and the chicken is cooked through.
4. Meanwhile, steam or blanch the bok choy in a saucepan of boiling water for 1–2 minutes, until just tender. Drain well.
5. Serve the chicken sprinkled with sesame seeds and coriander, if using, and with the bok choy and steamed rice alongside.

NUTRITION NOTE Asian-style meals are popular with little kids due to their sweet and salty flavour, and can be a familiar way to encourage them to try new foods. However, be mindful of the high salt content of Asian sauces and limit the amount served alongside the meals of younger children.

STORAGE This recipe is best enjoyed fresh, though leftovers will keep in an airtight container in the fridge for up to 2 days.

ALLERGIES/INTOLERANCES Replace the honey for babies under 12 months with additional maple syrup. ***Gluten/wheat:*** use gluten-free soy sauce. ***Sesame:*** omit the sesame seeds.

PIZZA WITH THREE TOPPINGS

MAKES 3 x 30 CM PIZZAS
PREP TIME 10 minutes
(+ 1 hour 10 minutes resting)
COOKING TIME 15 minutes

2 teaspoons (15 g) dried yeast
1 teaspoon caster sugar
1½ cups (375 ml) lukewarm water
3½ cups (525 g) '00' or baker's plain flour, plus extra for dusting
1 teaspoon salt
1 tablespoon olive oil

Cooking pizza with your kids is a lovely bonding activity that encourages respect of food and nutrition, and teaches life skills such as activating yeast, kneading and rolling dough, and being creative with toppings.

1. Place the yeast, sugar and water in a bowl and mix well to combine. Set aside in a warm, draught-free place for 10 minutes or until frothy (if it isn't frothy, the yeast has not activated and you'll need to start again).
2. Sift the flour and salt together into a bowl. Add the yeast mixture and use floured hands to mix to a soft dough. Turn out onto a lightly floured surface and knead for a few minutes or until smooth and elastic. If the mixture is too sticky to handle, add more flour, 1 tablespoon at a time.
3. Divide the dough into three equal balls. Place on a floured tray and cover with a clean tea towel. Set aside in a warm, draught-free place to prove for 1 hour or until the balls have doubled in size.
4. Preheat the oven to 220°C (200°C fan-forced) and lightly dust a pizza tray with flour.
5. Use a floured rolling pin to roll out a ball of dough on a lightly floured surface to a rustic circle, about 2–3 mm thick. Place on the tray and spread with Hidden veggie sauce (see page 236), Basil pesto (see page 232), Spinach, broccoli and cashew pesto (see page 236) or no-added-salt tomato paste (puree), then add your desired toppings. (Alternatively, see recipes on opposite page.) Bake for 15 minutes or until the base is crisp.

NUTRITION NOTE Pizzas are usually a popular dinner option and you can use lots of fresh and wholesome ingredients for the toppings, so take the chance to introduce your kids to a range of healthy foods in a positive way.

STORAGE Par-bake the pizza bases for 10 minutes or until light golden and starting to crisp. Set aside to cool, then wrap individually in plastic film, place in large freezer bags and freeze for up to 1 month.

ALLERGIES/INTOLERANCES ***Gluten/wheat:*** Use bought gluten-free pizza bases instead of making the dough.

SPINACH, HAM AND CHEESE

MAKES ENOUGH FOR A 30 CM PIZZA

¼ cup (70 g) Hidden veggie sauce (see page 236)
1 cup (120 g) grated cheddar cheese
½ cup (10 g) baby spinach
80 g thickly sliced good-quality ham, finely chopped

1 Preheat the oven to 220°C (200°C fan-forced).
2 Spread the pizza base with the hidden veggie sauce, then top with cheese, spinach and ham. Bake for 15 minutes or until the base is crisp.

SWEET POTATO, MUSHROOM AND CHEESE

MAKES ENOUGH FOR A 30 CM PIZZA

200 g sweet potato, peeled and cut into 1 cm cubes
1 tablespoon olive oil
¼ cup (80 g) Spinach, broccoli and cashew pesto (see page 236)
1 cup (120 g) grated cheddar cheese
60 g button mushrooms, thinly sliced

1 Preheat the oven to 220°C (200°C fan-forced).
2 Place the sweet potato cubes on a lined baking tray. Drizzle with the olive oil and toss to coat. Bake for 10–15 minutes or until softened.
3 Spread the pizza base with the pesto, then top with cheese, mushrooms and sweet potato. Bake for 15 minutes or until the base is crisp.

PRAWN AND PESTO

MAKES ENOUGH FOR A 30 CM PIZZA

150 g raw prawns, peeled and deveined
1 clove garlic, crushed
1 tablespoon olive oil
2–3 tablespoons Basil pesto (see page 232)
1 cup (120 g) grated cheddar cheese
1 tablespoon finely chopped red onion
¼ cup (50 g) feta (optional)

1 Preheat the oven to 220°C (200°C fan-forced).
2 Combine the prawns and garlic in a bowl. Heat the oil in a small heavy-based frying pan over medium heat. Cook the prawns, stirring, for 2 minutes or until cooked through. Remove from the heat.
3 Spread the pizza base with the basil pesto, then top with cheese, onion, prawns and feta, if using. Bake for 15 minutes or until the base is crisp.

APPLE AND PEAR CRUMBLE

SERVES 4–6
PREP TIME 10 minutes
COOKING TIME 40 minutes

3 granny smith apples, peeled, cored and cut into chunks or slices
1½ tablespoons brown sugar
¾ teaspoon ground cinnamon
2 firm, ripe pears, peeled, cored and cut into chunks or slices
½ cup (80 g) wholemeal plain flour
1 cup (90 g) rolled oats
75 g butter, chilled and cubed
Simple custard (see page 241), to serve

We challenge any child to resist this scrumptious apple crumble, naturally sweetened with ripe fruit and topped with a fragrant and crunchy cinnamon crumble. Finish it off with a drizzle of homemade custard and you are sure to delight even the fussiest eater.

1. Preheat the oven to 180°C (160°C fan-forced).
2. Place the apple in a small heavy-based saucepan with 2 teaspoons of the sugar, ¼ teaspoon of the cinnamon and ¼ cup (60 ml) water. Cover and cook over medium heat for 5 minutes. Add the pear and cook, uncovered, stirring occasionally, for 5 minutes or until the apple is just tender. Remove from the heat.
3. Combine the flour, oats and remaining sugar and cinnamon in a bowl. Use your fingertips to rub in the butter until the mixture resembles coarse breadcrumbs.
4. Place the apple mixture in a 1.5-litre capacity baking dish. Scatter the crumble mixture over the top and bake for 30 minutes or until the crumble is golden. Serve the warm crumble with custard.

NUTRITION NOTE Simple swaps, such as wholemeal flour for white flour, and macadamia oil for butter (see Allergies/Intolerances, below) add a little more nutrition to this 'sometimes' food.

STORAGE Keep leftover crumble in an airtight container in the fridge for up to 2 days. The assembled, uncooked crumble can be made in a disposable pie dish and frozen, wrapped well in plastic film, for up to 2 months.

ALLERGIES/INTOLERANCES ***Gluten/wheat:*** use quinoa flakes instead of oats and gluten- or wheat-free flour. ***Dairy:*** use ¼ cup (60 ml) macadamia oil or melted coconut oil instead of butter.

CHAPTER 3

ACCEPT THE MESS

Every parent will attest that small children can make an extraordinary amount of mess at mealtimes. Food ends up on the floor, the chair, their clothes, face and hair, and on the walls if you're really unlucky! Children explore food by playing with it, so all that mess is usually a by-product of the learning process. Take a deep breath, accept it's a natural part of the feeding journey and stay positive, because anger and frustration do not make for happy mealtimes.

Young children have limited fine motor skills, so they learn how to eat by smelling, touching and feeling their food, as well as tasting it. While it may look as though they're just having fun with it, they are actually exploring all the sensory messages that each item of food brings. It can be frustrating to watch, but staying calm and encouraging them will pay off in the long run.

PLAYING WITH PURPOSE

The act of eating seems simple to us, but we are used to absorbing and processing all the sensory information we receive from food, such as the colours, aromas, textures and flavours. When children poke, touch, squish, squeeze, lick and even spit out food they are exploring it, and doing this without reproach makes the experience more relaxing and enjoyable. Scraping around their mouth with a spoon or attempting to wipe their face during the meal can negate the idea that mess is okay, and may even feel like punishment. This is particularly true for children who are sensitive to touch. (Of course, if they indicate that they'd like their hands or face cleaned during a meal, it's fine to do this.) So, next time they squish a meatball between their fingers, smear yoghurt over their face or shred a broccoli floret, just view it as a learning experience. Invest in a big splash mat, feeding smocks to keep their clothes a little cleaner and some wipe-clean bibs, and remember that, like all phases, this too shall pass.

SPITTING OUT FOOD

At some point in your babies' food journey, they may begin to spit out food after a single bite or just a few little chews. This may simply be a sign of distaste or fullness, but it can also be a natural part of the learning process. Once children have processed all the sensory information they've received about a food and feel comfortable enough to try it, they will put it in their mouth. They now need to process further information about how it feels in their mouth. If the texture is unfamiliar, they may spit it out straight away. If the flavour is unfamiliar, they may chew it a few times before they spit it out. Give them time to explore the food; they may want to try it again straight away or they may need to be exposed to it a few more times before they are ready to taste it again.

Spitting out food can also be a survival instinct. Children need to feel comfortable and safe getting food out of their mouth before they will want to swallow it. If they aren't able to spit a food out, they may be more likely to gag or choke on it. So if it is new, more textured or requires more effort to chew, they may spit out the first few mouthfuls before they attempt to swallow it. Babies and toddlers often struggle with harder-to-chew textures such as red meat and will spit it out while they are learning to eat until they have the oral motor skills required to chew and swallow it. Allowing your child to spit out food for this reason creates the secure environment they need to explore new tastes and textures. Provide a napkin or small bowl if necessary.

Another reason for spitting out food could be that their appetite is satisfied and they don't want anything more to eat. Being able to recognise this signal and respect their hunger and fullness cues (see page 165) by removing their plate of food will help keep mealtimes relaxed. Avoid giving this behaviour too much attention or they will do it more often. Instead, develop some simple sign language to help them communicate their feelings of fullness.

THROWING FOOD

Babies love to drop food on the floor at mealtimes – it's a little experiment to see what will happen. A frustrated parent is a guaranteed result, not only because it makes a mess, but also because it's a waste of food. But before you let the frustration show, consider what they're doing. If it is simply a game and they want your attention, pick up the food, place it just to the side of their meal and say, 'Food stays on the table'. On the other hand, if it seems that your baby is dropping food to indicate they have had enough to eat or are bored, remove the food and signal that the mealtime is over. Give minimal attention to the throwing of the food and praise positive eating behaviours instead. It takes patience and consistency, but eventually your baby will lose interest in throwing food.

If the behaviour continues, or your child begins refusing meals altogether or grazing, look at your mealtime schedule (see pages 164–165) – they may be having too many snacks or the meal could be too late and they are tired.

AVOID DISTRACTIONS

The use of distractions, such as the television, iPad, toys and books, should never be a solution for fussy eating behaviours. Children need to concentrate on the flavours and textures of the food they are eating, the etiquette of mealtimes and their feelings of hunger and fullness. This is essential for good eating habits, including self-regulation, in the long term. Discuss the mealtime routine with your children so they know what to expect and what is not allowed. Going over the rules together makes it more likely that they'll be obeyed. Ensure that all technology is switched off before coming to the table and then reward their good behaviour with lots of attention as you talk and enjoy the meal together. If your mealtimes are reliant on technology and you are worried about what may happen when the iPad or TV is switched off, make changes gradually, such as moving the meal from the couch to the table and allowing that to become routine before removing the technology. Make sure you keep mealtimes relaxed and fun, without any pressure or anxiety.

BABY-LED WEANING

This is a method of introducing solid foods to babies at around 6 months of age whereby they feed themselves without the need for spoons or pureed food of any kind. Always remember to choose age-appropriate nutritious foods, being mindful to avoid processed foods high in added salt and sugar.

Baby-led weaning (BLW) basics:

- Your baby must put food in their mouth themselves – nobody else should feed them
- Do not offer whole nuts or hard, inappropriate foods
- Never leave your baby alone with food
- The first foods you provide should be the same as parent-led weaning (regular feeding), but in finger food form. The food should be easy to pick up, such as long sticks of steamed sweet potato
- To adapt puree recipes, chop each ingredient into appropriate finger foods instead of pureeing or mashing. Some babies may like to scoop up mouthfuls of mixed-textured meals like spaghetti bolognese or risotto with their hands
- Introduce new shapes and textures gradually, so your baby can handle new foods at their own pace
- Where possible, offer your baby the same foods that you are eating. Include your baby in family mealtimes, so they can learn how to eat by copying you
- Explain BLW in detail to anyone caring for your baby.

INTRODUCING THE SIPPY CUP

When your baby is 6 months old, around the time of starting solids, it is recommended you introduce a sippy cup of cooled, boiled water. The sippy cup is important for your baby's oral motor skills as it teaches them how to drink from a cup. They already know how to suck, so learning how to sip is the next step.

Choose a cup without an anti-leak valve or one with a valve that can be easily removed, so it encourages your child to sip rather than suck. At first, they will probably spit out more water than they swallow, but as they develop the skill they will become much more capable. When they're ready, progress to a cup with a straw. When you're at home or outside and spillages aren't a worry, offer them an open cup so they can practise with it from an early age.

When they first start with the sippy cup, breastmilk and/or infant formula will continue to be their main drink so they may not drink much from the cup. But as they become more established on solids, offering water at every meal and snack time, and occasional sips in between, helps with hydration and can prevent constipation. After 12 months, whether you are continuing to breastfeed or have transitioned to cow's milk, water will become your baby's main drink. Steer clear of sugary drinks such as juices, cordials, soft drinks and sport drinks, as they may reduce their appetite for food and contribute to dental caries and childhood obesity.

BLW is messy, as your child is navigating different foods and mastering their fine motor skills. It can be very tiring at first, but try not to rush or distract them while they are experimenting with food.

CHICKEN AND ZUCCHINI NUGGETS

MAKES 25–30
PREP TIME 10 minutes
COOKING TIME 16 minutes

500 g free-range chicken mince
2 tablespoons milk
1 cup (100 g) packaged wholemeal breadcrumbs
1 small zucchini (courgette), coarsely grated
1 golden shallot, finely diced
1 heaped tablespoon finely chopped flat-leaf parsley
1 tablespoon olive oil or rice bran oil

Nuggets are a popular choice for kids because they are bite-sized and delicious, and when you make your own you can choose what goes in them. You can also use this mixture to make six large burger patties for older children and adults. Pan-fry until cooked through and serve on a roll with avocado, rocket and mayonnaise.

1. Combine all the ingredients, except the oil, in a large bowl. Use your hands or a wooden spoon to mix until thoroughly combined.
2. Shape tablespoons of the mixture into nuggets and place on a tray lined with baking paper.
3. Heat the oil in a large heavy-based frying pan over medium heat. Cook the nuggets, in batches to avoid overcrowding the pan, for 4 minutes each side or until light golden and cooked through. Transfer to paper towel to drain.

FUSSY EATING TIP Chicken nuggets are a great vessel for introducing new flavours. Try adding grated carrot, sautéed chopped mushrooms, finely chopped spinach and a variety of herbs, such as thyme and basil.

TIP You can lightly fry the shallot before adding it to the mixture, if desired.

STORAGE Keep in an airtight container in the fridge for up to 2 days. To freeze, place uncooked or cooked nuggets on a baking tray lined with baking paper and freeze for 3–4 hours, then transfer to a freezer bag and freeze for up to 2 months.

*ALLERGIES/INTOLERANCES ***Gluten/wheat:*** use gluten- or wheat-free breadcrumbs, or a cup of quinoa flakes or cooked quinoa instead of the breadcrumbs. ***Dairy:*** use a dairy-free milk alternative.

(F)

CREAMY CHICKEN AND CAULIFLOWER CREPES

MAKES 8
PREP TIME 15 minutes
COOKING TIME 50 minutes

- 2 eggs
- 2 cups (500 ml) milk
- 1 tablespoon olive oil
- 1½ cups (225 g) wholemeal plain flour or plain flour
- 1 teaspoon unsalted butter or olive oil, plus extra for greasing
- 200 g chicken breast fillet, fat trimmed, finely chopped
- ½ leek, white part only, thinly sliced
- 1 small clove garlic, crushed
- 1 cup (250 ml) salt-reduced chicken stock, homemade chicken stock (see page 240) or water
- 1½ cups (160 g) finely chopped cauliflower florets
- 2–3 tablespoons pouring cream
- pinch of dried thyme
- ½ cup (100 g) fresh ricotta (optional)
- ½ cup (60 g) grated cheddar cheese

Crepes make a delicious savoury meal for kids of all ages, from a soft first finger food to substantial family dinner. Adapt the filling to include your favourite veggies or protein.

1. Whisk the eggs, milk, olive oil and flour together in a jug until smooth. Place the batter in the fridge to rest.
2. Meanwhile, heat the butter or oil in a heavy-based saucepan or frying pan over medium heat. Add the chicken and cook for 2–3 minutes or until light golden. Add the leek and garlic and sauté for 3 minutes or until soft. Pour in the stock or water, add the cauliflower and bring to the boil. Cook for 10 minutes or until the chicken is cooked through and the cauliflower is tender. Add the cream and thyme and stir to combine. Turn off the heat, but leave the pan on the stovetop as the sauce will continue to thicken.
3. Preheat the oven to 200°C (180°C fan-forced) and line a baking tray with baking paper.
4. Heat a non-stick frying pan over medium heat. Grease the pan with some butter or oil. Pour in ¼ cup (60 ml) of batter and quickly tilt the pan in a circular motion until it covers the base. Cook until the edges begin to curl, then flip and cook until golden. Place on a plate and cover with foil. Repeat with the remaining batter to make 8 crepes in total.
5. Spoon one-eighth of the chicken mixture over the edge of a crepe. Gently roll the crepe over once, then add a dollop of ricotta and continue to roll. Place the crepe, seam-side down, on the lined tray. Repeat to fill the remaining crepes. Sprinkle the rolled crepes with cheese and bake for 10 minutes or until melted. Remove from the oven and serve.

FUSSY EATING TIP Children may need to be exposed to a new food up to 20 times before they become familiar with it and accept it. To help reduce anxiety around new meals, serve foods you know they love and enjoy alongside them. Knowing there is something on their plate that they will eat can also help reduce your own stress levels.

STORAGE Keep leftovers in an airtight container in the fridge for up to 1 day. Cooked, unfilled crepes can be frozen in a freezer bag, separated with freezer paper, for up to 2 months.

✱ALLERGIES/INTOLERANCES ***Gluten/wheat:*** use gluten- or wheat-free flour.

(F)

BABY LASAGNE FINGERS

MAKES 6
PREP TIME 20 minutes
COOKING TIME 30 minutes

25 g butter
1 tablespoon plain flour
1½ cups (375 ml) milk
100 g grated cheddar cheese
ground black pepper, to taste (optional)
2¼ cups (560 g) Basic Bolognese (see page 237)
250 g dried lasagne sheets
steamed vegetables and chopped fruit, to serve

Lasagne is a popular 'first' family meal for many babies. When you use a veggie-packed homemade bolognese sauce, it's also a nutrient-rich choice. Simply mash a portion and spoon-feed to your baby or slice into fingers for independent self-feeders.

1. Preheat the oven to 190°C (170°C fan-forced).
2. Melt the butter in a small heavy-based saucepan over medium heat. Add the flour and stir to form a smooth paste. Gradually whisk in the milk and continue whisking until the sauce boils and thickens. Add ⅓ cup (40 g) of the cheese and season with pepper, if using, then stir until smooth and combined. Remove from the heat.
3. Spread ¼ cup (60 g) of the bolognese sauce over the base of a 22 cm × 12 cm loaf tin. Top with a layer of lasagne sheets, then spread over half the remaining bolognese. Spoon over half the white sauce, sprinkle over half the remaining cheese, then add another layer of lasagne sheets. Repeat with the remaining bolognese, white sauce and cheese.
4. Bake the lasagne for 25–30 minutes or until golden brown. Remove from the oven and allow to cool a little, then slice into 6 fingers and serve with vegetables and fruit alongside.

FUSSY EATING TIP It's important to serve babies a variety of iron- and zinc-rich meals, as these nutrients are essential for normal growth and development.

STORAGE Keep in an airtight container in the fridge for up to 2 days. Alternatively, freeze individual portions in freezer bags or airtight containers for up to 2 months.

✱ALLERGIES/INTOLERANCES ***Gluten/wheat:*** use gluten- or wheat-free lasagne sheets or use thin slices of zucchini as an alternative to pasta. ***Dairy:*** serve the bolognese sauce with small pasta, such as risoni or star pasta, instead of making lasagne. ***Egg:*** use egg-free lasagne sheets.

CRISPY POLENTA PORK FINGERS

MAKES 12
PREP TIME 15 minutes
COOKING TIME 10 minutes

2 free-range pork fillets, halved lengthways and each piece cut into three long strips
¼ cup (60 ml) your preferred milk
¼ cup (40 g) polenta
1 teaspoon smoked paprika
2 tablespoons olive oil or rice bran oil

A fabulous finger food for busy weeknights, babies and young toddlers can enjoy these as is, while older children might enjoy them burger-style with our yummy Carrot, apple and fennel coleslaw (see page 241).

1 Use a rolling pin or meat mallet to pound the pieces of pork until they are about 1 cm thick. Place the milk and combined polenta and paprika in separate shallow bowls.

2 Dip a piece of pork in the milk, then in the polenta mixture, turning to coat evenly. Place on a plate and repeat to coat the remaining pieces of pork.

3 Heat the oil in a large heavy-based frying pan over medium heat. Cook the pork, in batches if necessary to avoid overcrowding the pan and adding a little more oil if required, for 1–2 minutes each side or until golden and cooked through.

FUSSY EATING TIP While minced meat is an easy option for babies, giving them strips of meat that are cooked until tender (not overcooked and tough) as finger food helps them become more accepting of, and capable of eating, a wider variety of meats.

STORAGE Keep in an airtight container in the fridge for up to 2 days. Crumbed, uncooked pork can be frozen in a freezer bag, separated with sheets of freezer paper, for up to 2 months.

ALLERGIES/INTOLERANCES ***Dairy:*** use water instead of milk.

CRUMBED FISH BITES

Making your own fish fingers is really easy and they're miles tastier and healthier than the commercial ones.

SERVES 3–4
PREP TIME 15 minutes
COOKING TIME 10 minutes

½ cup (75 g) plain flour
1 egg, lightly whisked
½ cup (35 g) fresh multigrain breadcrumbs
¼ cup (50 g) quinoa flakes
220 g flathead fillets or other firm white fish fillets, cut into 2–3 cm pieces
¼ cup (60 ml) olive oil or rice bran oil
roasted vegetable fingers and chopped fruit, to serve

1 Place the flour, egg and combined breadcrumbs and quinoa in three separate shallow bowls.

2 Working with one piece of fish at a time, add to the flour and toss to coat, then dust off the excess and dip in the egg, then coat in the breadcrumb mix.

3 Heat the oil in a large heavy-based frying pan over medium–high heat. Cook the fish bites, in batches, for 1–2 minutes each side or until golden and cooked through. Transfer to paper towel to drain. Serve with the vegetable fingers and fruit.

NUTRITION NOTE High in protein and a source of selenium and omega-3 fatty acids, fish is an immune-boosting food that helps keep kids fit and well.

STORAGE Keep in an airtight container in the fridge for up to 2 days. Crumbed, uncooked fish can be frozen in a freezer bag, separated with sheets of freezer paper, for up to 2 months.

*ALLERGIES/INTOLERANCES ***Gluten/wheat:*** use gluten-free flour, such as rice flour, and replace the breadcrumbs with additional quinoa flakes or gluten-free breadcrumbs. **Egg:** use plain Greek-style yoghurt instead of the egg.

RAINBOW VEGETABLE SHREDDIES »

Vegetable shreddies are a well-loved recipe on the One Handed Cooks website. You can mix up the selection of veggies to take advantage of seasonal produce or cater to your child's preferences.

MAKES 16
PREP TIME 10 minutes
COOKING TIME 16 minutes

1 zucchini (courgette), coarsely grated
½ small sweet potato, coarsely grated
50 g broccoli florets, finely chopped
½ small onion, finely chopped
1 tablespoon finely chopped herb (such as parsley, coriander or thyme)
1 egg, lightly whisked
2 tablespoons wholemeal plain flour
2 tablespoons rice bran oil

1 Squeeze out the excess liquid from the zucchini and sweet potato and pat dry with paper towel. Place all of the vegetables in a bowl, add the herb, egg and flour and stir until well combined.

2 Heat the oil in a large non-stick frying pan over medium heat. Dollop heaped tablespoons of mixture into the pan and carefully flatten each with a spatula. Cook for a few minutes or until the mixture holds together. Gently flip and continue cooking until both sides are golden and crisp. Remove from the pan and transfer to paper towel to drain. Continue to cook the remaining mixture. Serve.

STORAGE Keep in an airtight container in the fridge for up to 24 hours. Alternatively, place in a freezer bag, separated with sheets of freezer paper, and freeze for up to 1 month. Reheat in a 180°C oven (160°C fan-forced) for 10–15 minutes or pan-fry until warm and crisp.

*ALLERGIES/INTOLERANCES ***Gluten/wheat:*** use gluten- or wheat-free flour. ***Egg:*** omit the egg.

NUTRITION NOTE

Offering lots of colourful vegetables ensures your child gets the health-promoting natural plant chemicals called phytochemicals that they provide.

MINI QUICHES

MAKES 12
PREP TIME 10 minutes
COOKING TIME 30 minutes

3 eggs
⅓ cup (80 ml) pouring cream
1 golden shallot, finely diced
1½ sheets (25 cm × 25 cm) frozen ready-rolled puff pastry, just thawed
50 g thinly sliced good-quality ham, finely chopped
1 small zucchini (courgette), coarsely grated, liquid squeezed out
¾ cup (90 g) grated cheddar cheese

Serving eggs in a variety of ways, including hard-boiled, scrambled or in an irresistible mini quiche like this, will help to encourage the acceptance and enjoyment of this nutritious food. You can play with flavours and add different herbs and vegetables if you like. See the allergy notes below for an egg-free version and you can make them without the pastry, too.

1. Preheat the oven to 180°C (160°C fan-forced).
2. Whisk the eggs and cream together in a bowl. Whisk in the shallot.
3. Use a round 8 cm cutter to cut 12 rounds from the pastry. Ease the pastry rounds into the holes of a non-stick 12-hole regular muffin tin. Evenly distribute the ham, zucchini and cheese among the pastry cases and spoon 1–2 tablespoons of egg mixture over the top of each.
4. Bake the quiches for 30 minutes or until the pastry is golden and filling is set. Remove from the oven and transfer to a wire rack to cool. Serve warm or at room temperature.

NUTRITION NOTE Eggs are high in protein, offer over 10 essential vitamins and minerals, and are a source of omega-3 fatty acids.

STORAGE These are best enjoyed fresh, but can be kept in an airtight container in the fridge for up to 2 days. Alternatively, freeze in freezer bags for up to 1 month. There's no need to thaw them before reheating.

✱ALLERGIES/INTOLERANCES ***Gluten/wheat:*** use gluten-free pastry or simply omit the pastry. ***Dairy:*** use coconut cream instead of cream and omit the cheese. ***Egg:*** substitute 150 g firm tofu, ¼ cup (60 ml) thickened cream and ¼ cup (60 ml) milk for the eggs and pouring cream. Blend together, then add the shallot, ham, zucchini and cheese. Spoon the mixture into the pastry cases and cook for 30–40 minutes or until the filling is set.

BAKED FALAFELS

MAKES 25
PREP TIME 15 minutes
(+ overnight soaking; optional)
COOKING TIME 30 minutes

1 cup (200 g) dried chickpeas (or 400 g tin chickpeas, drained and rinsed)
¼ cup (60 ml) extra virgin olive oil, plus extra for brushing
½ onion, quartered
1 small carrot, coarsely grated
2 tablespoons chopped flat-leaf parsley
1 tablespoon fresh lemon juice
1 clove garlic, chopped
1 teaspoon ground cumin
½ teaspoon ground coriander
toasted pita bread, cucumber sticks and cheese, to serve

YOGHURT DIPPING SAUCE
200 g plain Greek-style yoghurt
1 teaspoon hulled tahini
2 teaspoons fresh lemon juice
½ clove garlic, crushed (optional)
freshly ground pepper, to taste

Including a meat-free meal in your weekly meal plan will encourage your child to increase their intake of vegetables and help them become more familiar with vegetarian protein sources, such as legumes. These little falafels make a lovely snack, sandwich or wrap filling, or finger food.

1 If using dried chickpeas, place in a large bowl and cover with plenty of cold water. Cover the bowl with a clean tea towel and set aside overnight to soak.
2 Preheat the oven to 200°C (180°C fan-forced) and line a baking tray with baking paper.
3 Drain and rinse the chickpeas, then place in a food processor with the olive oil, onion, carrot, parsley, lemon juice, garlic, cumin and coriander. Process to a coarse paste, being careful not to overmix. Roll tablespoons of the mixture into balls and place on the lined tray. Brush with the extra oil and bake for 25–30 minutes or golden brown.
4 Meanwhile, to make the yoghurt dipping sauce, combine all the ingredients in a small bowl.
5 Serve the falafels with the toasted pita bread, cucumber sticks, cheese and yoghurt dipping sauce.

NUTRITION NOTE These falafels are high in protein and fibre, and are a vegetarian source of iron and zinc.

STORAGE Keep leftovers in an airtight container in the fridge for up to 3 days. Alternatively, freeze individual portions of uncooked or cooked falafels in freezer bags or airtight containers for up to 3 months.

ALLERGIES/INTOLERANCES ***Gluten/wheat:*** omit the pita bread. ***Dairy:*** omit the yoghurt dipping sauce. ***Sesame:*** omit the tahini from the dipping sauce.

'CHOOSE YOUR OWN' SMOOTHIE

SERVES 2
PREP TIME 5 minutes
COOKING TIME Nil

½ frozen chopped banana
1 cup (250 ml) your preferred milk
½ cup (140 g) plain Greek-style yoghurt
75–150 g fruit and/or vegetables (such as berries, passionfruit, mango, pear, grated apple, pineapple, orange, kiwifruit, spinach, kale, avocado)

OPTIONAL EXTRAS

1 teaspoon sweetener (such as pure maple syrup or honey)
1 tablespoon pure nut butter
1 tablespoon chia seeds
2 tablespoons rolled oats
2 teaspoons cacao or cocoa powder

We've made many smoothies in our time and trying to narrow down our favourites to just one was simply too hard. So, here's a base recipe instead, and you can use it to encourage your kids to create their own delicious concoctions. They will love the independence and may even be inspired to try a new food in the process.

1 Place all the ingredients in a blender and blend until smooth. Serve.

NUTRITION NOTE An easy breakfast idea or nutritious snack, smoothies are high in calcium, a good source of protein and fibre, and often contain a serve or two of fruit and veg.

STORAGE Any leftover smoothie will keep, covered, in the fridge for up to 24 hours. Alternatively, freeze leftovers in small reusable pouches or covered ice cube trays for up to 1 month.

ALLERGIES/INTOLERANCES Do not use honey for babies under 12 months. ***Gluten/wheat:*** avoid oats as an optional extra. ***Dairy:*** choose a dairy-free milk alternative and omit the yoghurt.

TRI-FRUIT ICY POPS

MAKES 10
PREP TIME 10 minutes
(+ 5½ hours freezing)
COOKING TIME Nil

300 g seedless watermelon, rind removed and flesh chopped
honey or pure maple syrup, to taste (optional)
3 kiwifruit, peeled and diced
2 sweet oranges (such as navel), peeled and diced

Icy pops are a great way to serve fruit in a new and interesting way, let alone keep little bodies hydrated on a hot day. Ripe, seasonal fruit will have the most natural sweetness.

1. Place the watermelon in a food processor or blender and blend until smooth. Add a little honey or maple syrup to sweeten slightly, if required. Spoon into 10 popsicle moulds and place in the freezer for 30–45 minutes, until just set.
2. Place the kiwifruit in the cleaned food processor or blender and blend until smooth. Add a little honey or maple syrup to sweeten slightly, if required. Spoon into the popsicle moulds and return to the freezer for a further 30–45 minutes, until the kiwifruit layer is just set.
3. Place the orange in the cleaned food processor or blender and blend until smooth. Add a little honey or maple syrup to sweeten slightly, if required. Spoon into the popsicle moulds, being careful not to overfill them, then place the sticks or lids on and return to the freezer until frozen solid (this will take about 4 hours).
4. To remove, dip the moulds into warm water for a few seconds and then ease the icy pops out.

FUSSY EATING TIP Use whatever three fruits your child loves most. Or, try including two they love and one that might be new.

STORAGE Keep in the freezer for up to 2 months.

CHAPTER 4

LET PHASES COME AND GO

Every child goes through phases of eating less or refusing food. This may occur for many reasons – their body may be concentrating on growing, they may be mastering a new skill, a tooth could be pushing through or they may be feeling unwell. Try to pick up on these cues so you can work through the phase together, rather than getting upset and turning mealtimes into a negative experience.

These are eight of the most common reasons for food refusal or selective eating, and we've given suggestions to help you deal with each. As always, seek professional medical advice if you have any concerns regarding your child's food intake, behaviour or general wellbeing (see When to seek help on page 3 for more information).

SPOON REFUSAL

Although it's a common behaviour in babies, spoon refusal is very frustrating, especially in a young baby who has only recently started solids. The first thing to do is try to work out the reason behind it. Could they have developed a negative association with being spoon-fed, because the spoon has been overloaded, pushed into their mouth when they are not ready or used to clean around their mouth? Are they trying to assert some independence (this often happens when there are older siblings) or are they just not hungry? Identifying the cause can help you find a solution.

It may help to stop offering the spoon for a few days to reduce anxiety. Give age-appropriate finger foods instead and let your baby explore them. Reintroduce a spoon-fed meal alongside the finger food and brush up on your spoon technique (see page 8) to encourage acceptance. Giving your child a spoon to hold as well may help satisfy their independence and develop their self-feeding skills.

NUTRITIONAL DEFICIENCIES

It can be hard to work out whether fussy eating behaviours have caused nutritional deficiencies, or whether the deficiencies came first, resulting in food refusal and fussy eating. In most cases it is a bit of both. Iron and zinc are the most common nutritional deficiencies in children, as their stores begin to deplete from around 6 months of age. Both of these can cause a decreased appetite and unwillingness to accept a variety of nutritious foods.

To minimise the risk of deficiencies, introduce a wide variety of nutrient-rich foods, particularly those containing iron and zinc, from around 6 months of age. Foods rich in iron include red meat, chicken, fish, eggs, legumes, wholegrain cereals and dark-green leafy vegetables. Foods rich in zinc include red meat, chicken, seafood, milk, legumes and nuts. It also helps to include foods rich in vitamin C at mealtimes to boost iron absorption.

Foods rich in calcium can decrease the absorption of iron, so offer dairy foods at snack times, rather than with main meals. Limit milk to 600 ml per day for children over 12 months, because it can reduce their appetite for solid foods and interfere with iron intake and absorption.

If you suspect your child may have a nutrient deficiency, visit your doctor. Nutritional supplementation should only be commenced when advised by a health professional, as inappropriate use of some dietary supplements, including iron, may do your child more harm than good.

REFLUX

Gastro-oesophageal reflux occurs when stomach contents are brought back up into the oesophagus (the tube that connects the mouth with the stomach) or the mouth. Many babies, often described as 'happy chuckers', regurgitate breastmilk and food without any problems, but some experience pain and distress due to stomach acid irritating the oesophagus. Babies who suffer pain due to reflux may begin to associate food and eating with discomfort, and start to refuse food or only accept food they know will not cause any pain, such as purees.

If you suspect your baby has reflux or 'silent reflux', in which they rarely vomit but often seem to be in pain due to an inflamed oesophagus, take them to the doctor. Children with reflux can be sensitive to different foods, but seek the advice of your doctor or an Accredited Practising Dietitian (APD) to avoid unnecessarily restricting nutritious foods.

CONSTIPATION

Most kids suffer a period of constipation at one time or another, particularly as infants when they're starting solids. This is because their developing digestive system is getting used to the variety of new foods – it's a big change from a liquid diet! Constipation can cause discomfort and reduce their appetite for breastmilk or formula, and solids. If your child is less than 6 months of age and has started solids, try reducing, or temporarily stopping, the introduction of solids for a few days, until symptoms improve.

The usual reasons for constipation in older babies and children are inadequate fibre and fluids. Some great ways to get more fibre into your child's diet include leaving the skin on fruits and vegetables whenever possible, as it provides additional fibre, and giving them foods rich in fibre, such as whole grains (try oats, quinoa and brown rice), multigrain bread, lentils, legumes, ground nuts, nut butters and seeds. Include fruits that help to soften stools in their diet, too, such as prunes, pears, papaya and apricots.

Be careful when introducing high-fibre foods or increasing the amount of fibre in your child's diet too quickly, as this can result in wind and even diarrhoea. Offer cooled, boiled water at mealtimes to ensure adequate fluid intake in addition to breastmilk or formula. Consider giving your baby an additional breastfeed, particularly in warm weather. For formula-fed babies, ensure your formula is made up correctly and offer additional drinks of water if required. Warm baths and gentle tummy massages in a clockwise direction can help relieve the pain, but if constipation persists, consult your doctor.

TEETHING

When teething is the reason behind food refusal, at least you know it's only a phase and their appetite will return. Adapt the temperature and texture of their meals to accommodate their symptoms, but maintain variety and return to their usual eating pattern as soon as possible.

Some babies constantly want to chew while teething, as the movement provides soothing counterpressure. If this sounds like your baby, offer hard munchables (see page 9), our Homemade teething rusks (see page 117), frozen food such as frozen banana or frozen fruit puree, chilled fruit or a chilled mango seed. You can offer these in a baby feeder mesh bag or as finger food. (Always supervise your baby when offering finger food.) You can also provide a soft spoon to chew on while you feed them. Some babies prefer cold food when they are teething – try plain Greek-style yoghurt mixed with fruit or vegetable purees.

FUSSY EATING

Most babies are willing to try all the new foods you offer them, but as they grow older they can become more selective in their food choices. There's no denying it's easier to cook and offer what you know they will eat, but this will only cement their fussy eating behaviours. Rather than forcing your child to eat their dinner or bribing them, try catering to their innate desire to choose. Offer a tasting plate (see pages 120–121) of a variety of nutritious foods and allow them to choose what and how much they want to eat. Give them something you know they'll eat alongside something new to help reduce anxiety about new foods.

SENSORY PREFERENCES

Eating would have to be the most difficult sensory task we undertake. A food's appearance, smell, flavour, texture and the way it feels all influence how we interact with it and how much we might enjoy it. Everyone interprets sensory information differently, depending on their genetics, experiences and lasting memories. Some people may be more sensitive with one sense, such as texture, and less sensitive with another, such as smell. What's more, our thresholds for tolerating different senses change depending on our level of illness, stress and fatigue.

Watch your child interact with food and tune into their signals, cues and feelings so that you can understand their sensory preferences and discover what they detect, tolerate, avoid and love. Don't simply assume their food preferences will be the same as yours. Understanding the way they process foods from a sensory perspective can explain aspects of their behaviour and why they like some foods and not others. It will allow you to cater to their needs and make mealtimes feel safe and secure.

If you feel your child's sensory preferences are affecting daily life or their health and wellbeing, seek advice from your doctor. Help and support, often from an occupational therapist, involves gradually helping them accept and tolerate different foods and food sensations.

POOR ORAL MOTOR SKILLS

If your child regularly coughs or chokes while eating, constantly spits out food, refuses to progress from smooth purees or only accepts foods that have a soft, easy-to-eat texture, they may be physically unable to chew and swallow food. Although these are all normal stages of development, they may also indicate inadequate oral motor skills.

From the moment children start solids they need to build on the suckle reflex and learn more complex oral motor skills, such as suck, munch and chew. These are learned behaviours, so if appropriate textures aren't offered, or aren't accepted, they can't practise these skills and develop them properly. Progressing to mixed-textured meals and harder-to-chew finger foods is essential to help them learn how to efficiently chew and safely swallow food.

If you suspect your child is significantly delayed in their oral motor abilities or they refuse food due to one or more of these reasons, take them to a qualified health professional to assess their oral motor skills.

SALMON AND LEEK POTATO CROQUETTES

MAKES 14
PREP TIME 20 minutes
(+ 20 minutes chilling)
COOKING TIME 30 minutes

- 2 waxy potatoes (such as Dutch cream), peeled and halved
- 1 tablespoon milk
- 20 g unsalted butter
- ½ small leek, white part only, thinly sliced
- 130 g tin skinless and boneless salmon in springwater, drained
- 1 tablespoon fresh lemon juice
- 1 tablespoon finely chopped flat-leaf parsley
- pinch of salt and pepper (optional)
- 2 slices multigrain bread, roughly torn
- ¼ cup (30 g) grated cheddar cheese
- ½ cup (75 g) plain flour
- 2 eggs, whisked
- 2 tablespoons rice bran oil

This recipe was an instant favourite with our kids. They just can't resist the subtle flavours of leek and salmon in an irresistible soft finger food. They are a great way to reintroduce fish to those who are rejecting it, too.

1. Place the potatoes in a saucepan and cover with water. Bring to the boil and cook for 10–12 minutes or until soft. Drain, add the milk and mash until smooth. Transfer to a large bowl.
2. Heat the butter in a small frying pan over low–medium heat. Add the leek and sauté for 5 minutes or until soft, stirring occasionally. Remove from the heat. Add to the potato along with the salmon, lemon juice and parsley. Season with a pinch of salt and pepper, if using. Mix until well combined, then take a small handful of mixture and shape it into a croquette. Place on a tray lined with baking paper and continue with the remaining mixture to make 14 croquettes in total. Place in the fridge for 20 minutes to chill.
3. Meanwhile, put the torn bread and cheese in a food processor and process to the consistency of fine breadcrumbs. Place in a shallow bowl and put the flour and whisked egg in two more shallow bowls.
4. Remove the croquettes from the fridge. Working with one croquette at a time, coat in the flour, then dip in the egg, coat in the breadcrumb mixture and return to the tray. Continue to coat the remaining croquettes.
5. Heat half of the oil in a large heavy-based frying pan over medium heat. Cook half the croquettes for 5–7 minutes, gently turning often, until they are browned all over and heated through. Drain on paper towel and repeat with the remaining oil and croquettes. (Alternatively, drizzle the croquettes with rice bran oil and bake in the oven at 180°C/160°C fan-forced for 20 minutes, then turn and cook for a further 10 minutes or until golden brown.)

NUTRITION NOTE A super source of omega-3, tinned salmon is an economical way to include these essential fatty acids in your family's diet.

STORAGE Keep in an airtight container in the fridge for up to 2 days or wrap individually and freeze in an airtight container for up to 2 months.

✱ALLERGIES/INTOLERANCES ***Gluten/wheat:*** use gluten- or wheat-free flour, and use gluten- or wheat-free breadcrumbs or quinoa flakes. ***Egg:*** use your preferred milk instead of the egg.

LITTLE QUINOA BITES

MAKES 24
PREP TIME 5 minutes
COOKING TIME 35 minutes

- 1 tablespoon olive oil, plus extra for greasing
- ½ cup (95 g) quinoa
- ½ small onion, very finely chopped or grated
- 1 cup (80 g) finely chopped broccoli florets
- 1 teaspoon finely chopped herb (such as thyme or parsley; optional)
- 2 eggs, lightly whisked
- ½ cup (40 g) grated cheddar cheese

These little bites are a wonderful finger food, soft enough for early feeders and gentle on teething gums. Your baby will delight in the flavours and textures, and you might find older children like the look of them, too.

1. Preheat the oven to 180°C (160°C fan-forced) and grease two 12-hole mini muffin tins with olive oil.
2. Place the quinoa in a fine-meshed sieve and rinse thoroughly under cold running water. Transfer to a heavy-based saucepan, add 1 cup (250 ml) water and bring to the boil over medium–high heat. Reduce the heat to low, cover and simmer for 10 minutes. Turn off the heat and set aside, without lifting the lid, for 4 minutes. Fluff the quinoa with a fork and set aside to cool slightly.
3. Meanwhile, heat the olive oil in a saucepan over medium heat. Add the onion and sauté for 3 minutes or until softened. Add the broccoli and herb, if using, and sauté for a further 3–5 minutes or until tender, reducing the heat to low if the onion is browning. Remove from the heat and set aside to cool slightly.
4. Place the quinoa, onion mixture, egg and cheese in a bowl and mix until combined. Spoon the mixture into the greased muffin holes and bake for 15 minutes or until set and light golden.

NUTRITION NOTE Quinoa is easy to digest and low in allergens, making it a great first food for your baby.

STORAGE Keep in an airtight container in the fridge for up to 2 days. To freeze, wrap individually and place in a freezer bag for up to 2 months.

ALLERGIES/INTOLERANCES ***Dairy:*** omit the cheese.

VEGGIE AND RICOTTA FRITTERS

MAKES 12
PREP TIME 10 minutes
COOKING TIME 18 minutes

1¼ cups (185 g) plain flour
1 teaspoon baking powder
½ cup (125 ml) milk
2 eggs
¼ cup (50 g) fresh ricotta
½ zucchini (courgette), finely grated, liquid squeezed out
½ carrot, finely grated
½ cup (60 g) grated cheddar cheese
¼ cup (60 ml) olive oil
fruit and ripe avocado, extra ricotta or dip, to serve (optional)

This is an excellent base recipe for a lovely savoury fritter. You can easily adapt it to include your child's favourite veggies and even some protein, such as tinned tuna or shredded leftover chicken.

1. Sift the flour and baking powder together into a large bowl. Whisk the milk, eggs and ricotta together in a separate bowl. Add the ricotta mixture to the flour and stir until just combined. Fold through the zucchini, carrot and grated cheese.
2. Heat the oil in a large heavy-based frying pan over medium heat. Add heaped tablespoons of batter to make fritters and cook, a few at a time, for 2–3 minutes each side or until golden and cooked through. Transfer to a plate and repeat to cook the remaining fritters.
3. Serve the fritters as a meal or snack, with fruit and avocado, extra ricotta or dip alongside, or slice into little fingers for young babies.

FUSSY EATING TIP These fritters provide a baby- and toddler-friendly way to incorporate veggies into the diet.

STORAGE Keep in an airtight container in the fridge for up to 2 days. Alternatively, freeze individual portions wrapped in plastic film for up to 3 months.

ALLERGIES/INTOLERANCES ***Gluten/wheat:*** use gluten- or wheat-free flour. ***Dairy:*** substitute a 75 g tin of creamed corn for the ricotta, omit the cheese and use your preferred dairy-free milk. ***Egg:*** substitute a large, mashed overripe banana for the eggs.

PUMPKIN, PEAR AND SPELT BABY BARS

MAKES 44
PREP TIME 15 minutes
COOKING TIME 45 minutes

75 g unsalted butter, softened, plus extra for greasing
1 pear, peeled, cored and diced
1 cup (150 g) diced pumpkin
½ cup, firmly packed (110 g) brown sugar
1 teaspoon pure vanilla extract
1 egg
2 cups (300 g) spelt (or wholemeal) plain flour
1 teaspoon baking powder

There's an overwhelming array of snack foods for babies and toddlers on the supermarket shelves, and many contain ingredients you've probably never heard of. Steer clear of them and make these bars instead. They are easy to chew, freeze well and are all-natural. You could use less sugar for younger babies, as the pear and pumpkin provide plenty of sweetness.

1. Preheat the oven to 180°C (160°C fan-forced). Grease a square 22 cm cake tin with butter and line with baking paper.
2. Place the pear, pumpkin and 1 cup (250 ml) water in a small heavy-based saucepan and bring to the boil over medium–high heat. Reduce the heat and simmer, covered, for 10–15 minutes or until tender. Drain, then mash until smooth and set aside.
3. Use an electric mixer to beat the butter and sugar for 2–3 minutes or until thick and pale. Add the vanilla and egg and beat until combined (the mixture will look slightly curdled at this point, but that's okay).
4. Stir in the mashed pear and pumpkin until combined. Add the combined sifted flour and baking powder and mix until just combined.
5. Spoon the mixture into the prepared tin, smooth the surface and bake for 25–30 minutes or until a skewer inserted into the centre comes out clean. Remove from the oven and cool in the tin for 5 minutes before transferring to a wire rack to cool completely. Slice into 5.5 cm × 2 cm bars or small squares. (Alternatively, shape the mixture into individual bars or balls and bake for 10–15 minutes.)

NUTRITION NOTE Some people find spelt easier to digest than wheat, even though they are related. Spelt flour is higher in fibre and some nutrients, such as B vitamins, than regular wheat flour. Choose a wholemeal variety to maximise nutrient content.

STORAGE Keep in an airtight container for up to 5 days. Alternatively, freeze individual portions in airtight containers for up to 3 months.

ALLERGIES/INTOLERANCES ***Gluten/wheat:*** use gluten- or wheat-free flour. ***Dairy:*** use 75 g coconut oil instead of the butter. **Egg:** replace the egg with a mashed overripe banana.

PEA AND HAM COUSCOUS SQUARES

MAKES 24
PREP TIME 15 minutes
COOKING TIME 45–55 minutes

- 20 g unsalted butter
- ½ leek, white part only, thinly sliced
- 1 carrot, diced
- 1 cup (120 g) frozen peas
- 100 g good-quality ham off the bone, chopped
- 1 cup (250 ml) no-added-salt vegetable stock, homemade vegetable stock (see page 240) or water
- 1 cup (200 g) couscous
- 1 cup (120 g) grated cheddar cheese

A play on the traditional flavour combination of pea and ham, this recipe makes a hearty soft finger food. You could use any single or mixed purees you may have in the fridge or freezer instead of making the pea and ham mixture. Simply use 1½ cups of the puree and start the recipe at step 4 (you only need the couscous and grated cheese in this case).

1. Preheat the oven to 180°C (160°C fan-forced) and line a square 18 cm cake tin with baking paper, allowing it to overhang two sides.
2. Heat the butter in a heavy-based saucepan over low–medium heat. Add the leek and sauté for 5 minutes or until soft. Add the carrot, peas and ham and stir to combine. Pour in the stock or water – it should just cover the mixture. Bring to the boil, then reduce the heat and simmer for 10 minutes or until the carrot is tender. Remove from the heat and leave to cool. Once cool, use a stick blender to process the mixture in the saucepan to a puree consistency.
3. Return the saucepan to medium heat and bring the mixture to the boil. Stir in the couscous, then turn off the heat and cover the pan. Set aside for 3–5 minutes, until the couscous has absorbed all the liquid and is soft. Stir through the cheese.
4. Press the couscous mixture into the lined tin and bake for 25–35 minutes or until firm to touch. Remove from the oven and transfer to a wire rack to cool completely – this is when the slice will firm up. To serve, use the overhanging paper to lift the slice out of the tin and cut into 24 pieces.

NUTRITION NOTE For younger babies, avoid the higher salt content of ham and use shredded cooked chicken or drained tinned tuna instead.

STORAGE Keep in an airtight container in the fridge for up to 2 days. Alternatively, freeze individual portions wrapped in plastic film for up to 2 months.

ALLERGIES/INTOLERANCES ***Gluten/wheat:*** Use 2 cups (280 g) cooked quinoa instead of the couscous, use gluten-free stock and reduce it to ¼ cup (60 ml). ***Dairy:*** use olive oil instead of the butter and omit the cheese.

BROAD BEAN AND PEA DIP

MAKES 1¼ CUPS (310 G)
PREP TIME 15 minutes
COOKING TIME 5 minutes

2 cups (300 g) frozen broad beans or 1 kg fresh broad beans, podded
¾ cup (90 g) frozen peas
¼ cup (60 ml) extra virgin olive oil
1 clove garlic, crushed
1 tablespoon fresh lemon juice
½ cup (40 g) grated parmesan
vegetable sticks (such as capsicum [pepper], carrot, celery, cucumber), to serve

This dip can be served as part of a tasting plate with toast fingers or raw or steamed vegetable sticks. If serving to a baby between 6 and 12 months of age, you can offer hard munchables alongside (see page 9). These are raw veggie sticks that are approximately the size of a thick permanent marker, so babies can't bite or swallow them. Hard munchables help babies learn more about the characteristics of foods, such as their shape and colour, and gumming them helps develop their oral motor skills.

1. Bring a saucepan of water to the boil over high heat. Add the broad beans and peas and cook for 2–3 minutes or until the peas are bright green and both vegetables are tender. Drain and rinse under cold water.
2. Use your fingernail to split the skin of each broad bean and gently squeeze out the bright-green bean, discarding the skin. Place the beans and peas in a food processor or blender with the olive oil, garlic and lemon juice and process until combined.
3. Stir through the parmesan and serve with the vegetable sticks for dipping.

NUTRITION NOTE Broad beans are a member of the legume family and are a quality source of slow-releasing carbohydrates, protein and B vitamins.

TIP You can replace the parmesan with ricotta, stirred through after processing, or feta, crumbled over the top of the dip, if you like.

SAFETY NOTE It is essential to supervise children while they are eating to prevent choking.

STORAGE Keep in an airtight container in the fridge for up to 3 days.

✱ALLERGIES/INTOLERANCES ***Dairy:*** omit the parmesan.

SESAME-CRUMBED CHICKEN FINGERS

MAKES 6
PREP TIME 10 minutes
COOKING TIME 10 minutes

6 chicken tenderloins
1 cup (70 g) fresh multigrain breadcrumbs
¼ cup (15 g) grated parmesan
1 tablespoon sesame seeds
⅓ cup (50 g) plain flour
1 egg, lightly whisked
2 tablespoons olive oil
20 g unsalted butter

When you give babies the opportunity to munch on a wide variety of foods and textures, it's surprising what they can manage to eat. These tender chicken fingers are easy for babies to hold while they suck and chew.

1. Place the chicken between 2 sheets of baking paper and flatten slightly with a meat mallet. Combine the breadcrumbs, parmesan and sesame seeds in a shallow bowl. Place the flour and egg in separate shallow bowls.
2. Working with one tenderloin at a time, toss in the flour to coat, then dip in the egg, allowing any excess to drip off, and coat in the breadcrumb mixture.
3. Heat half each of the oil and butter in a large heavy-based frying pan over medium–high heat. Cook half the tenderloins for 2 minutes each side or until golden brown and cooked through. Transfer to a plate lined with paper towel. Add the remaining oil and butter to the pan and cook the remaining tenderloins. Serve whole or sliced into 1 cm-thick strips.

NUTRITION NOTE Adding seeds, parmesan, nut meals or herbs to breadcrumbs is a great way to boost nutrients, fibre and antioxidants.

STORAGE Keep in an airtight container in the fridge for up to 2 days. Alternatively, freeze cooked or uncooked crumbed chicken fingers, wrapped in plastic film, for up to 2 months.

✱ALLERGIES/INTOLERANCES ***Gluten/wheat:*** use gluten- or wheat-free breadcrumbs, or quinoa flakes instead of the breadcrumbs. Replace the flour with rice flour. ***Dairy:*** omit the parmesan and replace the butter with extra oil. ***Sesame:*** simply omit the sesame seeds or substitute a tablespoon of chopped parsley instead.

HERBY LAMB CUTLETS

MAKES 6
PREP TIME 5 minutes
(+ 2 hours marinating)
COOKING TIME 8 minutes

1½ tablespoons extra virgin olive oil or macadamia oil
1½ tablespoons fresh lemon juice
1 clove garlic, crushed
1 tablespoon chopped flat-leaf parsley
2 teaspoons thyme leaves
freshly ground pepper, to taste (optional)
6 French-trimmed lamb cutlets
roasted or steamed vegetables or Roast vegetable couscous salad (see page 138), to serve

Lamb cutlets are a great first finger food (even if your baby is just sucking the juices to begin with), as they're easy to hold and rich in iron and zinc.

1 Combine the olive or macadamia oil, lemon juice, garlic, parsley, thyme and pepper, if using, in a shallow dish. Add the lamb cutlets and rub the oil mixture evenly over the meat to coat. Cover and refrigerate for 2 hours to marinate. Remove from the fridge 30 minutes before cooking.

2 Preheat a barbecue plate or heavy-based frying pan over medium–high heat. Cook the lamb cutlets for 3 minutes each side for medium or until cooked to your liking.

3 Serve with vegetables or roast vegetable couscous salad, if desired.

FUSSY EATING TIP When you first offer finger food to your baby, don't be worried if all they do is play with it. You are helping to make eating fun, develop their eating skills and form positive associations with eating.

STORAGE Keep in an airtight container in the fridge for up to 2 days.

ARROWROOT BISCUITS

MAKES ABOUT 24
PREP TIME 15 minutes
COOKING TIME 10 minutes

1½ cups (225 g) arrowroot flour (tapioca flour)
1 cup (150 g) plain flour, plus extra for dusting
1 teaspoon baking powder
¼ cup (55 g) caster sugar
pinch of salt
½ cup (125 ml) olive oil
⅓ cup (80 ml) your preferred milk
1½ teaspoons pure vanilla extract
1 egg

Arrowroot biscuits are a classic treat for toddlers. Make your own with this simple recipe where the authentic arrowroot flavour shines through.

1. Preheat the oven to 180°C (160°C fan-forced). Line a large baking tray with baking paper.
2. Sift the arrowroot flour, plain flour and baking powder together into the bowl of an electric mixer fitted with a paddle attachment. Add the sugar and salt. Place the olive oil, milk, vanilla and egg in a jug and whisk until well combined.
3. Beating on medium speed, slowly pour the wet ingredients into the bowl and mix until a soft dough forms. If the mixture is too dry, add a tablespoon of milk; if it is too wet, add a tablespoon of plain flour.
4. Turn the dough onto a lightly floured surface and knead for 1–2 minutes or until smooth. Use a floured rolling pin to roll out the dough until it is 5 mm thick. Use shaped biscuit cutters to cut out shapes and place on the lined tray. Lightly prick each biscuit once with a fork.
5. Bake the biscuits for 10 minutes or until they are a pale golden brown. Remove from the oven and set aside on the tray for 5 minutes, then transfer to a wire rack to cool. The biscuits will harden further upon cooling.

NUTRITION NOTE Arrowroot flour is easily digested and allergy-friendly, so it's a great choice in baked goods for babies.

TIP For a sweeter biscuit, increase the sugar to ½ cup (110 g) sugar.

STORAGE Keep in an airtight container for up to 5 days. Alternatively, wrap biscuits individually and freeze in a freezer bag for up to 1 month. Or, you can freeze the uncooked dough, wrapped in plastic wrap, for up to 1 month.

✱ALLERGIES/INTOLERANCES ***Gluten/wheat:*** use gluten- or wheat-free flour instead of plain flour. ***Dairy:*** use your preferred dairy-free milk. ***Egg:*** use ⅓ cup (100 g) unsweetened apple puree or a 'chia egg' (see page 5) instead of the egg.

HOMEMADE TEETHING RUSKS

MAKES 12
PREP TIME 10 minutes
COOKING TIME 40 minutes

20 g unsalted butter, chilled and chopped
1 cup (160 g) wholemeal plain flour, plus extra for dusting
¼ cup (60 ml) your baby's preferred milk
1 tablespoon fruit puree
pinch of ground cinnamon, or to taste

There's something therapeutic about making your own baby rusks – perhaps it's the act of rubbing the butter into the flour, or just the happy feeling that comes from knowing exactly what's going in your baby's mouth. Our babies love these flavoursome rusks and, unlike the store-bought variety, they're rarely ditched over the side of the pram.

1. Preheat the oven to 160°C (140°C fan-forced) and line a baking tray with baking paper.
2. Use your hands to rub the butter into the flour until it resembles very fine breadcrumbs. Add the milk, fruit puree and cinnamon and use a spoon to mix together to form a soft dough. If the dough is too dry, add another teaspoon of milk; if it is too wet, add another teaspoon of flour.
3. Turn the dough onto a floured surface and knead until the mixture comes together. Divide the mixture into 3 equal balls. Roll each ball into a long, thin rope, about 1.5 cm wide. Flatten the top slightly and then cut into 4 long pieces. Place on the lined tray and repeat with the remaining dough.
4. Bake the rusks, turning halfway through cooking, for 40 minutes or until they are light golden and firm. Turn off the oven and leave the rusks inside for a further 10 minutes to dry out. Remove from the oven and transfer to a wire rack to cool and harden further.

NUTRITION NOTE Hard finger foods, such as teething rusks, help to desensitise your baby's gag reflex and also encourage them to strengthen their jaw muscles and oral motor skills.

SAFETY NOTE It is essential to supervise children while they are eating to prevent choking.

STORAGE Keep in an airtight container for up to 2 weeks or freeze in a freezer bag for up to 2 months.

*ALLERGIES/INTOLERANCES ***Gluten/wheat:*** use gluten- or wheat-free flour instead of plain flour. ***Dairy:*** use a dairy-free spread instead of butter, and dairy-free milk.

CHAPTER 5

STAY IN CONTROL

You are in charge of what your children eat (for a good while at any rate), so it's up to you to equip them with healthy eating habits. Don't bring undesirable foods into the house – if healthy foods are all that's on offer, they will eat them. Serve a selection of nutritious foods with a variety of tastes and textures, eat with them whenever possible and they'll be off to a great start.

Food preferences are established early on in life, so children who are offered wholesome, home-cooked foods with a variety of ingredients are more likely to adopt long-term healthy eating habits. When your baby is ready for finger foods, you can start offering tasting plates, which are a wonderful way to expose them to a wide variety of flavours and textures, in a format that is both approachable and unintimidating. Serve a combination of protein, carbohydrates, fruit and vegetables.

THE BENEFITS OF FINGER FOODS

The introduction of finger foods is an important step in a baby's development and eating ability. They are ready for finger foods from about 7 months of age, although some are happy to explore them from 6 months. Finger foods help satisfy their desire to feed themselves and their curiosity about a food's texture, and benefits their oral motor development and development of speech.

Finger foods are helpful for:

- Oral motor skills: Building jaw strength and developing the tongue movement from a forwards-and-backwards suckling motion to a side-to-side movement. This allows the tongue to move food to the back molars so it can be chewed efficiently
- Gag reflex desensitisation: Babies are born with a highly sensitive gag reflex and this starts to desensitise and move further back in their mouth as they begin to orally explore both objects and solid foods
- Sensory processing: Meals involve all the senses, not just taste alone. Talk to your baby about what the food looks like, how it feels, what its texture is like and how it smells and tastes. Finger foods help babies learn more about food than when they are spoon-fed alone
- Fine motor skills: Picking up finger food and putting it in their mouth, or even playing with it, helps develop fine motor skills and self-feeding ability.

WHAT IS A TASTING PLATE?

The tasting plate is our preferred way to feed finger foods to small children, because it's simple, realistic and promotes all the positive aspects of eating and mealtimes. It's perfect for little ones who want to feed themselves, but it can just as easily be offered alongside a spoon-fed meal.

Frequently asked questions:

When should I introduce a tasting plate?

You can offer a basic plate as soon as finger foods are incorporated into your child's diet. This could comprise a few steamed vegetables, a variety of soft fruits or crust-less sandwiches, and can be offered after a spoon-fed meal.

How do I keep it nutritionally balanced?

Try to include something from each food group: vegetables and legumes, fruit, grains, meat or meat alternatives, and dairy or dairy alternatives. If you have a good variety of natural colours on the plate, chances are you're providing a good variety of essential nutrients and valuable antioxidants. Remember that every mealtime or food experience is an opportunity to reinforce positive eating habits.

What if I want to offer a spoon-fed meal, such as soup, casserole, risotto or pasta?

Serve the tasting plate alongside or after the spoon-fed meal. If children are capable of spoon-feeding themselves, offer the spoon-fed meal in one section of the plate or serve it in a separate small bowl.

How does it help a fussy eater?

Many parents find mealtime battles start when their children begin to test the boundaries. A tasting plate lets children feel they're in control of what they eat, even though you're still choosing the food on offer. The bite-sized portions and variety of colours, tastes and textures makes the tasting plate look fun and unintimidating, which encourages food exploration.

My child will only eat one thing, will this help?

The tasting plate is a non-confronting way to encourage your child to increase the variety of foods they eat. Involving them in meal planning and preparation, and eating with them, will also help.

When should I stop offering a tasting plate?

This will depend on your own family and how your child prefers to eat. Just keep adjusting the foods on the tasting plate to include more complex and flavoursome foods of varied textures until your child is ready to eat a simple extension of your own meal.

Introducing the tasting plate early in your solids journey has countless benefits for your children, such as encouraging the acceptance of finger foods, which are important for their oral motor development. But best of all, you decide what goes on the plate and your child decides what and how much they will eat. You can deconstruct your own meal (see One meal, three ways on pages 223–233), offer something you have cooked specifically with fruit and veggies alongside, or just put out a selection of whatever healthy foods you have on hand. Try to offer a range of different sensory experiences through textures and cooking methods, such as crunchy, raw vegetables (or steamed, according to age) along with soft, roasted vegetables. Always include a colourful fruit option, as the vitamin C in fruit boosts the absorption of iron from food, particularly vegetarian sources. This will remove the expectation that something sweet will follow the meal.

Tasting plates are a great vessel for introducing new foods, as you can team them with a selection of foods that your child is familiar with and enjoys to help reduce anxiety. Be sure to include at least one of their preferred foods on the plate when introducing any new foods. This also works for previously refused foods – if you keep adding them as a small component on a tasting plate, your child may begin to accept their presence and play with them, and at some point is likely to start eating them.

LET YOUR BABY SET THEIR OWN PACE

Just as every baby rolls, crawls and walks at different times, so too will their eating ability progress at their own pace. Some may be able to devour the meat from a lamb cutlet or chicken schnitzel at nine months of age, while others may prefer to be spoon-fed and only want to play with finger foods. Support your baby by praising good eating behaviour, offering foods appropriate to their ability and stage of development, and continuing to progress through a variety of textures by adding a small amount of quinoa, rice or couscous to their purees and offering simple finger foods alongside their spoon-fed meal.

If your baby is not yet eating the finger foods you offer, gently encourage positive interactions, such as touching, squishing and smelling. Removing any pressure to eat will help relax your baby and eventually they will be ready to try putting the food in their mouth. Pushing them or trying to force them to eat may increase their level of stress and anxiety, resulting in negative associations with eating and food refusal. If you are concerned about your child's developmental stage in relation to their age, seek the advice of your healthcare professional, such as your doctor, paediatrician, Accredited Practising Dietitian (APD), speech pathologist or child and family health nurse.

Remember that young children should never be left alone to eat. Constant supervision is essential and they should be seated appropriately to prevent choking.

A NOTE ABOUT SALT

Baby food may taste bland to you, but most babies have a heightened sense of taste so it will be full of flavour to them. Don't ever be tempted to add salt to give more flavour, as too much sodium can damage their kidneys. Babies can also quickly develop a taste for salty foods, which can contribute to fussy eating behaviours later on. Offer your baby foods that are naturally low in salt, such as fresh fruits, vegetables, lean meats, poultry, fish, eggs and legumes. Use herbs and/or spices to add flavour to purees, finger foods and family meals, beginning with small amounts and gradually adding more as they become used to them.

When buying packaged foods, always check the label – foods low in salt will contain less than 120 mg sodium per 100 g (over 600 mg per 100 g is considered high). For babies, choose products with less than 75 mg per 100 g. Salt goes by other names, too, so look out for baking soda, baking powder, celery salt, chicken salt, monosodium glutamate (MSG), meat or yeast extract, garlic salt, rock salt, sea salt, soy sauce, sodium, sodium bicarb, sodium sorbate, sodium nitrate, stock cubes and vegetable salt on the ingredients list. Ingredients are always listed in descending order by weight, so if salt is one of the first few ingredients the product is not a good choice.

YAKITORI SALMON SKEWERS

MAKES 5
PREP TIME 10 minutes
(+ 30 minutes soaking/marinating)
COOKING TIME 5 minutes

⅓ cup (80 ml) salt-reduced soy sauce
⅓ cup (80 ml) mirin
¼ cup (60 ml) salt-reduced chicken stock
1 clove garlic, crushed
1 teaspoon grated fresh ginger
2 × 200 g skinless salmon fillets, pin-boned and cut into 2.5 cm pieces
1 tablespoon rice bran oil
steamed brown rice, snow peas and cucumber sticks, to serve

It is really satisfying and rewarding when your child gets excited about a nutritious meal. Salmon and brown rice are two health-promoting foods that come together beautifully in this simple, delicious dish.

1. Soak 5 bamboo skewers in cold water for 30 minutes.
2. Place the soy sauce, mirin, chicken stock, garlic and ginger in a glass or ceramic bowl and stir to combine. Add the salmon pieces and refrigerate for 20 minutes to marinate.
3. Thread the salmon pieces onto the skewers, then use a large sharp knife to cut off the sharp ends for safety reasons.
4. Heat the oil in a large heavy-based frying pan over medium–high heat. Cook the salmon skewers, turning often and brushing with a little extra marinade, for 3–4 minutes or until just cooked through.
5. Serve the skewers with brown rice, snow peas and cucumber. For younger babies and toddlers, remove the salmon from the skewers before placing on their tasting plate.

FUSSY EATING TIP Don't underestimate the power of skewers! They immediately grab children's attention, and make food look easy and fun to eat.

STORAGE Keep leftover cooked salmon in an airtight container in the fridge for up to 2 days.

ALLERGIES/INTOLERANCES ***Gluten/wheat:*** use gluten-free soy sauce and stock.

F

TURKEY AND CAULIFLOWER TOTS

MAKES ABOUT 20
PREP TIME 15 minutes
(+ 30 minutes chilling)
COOKING TIME 30 minutes

2 cups (200 g) chopped cauliflower florets
1 tablespoon olive oil
1 small onion, finely chopped
½ cup (60 g) grated cheddar cheese
100 g turkey breast fillet, finely chopped
¼ cup (15 g) fresh multigrain breadcrumbs
2 tablespoons finely chopped flat-leaf parsley
1 tablespoon plain Greek-style yoghurt
1 egg, lightly whisked
1 tablespoon cornflour
pinch of salt and pepper
olive oil, for brushing
1 tablespoon sesame seeds (optional)
fruit and steamed vegetables, to serve

Crisp and golden with a soft and delicious filling, these tots make a hearty finger food for your child's tasting plate. Young babies will love practising chewing on them, while preschoolers and older kids will enjoy their flavour. You can easily adapt the filling to include more veggies, tofu or chicken.

1 Use a food processor to pulse the cauliflower florets a few times, until chopped into pieces the size of rice grains. Bring a saucepan of water to the boil, add the cauliflower and cook for 5 minutes or until tender. Drain in a fine-meshed sieve and pat dry with paper towel.

2 Heat the oil in a frying pan over medium heat. Add the onion and sauté for 3 minutes or until softened. Remove from the heat.

3 Combine the cauliflower, onion, cheese, turkey, breadcrumbs and parsley. Add the yoghurt and egg and stir until well combined. Mix in the cornflour, salt and pepper. Shape heaped teaspoons of the mixture into 5 cm-long 'tots' or logs. Place on a large baking tray lined with baking paper and chill in the fridge for at least 30 minutes.

4 Preheat the oven to 200°C (180°C fan-forced). Brush the tots with a little olive oil and bake for 10 minutes. Turn the tots and sprinkle with the sesame seeds, if using, then return to the oven for a further 10 minutes or until golden brown. Serve with fruit and vegetables alongside.

NUTRITION NOTE Turkey has a lovely mild flavour and it is high in protein and offers many important nutrients, including vitamin B12, selenium and niacin, which are necessary for good health.

STORAGE The tots are best eaten fresh but will keep in an airtight container in the fridge for up to 2 days. To freeze uncooked tots, freeze on a lined tray until frozen, then place in a freezer bag and freeze for up to 3 months.

*ALLERGIES/INTOLERANCES ***Gluten/wheat:*** use gluten- or wheat-free breadcrumbs. ***Dairy:*** omit the cheese and yoghurt. ***Egg:*** use a 'chia egg' (see page 5) or 'linseed egg' (see page 5) instead of the egg.

MINI SUSHI ROLLS

MAKES 32
PREP TIME 30 minutes
(+ 25 minutes cooling)
COOKING TIME 30 minutes

⅔ cup (130 g) brown rice
1 teaspoon rice vinegar
pinch of salt
pinch of white sugar
2 nori sheets
vegetable fillings (such as cucumber or capsicum [pepper] sticks, julienned carrot, thinly sliced avocado, chopped roasted pumpkin [squash])
salt-reduced soy sauce, to serve (optional)
fruit and cheese, to serve

Sushi is a popular and healthy 'fast food' option for kids, and it's surprisingly easy to make at home. You will need a bamboo sushi rolling mat for this recipe.

1. Place the rice in a fine-meshed sieve and rinse well under cold running water. Place the rice and 1⅓ cups (330 ml) water in a small heavy-based saucepan and bring to the boil over high heat. Reduce the heat and simmer, covered, for 25 minutes. Turn off the heat and set aside, without lifting the lid, for 5 minutes. Fluff the grains with a fork, add the rice vinegar, salt and sugar and stir to combine. Set aside for 25 minutes to cool.
2. Cut each nori sheet in half. Place a piece of nori, shiny side down, on the middle of your bamboo mat. Spread ⅓ cup (55 g) of the rice evenly over the nori, leaving a 1 cm gap at the end furthest away from you.
3. Place your chosen filling ingredients across the centre of the rice – take care not to add too much. Using the bamboo mat, roll the nori over so that it just encloses the filling, then gently squeeze the roll to lightly pack the rice. Moisten the rice-free end of the nori sheet with water and finish rolling up the sushi. Squeeze the sushi roll gently to tighten, then set aside.
4. Repeat using the remaining nori, rice and vegetable fillings. Use a sharp knife to slice each roll into 8 small pieces and serve with soy sauce and fruit and cheese alongside.

FUSSY EATING TIP Give your children the opportunity to choose their own fillings so they feel they have some control over mealtimes. If they feel relaxed and secure, they'll be more likely to try, interact with and enjoy new foods.

STORAGE Keep in an airtight container in the fridge and eat within 24 hours.

✱ALLERGIES/INTOLERANCES ***Gluten/wheat:*** use gluten-free soy sauce.

SATAY CHICKEN SKEWERS

MAKES 10 SKEWERS + ¾ CUP (225 G) SAUCE
PREP TIME 10 minutes
(+ 30 minutes soaking)
COOKING TIME 10 minutes

2 teaspoons peanut oil
2 tablespoons crunchy pure peanut butter
1 tablespoon salt-reduced soy sauce
1 clove garlic, crushed
½ teaspoon sweet chilli sauce
1 tablespoon honey
½ cup (125 ml) pure coconut milk
400 g chicken breast fillet, fat trimmed, cut into 2 cm pieces
lightly toasted shredded coconut, to serve (optional)
fruit and steamed vegetables, to serve

Why do kids love food on sticks? Because they make the meal feel more casual, unintimidating, different and fun. All of that helps them form positive food associations. Serve the satay sauce poured over the chicken, as a dipping sauce or mixed through steamed rice, peas and chicken for those who like to be spoon-fed.

1. Soak 10 small bamboo skewers in cold water for 30 minutes.
2. Meanwhile, heat 1 teaspoon of the peanut oil in a small saucepan over medium heat. Add the peanut butter, soy sauce, garlic, sweet chilli sauce and honey and cook, stirring, for 1 minute. Reduce the heat to low, add the coconut milk and stir until well combined. Transfer to a small bowl, adding a little more coconut milk if you prefer a thinner sauce.
3. Thread the chicken onto the soaked skewers, then use a large sharp knife to cut off the sharp ends for safety reasons. Heat the remaining oil in a heavy-based frying pan over medium heat. Fry the chicken skewers for 2 minutes each side or until golden brown and cooked through.
4. Spoon the satay sauce over the chicken skewers, sprinkle with the coconut, if using, and serve with fruit and vegetables alongside.

NUTRITION NOTE Soy sauce and sweet chilli sauce are very high in salt, so stick to the small amounts given in the recipe. For younger babies, simply melt pure peanut butter and serve over a few pieces of cooked chicken.

SAFETY NOTE Always supervise young children when they are eating food on skewers.

STORAGE Keep leftover chicken skewers and sauce in separate airtight containers in the fridge for up to 2 days. Alternatively, freeze the uncooked chicken skewers in a freezer bag for up to 2 months.

ALLERGIES/INTOLERANCES ***Gluten/wheat:*** use gluten-free soy sauce.

(F) (EF)

CHICKEN, PUMPKIN AND SPINACH BREAD PIES

MAKES 6
PREP TIME 10 minutes
COOKING TIME 45 minutes

- 2 tablespoons olive oil, plus extra for greasing
- 250 g chicken breast or thigh fillet, fat trimmed, cut into small pieces
- 1 tablespoon plain flour
- 1 teaspoon sweet paprika
- 200 g butternut pumpkin (squash), peeled, seeded and cut into 1 cm pieces
- 1 small leek, white part only, thinly sliced
- 80 g frozen spinach or curly kale (3 single-serve cubes)
- pinch of thyme leaves (optional)
- ½ cup (125 ml) salt-reduced chicken stock or homemade chicken stock (see page 240)
- ¼ cup (60 ml) pouring cream
- ½ teaspoon pure maple syrup (optional)
- 6 slices multigrain bread, crusts removed

Our kids would eat pie all day, every day if they could. So in an effort to make them more of an everyday option, we've been using bread for the crust instead of pastry. We like to mix all kinds of veggies into the filling, too.

1. Preheat the oven to 180°C (160°C fan-forced). Grease 6 holes of a regular muffin tin with olive oil.
2. Put the chicken in a bowl, add the flour and paprika and toss to coat. Heat 1 tablespoon of the oil in a heavy-based saucepan over high heat. Add the chicken and cook, stirring occasionally, for 2–3 minutes or until browned all over and just cooked through. Transfer to a clean bowl and set aside.
3. Reduce the heat to medium and heat the remaining oil in the pan. Add the pumpkin and leek and cook, stirring often, for 10 minutes. Add the spinach or kale, thyme, stock and cream and bring to a simmer. Simmer gently for 10 minutes or until the pumpkin is tender. Add the cooked chicken and maple syrup, if using, and stir to combine. Turn off the heat.
4. Place the bread slices in the greased muffin holes and use your fingers to mould them into cup shapes. Divide the chicken mixture among the bread cups. Bake for 15–20 minutes or until the bread is crisp and filling is hot.

NUTRITION NOTE Experiment with different, healthier pie crusts as an alternative to pastry. Multigrain bread, pita and mountain bread all work well.

STORAGE Cooked pies will keep in an airtight container in the fridge for up to 2 days. Alternatively, freeze the cooked filling in small portions for up to 2 months. Simply thaw in the fridge overnight, reheat and continue with step 4.

✱ALLERGIES/INTOLERANCES ***Gluten/wheat:*** use gluten- or wheat-free bread, substitute cornflour for the plain flour and use gluten-free stock. ***Dairy:*** replace the cream with chicken stock.

BOLOGNESE FILO TRIANGLES

MAKES 12
PREP TIME 20 minutes
COOKING TIME 20 minutes

1 cup (250 g) leftover Basic Bolognese (see page 237)
½ cup (60 g) grated cheddar cheese
20 g baby spinach leaves, chopped
4 sheets filo pastry
⅓ cup (80 ml) olive oil

Transform leftover bolognese into these crispy, cheesy filo triangles – we guarantee children won't be able to resist them.

1. Preheat the oven to 180°C (160°C fan-forced) and line a large baking tray with baking paper.
2. Combine the bolognese, cheese and spinach in a bowl.
3. Place a sheet of filo pastry on your benchtop and cut into 3 equal rectangles. (Keep the remaining sheets of pastry covered with a damp tea towel so they don't dry out.) Gently brush one rectangle with olive oil. Spoon a tablespoon of the bolognese mixture onto one corner of the rectangle and fold the pastry diagonally, creating a triangle. Continue folding, keeping the triangle shape. Brush with olive oil and place on the lined tray. Repeat with the remaining bolognese mixture and pastry. Bake for 15–20 minutes or until golden.

NUTRITION NOTE Safe food preparation and handling is essential to ensure food safety and prevent food poisoning, particularly when serving leftovers to your children. Leftover bolognese needs to be stored in the fridge and used within 2 days.

STORAGE These are best enjoyed on the day of cooking if you use bolognese that has been stored in the fridge or freezer. If you are using freshly cooked bolognese, cooked and/or uncooked filo triangles will keep in an airtight container in the fridge for up to 2 days or in the freezer for up to 2 months.

ALLERGIES/INTOLERANCES ***Dairy:*** omit the cheese.

BEEF BURGERS WITH HIDDEN VEGGIES

SERVES 6
PREP TIME 10 minutes
COOKING TIME 20 minutes

300 g premium lean beef mince
1 small onion, finely chopped
1 small zucchini (courgette), finely grated, liquid squeezed out
3 button mushrooms, finely chopped
1 tablespoon finely chopped flat-leaf parsley
1 egg, lightly whisked
1 teaspoon Worcestershire sauce
1 tablespoon olive oil or rice bran oil
¾ cup (90 g) grated cheddar cheese
Roast beetroot dip (see page 50) or Tomato sauce (ketchup) (see page 238)
6 multigrain bread rolls, split
1 cup (60 g) shredded iceberg lettuce
1 tomato, thinly sliced

Most kids will be thrilled to hear they're having burgers for dinner. You might even find they are already sitting patiently at the table as you serve (we wish!). For younger children who might not manage a proper burger, make 12 small patties (instead of 6 larger ones) and serve as finger food, with homemade potato chips or Sweet potato fries (see page 65).

1. Place the beef, onion, zucchini, mushroom, parsley, egg and Worcestershire sauce in a large bowl. Use your hands to mix until well combined.
2. Divide the mixture into 6 equal portions and shape into flat, round patties. Use your finger to make a small dimple in the middle of each patty – this helps them stay flat during cooking.
3. Heat the oil in a large, non-stick, heavy-based frying pan over low–medium heat. Cook the patties, in batches if necessary, for 5 minutes (avoid pressing on them as this will force out the juices) and then turn, sprinkle each patty with cheese, and cook for a further 5 minutes or until well browned and cooked through. If the cheese hasn't melted, place a lid over the frying pan and cook for 1 minute. Transfer to a plate.
4. To assemble the burgers, spread the beetroot dip or tomato sauce over the base of each roll and top with shredded lettuce, tomato and a beef patty. Cover with the top of the roll.

NUTRITION NOTE Whenever you make burger patties, add grated veggies to pack them with goodness.

TIP Serve the burger tasting-plate-style by deconstructing the elements and letting your child create their own meal.

STORAGE Keep cooked beef patties in an airtight container in the fridge for up to 2 days. Alternatively, freeze the uncooked patties on a lined tray until frozen, then place in a freezer bag, separated with freezer paper, and freeze for up to 2 months.

ALLERGIES/INTOLERANCES ***Gluten/wheat:*** use gluten- or wheat-free bread or bread rolls. ***Dairy:*** omit the cheese. ***Egg:*** omit the egg or substitute a 'chia egg' (see page 5).

(F)

LAMB AND PESTO SAUSAGES

MAKES 12
PREP TIME 10 minutes
(+ 30 minutes chilling)
COOKING TIME 10 minutes

500 g premium lamb mince
2 tablespoons Basil pesto (see page 232)
1 egg
½ cup (35 g) fresh multigrain breadcrumbs
⅓ cup (25 g) finely grated parmesan
1 tablespoon olive oil
fruit and steamed vegetables, to serve

These super-easy homemade sausages are a firm favourite. Oh, and they're not just for the kids! We think they're delicious.

1. Place the lamb mince, pesto, egg, breadcrumbs and parmesan in a large bowl and use your hands to mix until well combined. Shape the mixture into 12 small sausages and place on a lined tray in the fridge for 30 minutes to chill.
2. Preheat a barbecue grill plate on high, or a heavy-based frying pan over medium–high heat. Drizzle the olive oil over the sausages and cook, turning regularly, for 8–10 minutes or until browned and cooked through. (Alternatively, place on a baking tray lined with baking paper and bake in an oven preheated to 180°C/160°C fan-forced for 20–25 minutes, turning halfway through cooking, until cooked through.) Serve with fruit and vegetables alongside.

FUSSY EATING TIP For toddlers who love sausages (and little else), shape homemade rissoles into the shape of a sausage. It might be just the thing that helps them overcome their fear of trying something new.

STORAGE Keep in an airtight container in the fridge for up to 2 days. To freeze, wrap uncooked sausages in plastic film and freeze for up to 2 months.

*ALLERGIES/INTOLERANCES ***Gluten/wheat:*** use gluten or wheat-free breadcrumbs or substitute quinoa flakes for the breadcrumbs. ***Dairy:*** omit the parmesan from both the pesto and sausages. ***Egg:*** omit the egg or replace with a 'chia egg' (see page 5).

SPINACH AND RICOTTA NUDIES

MAKES 12
PREP TIME 15 minutes
COOKING TIME 10 minutes

250 g baby spinach leaves
1 cup (200 g) fresh ricotta
25 g grated parmesan, plus extra to serve
⅓ cup (50 g) plain flour, plus extra for dusting
2 egg yolks, lightly whisked
½ cup (120 g) Tomato and basil pasta sauce (see page 237) or Hidden veggie sauce (see page 236)
cooked pasta, fruit and vegetable sticks, to serve

Kids love the fillings in cannelloni and ravioli, so we like to serve them up as little 'nudies' (minus the pasta). These spinach and ricotta balls are a delicious vegetarian finger food that's perfect for the tasting plate.

1. Place the spinach and 1 tablespoon of water in a large frying pan over medium heat and cook, stirring, for 2–3 minutes or until wilted. Drain the spinach and squeeze out as much as liquid as possible, then finely chop and place in a large bowl.
2. Add the ricotta, parmesan, flour and egg yolk to the spinach and mix well to combine. Shape the mixture into dumplings the size of golf balls, or smaller if you prefer, flatten them slightly and dust lightly with flour.
3. Bring a large saucepan of water to the boil over high heat. Reduce the heat to hold at a simmer. Use a slotted spoon to lower half the nudies into the pan and scoop them out when they rise to the surface. Transfer to a plate lined with paper towel to drain. Repeat to cook the remaining nudies. (The nudies can be served as finger food, without sauce, at this point.)
4. Gently heat the tomato and basil pasta sauce or hidden veggie sauce in a saucepan or frying pan until warm. Add the nudies and very gently turn to coat in the sauce. Serve sprinkled with extra grated parmesan, if desired, and with pasta, fruit and vegetable sticks alongside.

NUTRITION NOTE If your baby or toddler tends to overstuff their mouth with food, make smaller balls to help them eat appropriately sized mouthfuls.

STORAGE These are best enjoyed fresh, but leftovers will keep in an airtight container in the fridge for up to 2 days.

ALLERGIES/INTOLERANCES ***Gluten/wheat:*** use gluten- or wheat-free flour and pasta.

ROAST VEGETABLE COUSCOUS SALAD

SERVES 4–6
PREP TIME 10 minutes
COOKING TIME 45 minutes

500 g butternut pumpkin (squash), peeled, seeded and cut into 2 cm cubes
1 red onion, cut into 8 wedges
2 tablespoons olive oil
2 cups (170 g) chopped broccoli florets
150 g cherry tomatoes, halved
pinch of salt
1 tablespoon pure maple syrup
¼ cup (40 g) pine nuts
1 cup (200 g) couscous
40 g baby spinach leaves
60 g feta, for older children or adults (or fresh ricotta for a lower-salt option)
fruit and steamed vegetables, to serve

A roast vegetable salad makes a nice change to simple steamed vegetables, and the addition of couscous, feta and pine nuts makes it substantial enough to enjoy as a light meal. Adapt it to include your family's favourite vegetables or experiment with some your child might not regularly eat.

1. Preheat the oven to 200°C (180°C fan-forced). Line a large baking tray with baking paper.
2. Place the pumpkin and onion on the lined tray, drizzle with 1 tablespoon of the olive oil and toss to coat. Bake for 30 minutes, then carefully toss and add the broccoli and cherry tomatoes to the tray. Drizzle the remaining olive oil over the broccoli and tomatoes, and sprinkle all the vegetables with salt. Return to the oven for a further 10 minutes.
3. Drizzle the maple syrup over the roasted vegetables and gently toss to coat. Scatter over the pine nuts and bake for a further 3–5 minutes or until the vegetables are sticky and tender, and the pine nuts are golden.
4. Meanwhile, cook the couscous according to the instructions on the packet.
5. Carefully toss the roasted vegetables and couscous together in a bowl. Stir through the baby spinach, scatter the crumbled feta over the top and serve with fruit and vegetables alongside.

FUSSY EATING TIPS Enjoy the salad together as a family, as parents are the best role models when it comes to eating. For younger children, deconstruct the salad into elements they can eat with their fingers.

STORAGE Keep in an airtight container in the fridge for up to 2 days.

ALLERGIES/INTOLERANCES ***Gluten/wheat:*** replace the couscous with cooked quinoa. ***Dairy:*** omit the feta. ***Nuts:*** replace the pine nuts with pepitas (pumpkin seed kernels) or sunflower seeds.

CHAPTER 6

EAT MEALS AT THE TABLE

Eating on the go is a real sign of the times. In our rush to get from one thing to the next we're feeding the kids in the car or pram, while they walk or play, standing at the kitchen bench – you name it. But the benefits of eating at the table are numerous and far-reaching, so pull up a chair and sit with them to eat whenever you get the chance.

When children are eating, the location and atmosphere can affect the amount they eat, whether they feel comfortable to try something new and how they behave during the meal. All these things can have a knock-on effect on their sleeping patterns, too, so there are some pretty good reasons to make mealtimes calm and enjoyable. Serve every meal at the table, eat with them if possible and give them 5 minutes to relax beforehand.

BREAKFAST

Breakfast is particularly important for kids, especially toddlers, as they need lots of energy so they can spend the day being active and absorb all the information they will be exposed to. It helps them concentrate, focus and remember new skills. Plenty of studies have shown that older children who enjoy a nutritious breakfast have better attendance levels at school, improved concentration and mental performance. They're also more likely to make better food choices during the day than those who don't eat breakfast.

A nutritious breakfast provides your child with a significant amount of the vitamins and minerals they require each day, including calcium, iron, B vitamins and fibre. It is also a great time to introduce new foods, especially for children who tend to refuse their dinner because they are tired or not hungry enough.

Creating a morning routine can help you get every day off to a good start. Sure, it can be a scramble to get out the door in time for daycare, school, work or an activity, but if you set the table the night before, think about the foods you're going to offer and prepare them as best you can, things will run more smoothly. Boil eggs in advance and keep them in the fridge, freeze leftover smoothies in reusable pouches and thaw in the fridge overnight, make bircher muesli, soak oats in milk overnight for a quick-cooking porridge or cook a batch of baked beans on the weekend and freeze individual portions to defrost overnight. Set your alarm so you have enough time to get ready, and try to keep the timing of the meal consistent.

If your child is tiring of cereal and toast, give them a breakfast tasting plate alongside (see pages 120–121). You could include a boiled egg, fruit, cheese or a little yoghurt or smoothie. Some kids, usually babies, will happily eat leftover cooked vegetables for breakfast.

BUILD A NUTRITIOUS BREAKFAST

A suitable breakfast offers a range of nutrients including slow-releasing carbohydrates, protein, fibre and essential vitamins and minerals, including calcium, B vitamins, iron, zinc and antioxidants. Follow these steps to put together a breakfast that ticks all the boxes.

1. Start with wholegrains, such as wholegrain bread, multigrain flakes, rolled oats, quinoa or quinoa flakes
2. Add a dairy food (or calcium-fortified alternative), such as full-fat milk, yoghurt or cheese. You can use expressed breastmilk or infant formula for babies
3. Include fruit or vegetables, like pear, banana, berries, mango, corn, avocado, roast tomato or green veggies
4. Include protein, such as milk, yoghurt, cheese, eggs, nuts or legumes.

To get you started, we've put together some nutritious breakfast tasting plate ideas:

- Veggie and ricotta fritters (page 106), a small bowl of plain Greek-style yoghurt and fresh fruit
- Fruit smoothie and wholegrain toast spread with nut or seed butter
- Corn fritters with avocado salsa (page 157)
- Creamy banana and apple porridge (page 150) or bircher muesli (page 146) with a boiled egg
- Wholegrain toast fingers with scrambled egg and avocado, and fresh fruit
- Super-start toasted muesli (page 144) with milk and/or plain Greek-style yoghurt, and fresh fruit
- Wholegrain toast with ricotta and Stewed rhubarb and pear puree (page 16)
- Carrot and blueberry oatbran muffins (page 190), a boiled egg and fresh fruit
- Plain yoghurt mixed with kiwi-go puree (page 12) or Stewed rhubarb and pear puree (page 16), and wholegrain toast spread with avocado
- Cheesy baked beans on toast (page 159) and fresh fruit
- Hazelnut and oat baby bars (see page 45), plain Greek-style yoghurt and fresh fruit.

LUNCH

There's nothing wrong with eating lunch while you're out and about, but always try to find a calm, quiet place where you can sit together. If you're going to the park, look for a table or bench, or set down a picnic rug; if you're visiting friends or relatives, make sure you feed your child at a table, even if the adults will be eating separately. If you have an appointment that may run into lunch time, pack a lunchbox with a selection of healthy foods your child enjoys just in case. Wherever you are, when it's time for lunch, stop what you're doing, find a suitable place and take some time out to feed your child. See pages 186–201 for healthy lunch recipes.

DINNER

By the end of the day, kids tend to be tired and hungry. Try to keep dinner at a consistent time and avoid giving them snacks too close to the meal, even if they're pestering you for food. Offer some water and, if necessary, give them a small portion of their meal at the table while they wait, such as a piece of cheese, vegetable or fruit. Ask them to do whatever tasks they've been allocated to help prepare for the meal, then set them up with an activity that calms them while you finish getting it ready. During the meal, talk about the food they're eating – the tastes, textures and how it is good for them – and eat with them if you can.

MINDFUL EATING

When we eat mindfully, we are using all of our senses to enjoy the food, free of distraction and judgement, and are able to appropriately respond to our hunger and fullness cues. This is an important life skill for children, as it teaches them to be aware of what they are putting into their bodies and the positive impacts that food can have on their lives, in terms of both nourishment and enjoyment. Knowing when they are feeling hungry and when they are feeling full also means they'll be less likely to over-eat and eat for emotional reasons as adults.

The frenetic pace of modern life has had a detrimental impact on the mindfulness, or self-awareness, of eating. There's a tendency to eat on the run or standing at the bench, rather than sitting down together at the table. If this sounds like your household, do what you can to slow things down and serve meals at the table with at least one caregiver present for your children.

FIVE REASONS WHY YOU SHOULD SIT DOWN WITH YOUR KIDS TO EAT

1. To ensure their safety and wellbeing
2. To promote mindful eating (see below, left), which encourages awareness of hunger and fullness cues
3. To role-model positive eating behaviours and enjoyment of a wide variety of nutritious foods
4. To build positive associations around food and eating
5. To encourage social interaction and communication as a family.

IS FRUIT JUICE A HEALTHY CHOICE?

Don't be fooled by clever marketing and packaging – the truth is that babies, toddlers and even school-aged children do not need fruit juice. It can reduce the appetite of babies and toddlers for breastmilk, formula and solid food, without providing any of the nutrients they need for optimal growth and development. Fruit juice and fruit drinks also contribute to tooth decay in children and even excess weight gain. If your child's appetite is satisfied from drinks, they may develop fussy eating behaviours when more nutritious foods are offered, too.

Babies and toddlers don't actually need a lot of fruit – one serve per day as part of a healthy balanced diet is generally enough to meet their requirements. For older children and adults, two serves is adequate. Whole fruit is best, because the pulp and skins contain valuable amounts of fibre, nutrients and health-promoting antioxidants important for your child's health. The pulp and skins are removed during the juicing process, making juice a poor substitute.

   V

SUPER-START TOASTED MUESLI

MAKES 4 CUPS (400 G)
PREP TIME 10 minutes
COOKING TIME 40 minutes

3 cups (270 g) rolled oats
½ cup (40 g) flaked almonds, chopped
2 tablespoons sunflower seeds
2 tablespoons sesame seeds
1 teaspoon ground cinnamon
¼ cup (60 ml) macadamia oil (or coconut, sunflower or light olive oil)
¼ cup (90 g) pure maple syrup or honey
¼ cup (20 g) desiccated or shredded coconut
2 tablespoons linseeds (flaxseeds) or chia seeds
½ cup (80 g) chopped dried fruit (such as sultanas, raisins, dates, apricots; optional)

Breakfast is the most important meal of the day, so avoid offering commercial cereals that are overloaded with added sugars, salt, artificial colours and flavours. Making your own muesli is a simple, foolproof way to get all the family off to a great start every day.

1. Preheat the oven to 150°C (130°C fan-forced) and line a large baking tray with baking paper.
2. Place the oats, almonds, sunflower seeds, sesame seeds and cinnamon in a large bowl and mix to combine. Add the oil and maple syrup or honey and stir to combine. Spread the mixture evenly over the lined tray.
3. Bake for 30–40 minutes, stirring every 15 minutes, until the mixture is golden and aromatic. Add the coconut for the last 5 minutes of cooking. Remove from the oven and set aside to cool completely. Stir through the linseeds or chia seeds and the dried fruit.

NUTRITION NOTE Macadamia oil is a delicious, nutty-flavoured oil that's rich in heart-healthy monounsaturated fatty acids. It has a high smoking point, so it can be used for baking and frying, as well as simple dressings. When buying coconut products, check the label to ensure there no preservatives added.

TIP Crush the nuts and seeds to an appropriate size for young children.

STORAGE Store in an airtight container for up to 2 weeks. Alternatively, freeze individual portions in freezer bags for up to 3 months.

ALLERGIES/INTOLERANCES ***Gluten/wheat:*** use quinoa, quinoa flakes, hulled buckwheat or millet instead of the oats. ***Nuts:*** Replace the almonds with a nut that is tolerated, or pepitas (pumpkin seed kernels).

CREAMY CHIA BIRCHER MUESLI

A delicious summertime alternative to porridge, this bircher-style muesli can be adapted to suit whatever grains, seeds and nuts are in your pantry.

SERVES 3–4
PREP TIME 10 minutes
(+ 1 hour or overnight soaking)
COOKING TIME Nil

1 cup (90 g) rolled oats
½ teaspoon ground cinnamon
1 tablespoon chia seeds
2 teaspoons small seeds (such as sesame or sunflower)
2 tablespoons crushed unsalted nuts (such as almonds, walnuts, cashews)
1 cup (250 ml) preferred milk
½ cup (140 g) plain Greek-style yoghurt
1 apple or pear, grated, or 1 small banana, mashed
pure maple syrup or honey, to serve (optional)
stewed or chopped fruit, to serve (optional)

1. Place the oats, cinnamon, chia seeds, small seeds, nuts and milk in a bowl. Cover and refrigerate for 1 hour or overnight to soak.
2. Spoon into bowls and stir in the yoghurt and fruit. Drizzle with a little maple syrup or honey, if using, and serve topped with stewed or chopped fruit.

NUTRITION NOTE We soak the oats in milk (rather than juice) for extra calcium, protein and vitamin B2.

TIP Always ensure nuts and seeds are crushed to an appropriate size if serving to children.

STORAGE Keep (without adding the fruit) in an airtight container in the fridge for up to 3 days.

ALLERGIES/INTOLERANCES ***Dairy:*** use soy, rice, oat, almond or coconut milk and stir through a little extra after soaking (in place of the yoghurt). ***Gluten:*** replace the oats with rolled, flaked or cooked quinoa.

NO-SOAK QUINOA BIRCHER

It's always a good idea to make a little extra when cooking grains like quinoa, couscous and rice for dinner. You can then keep individual portions in the fridge or freezer to use as a base for 'instant' meals, such as this.

SERVES 2
PREP TIME 5 minutes
COOKING TIME Nil

1 cup (180 g) cooked quinoa
1 cup (280 g) plain Greek-style yoghurt
1 diced banana, grated apple or pear, or sliced fruit, to serve

1. Combine the quinoa and yoghurt in a small bowl. Spoon into bowls, top with the fruit and serve.

NUTRITION NOTE This high-protein, high-calcium and gluten-free breakfast provides long-lasting energy.

STORAGE Keep leftovers in an airtight container in the fridge for up to 3 days.

ALLERGIES/INTOLERANCES ***Dairy:*** use coconut yoghurt, or soy yoghurt if appropriate.

CREAMY CHIA
BIRCHER MUESLI
NO-SOAK QUINOA
BIRCHER

SMOOTHIE BOWL

SERVES 2
PREP TIME 5 minutes
COOKING TIME Nil

1 cup (135 g) berries (such as blueberries, strawberries, raspberries), plus extra, to serve
200 g frozen chopped banana
1 cup (250 ml) preferred milk
¼ cup (70 g) plain or vanilla-flavoured yoghurt
2 trimmed curly kale or English spinach leaves
1 tablespoon pure maple syrup or honey (optional)
¼ cup (30 g) Super-start toasted muesli (see page 144)
¼ cup (20 g) shredded or desiccated coconut
¼ cup (25 g) LSA

What's not to love about smoothie bowls? They look so pretty and have plenty of sweetness and delicious crunch. Use whatever fruits are in season and play around with the toppings to include favourite seeds and nuts. Check the label when buying coconut to ensure there are no preservatives.

1. Place the berries, banana, milk, yoghurt, kale or spinach, and maple syrup or honey, if using, in a food processor or high-speed blender. Process until smooth and well combined.
2. Serve the smoothie topped with extra berries, muesli, coconut and LSA.

NUTRITION NOTE Smoothies are a fun way to get more vegetables into your child's day, including the green leafy varieties which are often challenging. Green leafy vegetables, including kale and spinach, are an excellent source of important health-promoting antioxidants as well as vitamin A, vitamin C and beta-carotene, which are important for the immune system.

TIP Crush the nuts and seeds in the muesli to an appropriate size if serving to young children.

STORAGE Leftover smoothie bowl (without the toppings) will keep in an airtight container in the fridge for 24 hours. Stir or shake well before eating.

ALLERGIES/INTOLERANCES ***Gluten/wheat:*** omit the muesli or use a gluten- or wheat-free variety. ***Dairy:*** use a dairy-free milk and omit the yoghurt. ***Nuts:*** replace the LSA with ground linseed (flaxseed) or chia seeds.

CREAMY BANANA AND APPLE PORRIDGE

SERVES 2–3
PREP TIME 5 minutes
(+ 5 minutes soaking)
COOKING TIME 10 minutes

1 cup (90 g) rolled oats
1¼ cups (310 ml) boiling water
1¼ cups (310 ml) milk,
plus extra to serve
1 apple, peeled, cored and grated
1 banana, sliced
1 teaspoon pure maple syrup,
plus extra to serve (optional)
¼ teaspoon ground cinnamon
(optional)

'Sugar and spice and all things nice' comes to mind when thinking about this comforting porridge. Adding fresh fruit provides lots of sweetness and a good dose of nutrition.

1. Place the oats and boiling water in a saucepan and stir to combine. Set aside for 5 minutes to soften the oats.
2. Add the milk, apple, half the banana, the maple syrup and cinnamon to the pan and stir to combine. Bring to the boil over medium–high heat, then reduce the heat and simmer, stirring often, for 5–10 minutes or until it reaches your desired consistency. For young babies, you can puree the porridge for an even smoother texture.
3. Serve warm with the remaining sliced banana and a drizzle of extra milk and maple syrup, if desired.

NUTRITION NOTE Rolled oats are an extremely nutritious, versatile and cheap whole grain to include in your family's diet. Just one serve of this porridge will meet or exceed the daily whole grain target for a child up to 3 years of age, and over 50 per cent for everyone else – all before 9 a.m. (Whole grain daily targets are: 2–3 years: 24 g, 4–8 years: 32–40 g, 9+ years: 48 g.)

STORAGE Keep leftover porridge in the fridge for up to 2 days. Simply add a little extra milk or water before reheating.

ALLERGIES/INTOLERANCES ***Gluten/wheat:*** You can use quinoa, quinoa flakes, millet or rolled buckwheat as an alternative to oats, however the amount of liquid required and the cooking time will vary accordingly. ***Dairy:*** use dairy-free milk or substitute water.

BREAKFAST MUFFINS

MAKES 12
PREP TIME 10 minutes
COOKING TIME 25 minutes

¼ cup (60 ml) baking oil (such as coconut, macadamia, light olive), plus extra for greasing
2 eggs
1 cup (250 ml) buttermilk
2 tablespoons honey or pure maple syrup
1 apple, peeled, cored and coarsely grated
½ orange, zest finely grated
2 cups (260 g) Super-start toasted muesli (see page 144)
1 cup (160 g) wholemeal plain flour
½ teaspoon bicarbonate of soda
¼ cup (30 g) ground linseed (flaxseed)
poppy seeds, to sprinkle (optional)

We've created these wholesome muesli muffins for those busy times when you can't sit down at the breakfast table. They contain loads of goodness and freeze beautifully, so they're perfect for breakfast on the go. You can use store-bought muesli if you don't have any homemade muesli on hand, or substitute the same quantity of toasted rolled oats.

1. Preheat the oven to 180°C (160°C fan-forced). Grease a 12-hole regular muffin tin with your chosen oil.
2. Whisk the oil, eggs, buttermilk and honey or maple syrup together in a bowl. Stir in the grated apple, orange zest and a squeeze (about 1 tablespoon) of orange juice.
3. Combine the muesli, flour, bicarbonate of soda and ground linseed in a separate bowl. Add the apple mixture and mix until just combined – take care not to overmix or the muffins will be tough.
4. Spoon the mixture into the greased muffin holes and sprinkle with poppy seeds, if using. Bake for 20–25 minutes or until the muffin tops spring back when lightly pressed and a skewer inserted into the centre of a muffin comes out clean. Remove from the oven and set aside for 5 minutes before turning out onto a wire rack to cool.

NUTRITION NOTE Children who eat breakfast every day tend to have better attendance at school, improved concentration and mental performance.

STORAGE The muffins will keep in an airtight container for up to 2 days. Alternatively, wrap individually in plastic film and freeze for up to 3 months.

ALLERGIES/INTOLERANCES ***Gluten/wheat:*** use gluten- or wheat-free flour and muesli. ***Dairy:*** add 1 tablespoon lemon juice or vinegar to your preferred dairy-free milk to replace the buttermilk. ***Egg:*** use ⅔ cup (120 g) unsweetened apple puree, 1 overripe banana or 2 'chia eggs' (see page 5) to replace the eggs.

RASPBERRY PIKELETS

MAKES ABOUT 12
PREP TIME 10 minutes
COOKING TIME 20 minutes

1½ cups (225 g) spelt flour (or a mixture of wholemeal plain flour and plain flour)
1 tablespoon baking powder
pinch of salt
½ cup (50 g) hazelnut meal
2 eggs
1¼ cups (310 ml) your preferred milk
½ punnet (75 g) raspberries, plus extra to serve
butter or olive oil, for greasing
pure maple syrup, to serve (optional)

Pikelets can be as simple or as fancy as you like. These ones have the subtle nutty flavour of spelt and hazelnut meal combined with the sweetness of raspberries. The spelt flour and hazelnut meal provide a nutritious boost, too. If you have leftovers, we will be surprised, but they make a wonderful finger food for morning tea the next day.

1. Sift the flour and baking powder together into a bowl. Add the salt and hazelnut meal and stir to combine.
2. Whisk the eggs and milk together in a jug. Add to the dry ingredients with the raspberries and whisk until well combined.
3. Melt 1 teaspoon of butter or olive oil in a non-stick, heavy-based frying pan over medium heat. Add heaped tablespoons of the mixture to the pan to make pikelets and cook until bubbles appear and burst on the surface. Flip the pikelets and cook until they are golden brown underneath and cooked through. Transfer to a plate and cover loosely with foil to keep warm. Repeat to cook the remaining mixture, greasing the pan when necessary.
4. Serve the pikelets topped with extra raspberries and maple syrup, if desired. Cut them into manageable fingers for babies and young toddlers.

NUTRITION NOTE Spelt, an ancient grain, is a relative of wheat and, along with the hazelnut meal, gives a lovely nuttiness. Together, they provide protein, fibre, B vitamins, vitamin E, omega-3 fatty acids, copper and manganese.

STORAGE Keep in an airtight container in the fridge for up to 2 days. Alternatively, place in a freezer bag, layered with freezer paper, and freeze for up to 2 months.

ALLERGIES/INTOLERANCES ***Gluten/wheat:*** replace the spelt flour with buckwheat flour. ***Dairy:*** use your preferred dairy-free milk and use dairy-free spread or oil to grease the pan. ***Eggs:*** use 2 'chia eggs' (see page 5) instead of the eggs. ***Nuts:*** replace the hazelnut meal with almond meal if tolerated, or additional flour.

CORN FRITTERS WITH AVOCADO SALSA

MAKES 10 (SERVES 4)
PREP TIME 20 minutes
COOKING TIME 20 minutes

¾ cup (110 g) plain flour
1 teaspoon baking powder
pinch of salt
1 egg
½ cup (125 ml) milk
3 corn on the cobs, husks and silk removed
1 small zucchini (courgette), coarsely grated, liquid squeezed out
½ red capsicum (pepper), finely diced
3 spring onions, trimmed and thinly sliced
small handful of coriander, roughly chopped
⅓ cup (80 ml) olive oil or rice bran oil

AVOCADO SALSA

1 small ripe avocado, peeled, seeded and diced
1 small ripe tomato, seeded and finely chopped
1 tablespoon coriander leaves, chopped
1 tablespoon fresh lime juice
freshly ground black pepper, to taste

Corn fritters make a veggie-packed meal option. When served with a fresh avocado and tomato salsa they are a nutrient- and fibre-rich choice. For older children and adults, try adding rocket or baby spinach and some smoked salmon or cooked bacon for extra flavour and texture.

1. To make the avocado salsa, combine all the ingredients in a bowl. Set aside.
2. Sift the flour, baking powder and salt into a large bowl. Place the egg and milk in a jug and whisk to combine. Gradually whisk the milk mixture into the dry ingredients until smooth.
3. Cut the kernels from the corn cobs and combine with the zucchini, capsicum, spring onion and coriander in a large bowl. Add the batter and stir to combine.
4. Heat the oil in a large heavy-based frying pan over medium heat. Add ¼ cup (60 ml) quantities of the corn mixture to the pan and gently flatten to make fritters. Cook for 3–4 minutes each side, until golden and cooked through. Transfer to a plate lined with paper towel and repeat to cook the remaining corn mixture, greasing the pan as necessary.
5. Serve the fritters with the avocado salsa.

NUTRITION NOTE Including vegetables in your child's breakfast will get them one step closer to consuming their recommended intake and benefiting from all the vitamins, minerals, antioxidants and natural plant chemicals that promote good health and wellbeing.

STORAGE Keep leftover fritters and salsa in separate airtight containers in the fridge for up to 3 days. Alternatively, place fritters in a freezer bag, layered with freezer paper, and freeze for up to 3 months.

✱ALLERGIES/INTOLERANCES ***Gluten/wheat:*** use gluten- or wheat-free flour.
Dairy: use water or a dairy-free milk alternative in place of the milk.
Egg: replace the egg with a 'chia egg' (see page 5) or 'linseed egg' (see page 5).

NUTRITION NOTE

Legumes provide protein, iron and zinc, and make an excellent addition to your child's diet from the moment you introduce solids.

CHEESY BAKED BEANS ON TOAST

SERVES 2–4
PREP TIME 5 minutes
COOKING TIME 10 minutes

2 teaspoons olive oil
1 small onion, finely chopped
1 carrot, coarsely grated
1 clove garlic, crushed (optional)
1 tablespoon no-added-salt tomato paste (puree)
400 g tin no-added-salt chopped tomatoes
1 tablespoon Worcestershire sauce
1 teaspoon pure maple syrup
2 × 400 g tins cannellini beans, drained and rinsed
2 slices multigrain bread
½ cup (60 g) grated cheddar cheese

These baked beans are a delicious way to introduce babies and toddlers to legumes. We use cannellini beans here, but chickpeas, red kidney beans or four-bean mix will work well, too.

1. Heat the olive oil in a deep, heavy-based frying pan over medium heat. Add the onion, carrot and garlic, if using, and sauté for 2–3 minutes or until softened. Add the tomato paste, tomato, Worcestershire sauce, maple syrup and beans and cook, stirring occasionally, for 5 minutes.
2. If your child prefers a creamier texture or it needs to be smoother for younger babies, transfer a quarter of the mixture to a bowl and mash it with the back of a fork before returning to the pan with a tablespoon of water and stirring to combine.
3. Preheat the grill on high and place the bread in the toaster. When the bread is toasted, spread with a thin layer of the baked beans and top with grated cheese. (You will have leftover baked beans; see storage information, below.) Place under the grill and cook for 1 minute, until the cheese is melted and golden. Leave to cool slightly, then slice into fingers and serve.

STORAGE Leftover baked beans will keep for up to 3 days in an airtight container in the fridge. Alternatively, freeze individual portions for up to 3 months.

ALLERGIES/INTOLERANCES ***Gluten/wheat:*** use gluten-free Worcestershire sauce or replace with 1 tablespoon water, and use gluten- or wheat-free bread. ***Dairy:*** omit the cheese.

KALE AND MUSHROOM OMELETTE

SERVES 1
PREP TIME 5 minutes
COOKING TIME 6–10 minutes

20 g butter
¼ small red onion, finely chopped
3 button mushrooms, finely chopped
1 large curly kale leaf, stalk trimmed, finely chopped
½ clove garlic, crushed
2 eggs, lightly whisked
¼ cup (30 g) grated cheddar cheese
1 tablespoon crumbled feta (optional)
½ ripe small avocado, peeled and sliced (optional)

Break up the spoon-fed breakfast routine with a hearty and delicious omelette. Adding kale and mushrooms boosts the nutrient levels, making this a perfect start to the day, particularly if you can make time to sit down to enjoy breakfast together as a family. It works well as a dinner option, too.

1. Melt the butter in a non-stick, heavy-based frying pan over medium heat. Add the onion, mushrooms and kale and sauté for 3–5 minutes or until soft. Add the garlic and sauté for 1 minute more. Transfer to a bowl.
2. Add the egg to the pan and cook until it is beginning to set around the edges. Spoon the kale mixture over half the omelette, sprinkle with cheddar and feta, if using, and continue to cook until the egg is only slightly runny in the centre and the cheeses are beginning to melt. Fold the omelette over to enclose the filling and transfer to a plate. Top with slices of avocado, if desired, and serve.

NUTRITION NOTE Eggs provide high-quality protein and are rich in essential amino acids and many important micronutrients, including iron, zinc, folate, vitamin A and vitamin B12.

ALLERGIES/INTOLERANCES ***Dairy:*** omit the cheeses.

CHAPTER 7

SCHEDULE MEALTIMES AND SNACKS

Having a flexible schedule for meal and snack times can mean the difference between a child who asks for food all day long yet doesn't seem to eat anything and one who is happy to sit and devour their breakfast, lunch and dinner. Every child's appetite and routine is different, so devise a schedule that suits your child and offer wholesome, satisfying foods.

It can be hard to determine the cause of misbehaviour and fussy eating behaviours at mealtimes. The food on offer may not be the problem – leaps in development, feeling tired, bored or unwell can all be factors, too. Stick to a regular schedule for meals and snacks so you are offering food when your child is hungry and not too tired. You can then rule out these reasons for misbehaviour and tune into their cues to discover what the real problem is.

STRUCTURE MEALS

Some children prefer five or six smaller meals throughout the day, while others love the traditional three main meals and two snacks. Some may prefer a larger lunch than dinner, while others may make breakfast their biggest meal. Follow your child's cues and structure their meals accordingly. Whatever your child's preference, there are some tricks to keeping a good balance and maintaining a flexible schedule.

- Enjoy a nutritious breakfast at the same time each day. This consistency will offer a 'typical' start to the day
- Try to get home for lunch or find a quiet place where you can sit at a table if you're out and about. Children will find it easier to focus on their food and are likely to eat more, so they will be well fuelled for the afternoon
- Have a consistent dinnertime each day if possible. Overtired children will generally eat less, misbehave and be unwilling to try new foods
- Offer snacks at the same time each day, no less than 1 hour before the next meal to ensure they are hungry for it. It may need to be even earlier for children with small appetites or who are fussy with food
- Always ensure your children sit down to eat to prevent the risk of choking.

BALANCED SNACKING

Snacks keep kids well fuelled during the day – eating up to six times a day is perfectly normal for active, growing toddlers. Consider snack times as another opportunity to offer nutritious foods, create positive associations with eating and to role-model good behaviour. Try not to take the view that they're simply a tool for delaying a main meal. If your child starts to refuse their main meals or constantly nags you for snacks, reassess the time you're allowing between snacks and meals, as well as the type and amount of food you are offering.

Suggestions for a nutritious snack balance:

- Maintain a variety of foods at meal and snack times, and try to include two options for each snack, such as yoghurt and fruit, dip and vegetables, cheese and crackers, or a hard-boiled egg and a few strawberries
- Include a source of protein (eggs, cheese, yoghurt, legumes and nut butters are all good options) at snack times to help satisfy hunger, rather than using commercially processed 'filler' foods
- Pack healthy and appropriate snacks for your child when you know you are going to be out and about
- Make your own muffins, biscuits and muesli bars so you can control portion sizes, ensure the ingredients are nutritious, and avoid additives and preservatives
- Ensure your children sit down to eat to prevent the risk of choking and to encourage mindful eating
- Offer a drink of water at snack times (and throughout the day) for adequate hydration and dental health
- Avoid giving in to unhealthy requests that can become routine, such as a finger bun or lollies when you visit the shops, chips after school, ice cream after dinner or biscuits when you visit friends or family. It's fine to include these on occasion (see 'sometimes' foods on page 204), but not every day
- Serve appropriate portion sizes. The upsizing of portions, particularly snack foods, is a common culprit for overeating
- Respond appropriately to your child's hunger and fullness cues by offering additional food at mealtimes if they indicate they are hungry. Never force them to continue eating if they say they have had enough
- Talk to your children about feeling hungry and feeling full, so they can recognise these feelings and respond
- Avoid using food as a reward for good behaviour or as a distraction for boredom, as this can encourage both non-hungry and emotional eating
- If your child asks for something to eat outside of their meal or snack time, don't be afraid to say 'no'. If they refused food at the previous meal or snack time it is tempting to give in, as they could be genuinely hungry, but stand firm – if you give them something to eat, they may see it as a reward for food refusal and begin a pattern of this behaviour.

EXAMPLE MEALTIME SCHEDULE

8 a.m. breakfast	Creamy banana and apple porridge (page 150)
10 a.m. snack	Almond power balls (page 176) and a slice of cheese
12 p.m. lunch	Mini sushi rolls (page 126), halved cherry tomatoes and a small portion of chopped fruit
3 p.m. snack	plain Greek-style yoghurt and cucumber sticks
5 p.m. dinner	Lamb and pesto sausages (page 134), Sweet potato fries (page 65), steamed broccoli and chopped fruit

APPETITE AWARENESS

Overeating is a common problem, as many of us learn to ignore our innate hunger and fullness cues as we grow older. Distractions during mealtimes, emotional eating, non-hungry eating, mindlessness and being taught that it is good manners to eat everything on your plate all exacerbate the problem. If you watch a baby eat, you'll see they often indicate they have had enough when there is still food in their bowl, despite obviously enjoying the meal. Knowing, recognising and respecting your child's hunger and fullness cues will help you ensure they continue to recognise and respond to them.

Take care not to encourage non-hungry and emotional eating. Offering food to stop tears and tantrums, distract a tired or bored baby, or reward good behaviour teaches children to ignore what their body is telling them. This non-hungry and emotional eating can lead to undesirable eating behaviours as adolescents and adults, affect their ability to maintain a healthy weight and take away their ability to enjoy and take pleasure in food and social occasions that centre around a meal. Instead of food, offer a cuddle, a nap or quiet time with a book or puzzle, and always suggest they have a drink of water. Wait until the next regular meal or snack time to offer food.

Many parents worry that their child isn't eating enough to meet their dietary requirements, and encourage them to continue eating after they've indicated they are finished. Some children simply have small appetites. If they eat small amounts of a variety of nutritious foods and are achieving typical developmental milestones and tracking along the growth curve at a normal rate, you should feel reassured. It's also important to consider the food they have eaten over the course of the day (or even week), rather than focusing on individual meals and what they didn't eat. Having a structured daily routine of meals and snacks will make it easier to recognise when your baby or toddler is hungry, compared with when they are simply tired, bored or thirsty. Trust your instincts and see pages 100–101 for common reasons for food refusal or selective eating.

If you suspect your child has a medical concern that is affecting their appetite, growth or is influencing food refusal, consult your doctor for assessment and referral to an appropriate healthcare provider.

HEALTHY TEETH SUPPORT A HEALTHY CHILD

We need strong, healthy and appropriately positioned teeth to be able to chew and swallow a wide variety of nutritious foods. Poor oral hygiene and tooth decay can increase the likelihood of infection and pain in your child's mouth, contributing to difficulty chewing, as well as fussy and selective eating behaviours. Eating a healthy, nutritious diet helps to maintain healthy teeth, along with introducing good oral hygiene habits. Vegetables, dairy foods and water all help to protect the teeth from decay.

Foods that are high in refined carbohydrates and sugar, on the other hand, such as biscuits, lollies, dried fruit, fruit snacks, chips and sugary drinks, tend to stick to teeth and can contribute to the development of tooth decay. Try to limit these foods to sometimes only. When your child's teeth start coming through take them to the dentist for a check-up, and continue with regular visits as the dentist deems necessary. Visit the dentist immediately if you notice any sign of tooth decay, such as dull, white patches on the teeth close to the gums that can't be removed by brushing; grey, brown or black spots on the teeth; and red and swollen gums.

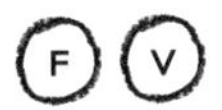

SAVOURY VEGGIE SLICE

MAKES 16 PIECES
PREP TIME 10 minutes
COOKING TIME 30 minutes

- 85 ml olive oil, plus extra for greasing
- 1 small onion, finely chopped
- ¾ cup (90 g) grated cheddar cheese
- 2 eggs, lightly whisked
- ¾ cup (180 ml) milk
- 1 carrot, coarsely grated
- 1 zucchini (courgette), peeled, coarsely grated, liquid squeezed out
- 2 tablespoons finely chopped mixed herbs (such as chives, parsley, thyme)
- 2 cups (320 g) wholemeal plain flour or plain flour (or a mixture of both)
- 3 teaspoons baking powder

If you are struggling to get your child to eat veggies, look for meals like this where you can 'hide' them. In addition, keep presenting vegetables to them in a variety of ways, such as growing them, visiting food markets and cooking together.

1. Preheat the oven to 200°C (180°C fan-forced). Lightly grease a square 22 cm cake tin with oil.
2. Heat 1 teaspoon of the olive oil in a small frying pan over medium heat. Add the onion and sauté for 2 minutes or until softened. Transfer to a large bowl. Add the cheese, egg, milk, carrot, zucchini, herbs and remaining ⅓ cup (80 ml) oil and whisk to combine.
3. Sift the flour and baking powder together into the bowl. Add the vegetable mixture and fold in gently until just combined. Spoon into the greased tin and bake for 25–30 minutes or until the slice is golden and set. Remove from the oven and leave to cool in the tin before cutting into 16 pieces.

FUSSY EATING TIP Bribing or forcing your child to eat their veggies (or any food) may result in a negative association with eating, decreased enjoyment of the food and greater anxiety and stress at mealtimes. Instead, look for positive motivations, such as serving new or previously refused foods when there are other children around who will eat them.

TIP You can save time by adding the onion raw, but cooking it first gives a sweeter flavour.

STORAGE Keep in an airtight container in the fridge for up to 3 days. Alternatively, wrap individually in plastic film, place in a freezer bag and freeze for up to 2 months.

✱ALLERGIES/INTOLERANCES ***Gluten/wheat:*** use gluten- or wheat-free flour. ***Dairy:*** omit the cheese and substitute a dairy-free alternative for the milk. ***Egg:*** use 2 'chia eggs' (see page 5) or 'linseed eggs' (see page 5) to replace the eggs.

SEEDED PESTO MUFFINS

MAKES 12
PREP TIME 10 minutes
COOKING TIME 20 minutes

- ⅓ cup (80 ml) macadamia or olive oil, plus extra for greasing
- 2 cups (320 g) wholemeal plain flour
- 1 tablespoon baking powder
- pinch of salt
- 1 cup (140 g) mixed seeds (such as sunflower seeds, sesame seeds, poppy seeds), plus extra for topping
- 2 eggs, lightly whisked
- 1 tablespoon pure maple syrup
- ¼ cup (60 g) Basil pesto (see page 232)
- ¾ cup (180 ml) milk
- ⅓ cup (25 g) grated parmesan, plus extra for topping

Our children love pesto and will attest that it's an irresistible element in these delicious muffins. The seeds on top provide a lovely crunch, too.

1. Preheat the oven to 200°C (180°C fan-forced) and grease a 12-hole regular muffin tin with macadamia or olive oil.
2. Sift the flour, baking powder and salt together into a bowl. Add the seeds and mix to combine.
3. Whisk the macadamia or olive oil, egg, maple syrup, basil pesto, milk and parmesan together in a separate bowl. Add to the dry ingredients and use a wooden spoon to mix until just combined.
4. Spoon the mixture evenly into the greased muffin holes. Sprinkle the muffins with extra seeds and parmesan. Bake for 20 minutes or until golden brown and a skewer inserted in the centre of the muffins comes out clean. Remove from the oven and transfer to a wire rack to cool.

NUTRITION NOTE Rich in healthy fats and essential vitamins and minerals, seeds offer children numerous health benefits. They are also a great alternative to nuts for those with allergies.

STORAGE Keep in an airtight container in the fridge for up to 3 days. Alternatively, wrap individually in plastic film, place in a freezer bag and freeze for up to 2 months.

*ALLERGIES/INTOLERANCES ***Gluten/wheat:*** use gluten- or wheat-free flour. ***Dairy:*** use a dairy-free milk and omit the parmesan. ***Egg:*** replace the eggs with 2 'chia eggs' (see page 5).

CAULIFLOWER HUMMUS

MAKES 2 CUPS (500 G)
PREP TIME 15 minutes (+ cooling)
COOKING TIME 5 minutes

3½ cups (350 g) chopped cauliflower florets
400 g tin chickpeas, drained and rinsed
¼ cup (60 ml) olive oil
¼ cup (60 ml) fresh lemon juice
2 tablespoons hulled tahini
1 small clove garlic, crushed
1 teaspoon ground cumin
pinch of salt

If you have a little hummus-lover in the house, use it as a vehicle to introduce new foods or flavours. Cauliflower is a great addition because it doesn't change the colour or texture too much, but you could also add leafy green vegetables, chia seeds or even avocado. Serve the hummus with steamed veggie sticks, crackers or as a spread on sandwiches and wraps.

1. Place the cauliflower in a steamer basket over a saucepan of boiling water and cook, covered, for 5 minutes or until tender. Remove from the pan and tip onto a clean tea towel to allow the excess water to drain off while it cools to room temperature.
2. Transfer the cauliflower to a food processor and pulse until finely chopped. Add the chickpeas, olive oil, lemon juice, tahini, garlic, cumin and salt and process until smooth, stopping once or twice to scrape down the side of the bowl. Process until the mixture forms a smooth paste, then transfer to a small bowl and serve.

NUTRITION NOTE Making your own hummus allows you to keep the salt content low and you can boost it with other nutritious ingredients such as vegetables, herbs, nuts and seeds.

STORAGE Keep in an airtight container in the fridge for up to 3 days.

ALLERGIES/INTOLERANCES ***Sesame:*** replace the tahini with extra olive oil and/or fresh lemon juice, adding enough to reach your desired consistency.

SCONES THREE WAYS

MAKES ABOUT 14
PREP TIME 10 minutes
COOKING TIME 15 minutes

2½ cups (375 g) self-raising flour, plus extra for dusting
25 g pure icing sugar
pinch of salt
75 g butter, chilled and chopped
1 cup (250 ml) buttermilk
milk, for brushing
jam and cream, to serve

Scones with jam and cream are a wonderful treat, or you can make our savoury or pumpkin variations to turn them into more of an everyday option.

1. Preheat the oven to 200°C (180°C fan-forced). Line a baking tray with baking paper.
2. Sift the flour, icing sugar and salt together into a bowl. Use your fingertips to rub in the butter until the mixture resembles very fine breadcrumbs.
3. Add the buttermilk and use a flat-bladed knife to mix using a cutting action until a soft dough forms. Turn the dough out onto a lightly floured surface. Gently knead, adding a little more flour if the dough is too sticky. Shape the dough into a disc, about 3 cm thick.
4. Use a lightly floured 5 cm cutter to cut out scones and place on the lined tray, leaving 5 cm between each. Brush the top of each scone lightly with milk. Bake for 12–15 minutes, until risen and lightly browned. Remove from the oven and transfer to a wire rack. Serve warm with jam and cream.

PUMPKIN VARIATION Add ¼ teaspoon ground cinnamon and ¼ teaspoon nutmeg when sifting the flour, icing sugar and salt. Add 1 cup (250 g) pumpkin (squash) puree to the mixture after rubbing in the butter, and use a flat-bladed knife to mix until partially combined. Reduce the buttermilk to ½ cup (125 ml).

SAVOURY VARIATION Add 1 coarsely grated small zucchini (courgette) with excess liquid squeezed out; 1 cup (120 g) grated cheddar cheese; and 1–2 tablespoons chopped herbs (such as chives, parsley or thyme) to the mixture after rubbing in the butter, then mix until combined. You can also add ½ cup (100 g) diced cooked bacon, ½ cup (80 g) lightly fried chopped onion or ½ cup (90 g) finely chopped capsicum (pepper), if you like.

NUTRITION NOTE Serve the scones with fresh berries for added nutrition.

STORAGE Keep in an airtight container for 1 day or in the fridge for up to 2 days.

*ALLERGIES/INTOLERANCES ***Gluten/wheat:*** use gluten- or wheat-free self-raising flour. ***Dairy:*** use coconut or macadamia oil or a dairy-free spread to replace the butter. Substitute dairy-free milk combined with 1 tablespoon lemon juice or vinegar for the buttermilk (if making the pumpkin scones, you'll only need to add 2 teaspoons lemon juice or vinegar). Omit the milk for brushing. Omit the cheese if making savoury scones.

TIP
For the basic recipe, mix in ½ cup (80 g) dried fruit or ½ cup (95 g) chocolate chips after rubbing in the butter, if desired.

TEENY TEDDIES

MAKES ABOUT 150
PREP TIME 40 minutes
(+ 30 minutes chilling)
COOKING TIME 12 minutes

125 g butter, chopped and softened
½ cup (110 g) caster sugar
1 teaspoon pure vanilla extract
1 egg
1½ cups (225 g) plain flour, plus extra for dusting
½ cup (80 g) wholemeal plain flour (or additional plain flour)
¼ teaspoon baking powder
1 tablespoon milk
1 tablespoon cacao or cocoa powder (optional)

These cute biscuits are perfect for a snack or lunchbox treat. This recipe makes a large quantity of teeny teddies, so we usually divide the dough into three portions and just cook one (about 50 biscuits), freezing the other portions of dough for another time. Or, we use the full quantity and make some teeny teddies, plus some larger biscuits.

1. Preheat the oven to 180°C (160°C fan-forced). Line a large baking tray with baking paper (if you are cooking the full quantity of biscuits, you will need to line 2–3 trays).
2. Use an electric mixer to beat the butter and sugar for 4–5 minutes or until pale and creamy. Add the vanilla and egg and continue to beat until well combined. Gradually add the flours, baking powder, milk and cacao or cocoa, if using, and beat on low speed until a dough forms. (If you want to make an equal quantity of vanilla and chocolate biscuits, transfer half the dough to a separate bowl and mix in 2 teaspoons of cacao or cocoa. Keep the vanilla and chocolate doughs separate from here on.)
3. Transfer the dough to a lightly floured bench and gently knead until smooth. Wrap in plastic film and place in the fridge for 30 minutes to chill.
4. Roll out the dough between 2 sheets of baking paper until it is 3–4 mm thick. Use a small teddy-shaped cutter to cut out shapes, placing them on the lined tray. Bake for 10–12 minutes or until just firm (and light golden for vanilla biscuits). They cook quickly because they are small, so take care not to overcook them. Remove from the oven and cool on the tray for 5 minutes before transferring to a wire rack to cool completely.

NUTRITION NOTE Offer 'sometimes' foods at a regular meal or snack time to ensure your child will enjoy the special food without distractions. This encourages mindful eating and nurtures positive eating behaviours.

STORAGE Keep in an airtight container for up to 1 week. Alternatively, freeze individual portions for up to 3 months. Uncooked dough, wrapped in plastic film, can be stored in the fridge for up to 1 week or frozen for up to 3 months.

✱ALLERGIES/INTOLERANCES ***Gluten/wheat:*** use gluten- or wheat-free flour. ***Dairy:*** use ½ cup (125 ml) olive oil or melted coconut oil instead of the butter, and use water or a dairy-free milk instead of the milk. ***Egg:*** substitute ⅓ cup (100 g) unsweetened apple puree or a 'chia egg' (see page 5) for the egg.

CHOC POPCORN BALLS

MAKES ABOUT 12
PREP TIME 10 minutes
(+ 1 hour chilling)
COOKING TIME 5 minutes

⅓ cup (80 ml) cooking oil (such as light olive, coconut or rice bran oil)
2 tablespoons popping corn
2 tablespoons pure maple syrup
1 teaspoon honey
1½ tablespoons cacao or cocoa powder
2 tablespoons pure nut or seed butter (such as peanut, almond, hulled tahini or sunflower)
pinch of salt

There's no reason to buy microwave popcorn with its synthetic flavours – it's easy to make your own, and a bag of popping corn is cheap and goes a long way. Serve it plain, with a little butter or make these sweet and nutty balls. The kids love to help squeeze and shape them, but make sure their hands (and yours!) are clean and wet as the mixture is really sticky.

1. Heat 2 tablespoons of the oil in a large heavy-based saucepan over medium–high heat until hot. Add the popping corn, cover and cook, shaking the pan often, for 3 minutes or until most of the kernels have popped. Remove from the heat and tip into a large bowl. Once cool enough to handle, remove any unpopped kernels (they usually fall to the bottom of the bowl). Use your hands to crumble the popcorn into smaller pieces.
2. Place the remaining 2 tablespoons of oil, the maple syrup, honey, cacao or cocoa, and nut or seed butter in a small saucepan over low heat and cook, stirring often, until melted and well combined. Pour the hot mixture over the popcorn, add a pinch of salt and use a flexible spatula to toss the popcorn to coat. Set aside until cool enough to handle.
3. Use wet hands to squeeze and shape heaped tablespoons of the popcorn mixture into balls, placing them on a tray as you go. Chill in the fridge for at least 1 hour or until set.

NUTRITION NOTE Popcorn is a terrific snack for older preschoolers and school-aged kids, but do not serve it to babies and toddlers as they can choke on unpopped kernels or swallow sharp sides if not chewed completely.

TIP If the mixture isn't holding together, put it in the fridge for 10 minutes and then try again.

STORAGE Keep in an airtight container in the fridge for up to 4 days. Alternatively, place on a tray and freeze just until frozen, then transfer to a freezer bag and store in the freezer for up to 1 month. Ensure the balls are completely thawed before serving.

✱ALLERGIES/INTOLERANCES ***Nuts:*** use sunflower seed butter or hulled tahini instead of nut butter.

ALMOND POWER BALLS

MAKES ABOUT 20
PREP TIME 10 minutes
COOKING TIME Nil

- ¾ cup (60 g) desiccated coconut, plus extra for coating (optional)
- ¾ cup (105 g) pitted dates
- 2 tablespoons pure almond butter
- 1 tablespoon chia seeds
- ¼ cup (10 g) puffed rice
- 1 teaspoon pure maple syrup
- 1 tablespoon cacao powder or chocolate chips (optional)

Most children love 'bliss balls' and so do we – they're easy to make and you can add lots of natural and nutritious ingredients they might otherwise refuse or that may be unsuitable for them to eat.

1. Place the coconut and dates in a food processor and process until finely chopped. Add the remaining ingredients and process until the consistency of fine crumbs, with no large pieces. Use your hands to squeeze some of the mixture – it should stick together. If it doesn't, try processing for a further 10–20 seconds. Add a little more almond butter or maple syrup, if needed. Transfer the mixture to a clean bowl.
2. Use wet hands to shape tablespoons of the mixture into balls, placing them on a tray as you go. Place the extra coconut in a shallow bowl and roll the balls in coconut to coat, if desired.

NUTRITION NOTE While whole nuts aren't appropriate for children under 3 years of age, you can still incorporate them into their diet with quality nut butters, nut spreads and finely ground nuts. Almonds are high in fibre and rich in health-promoting antioxidants and nutrients, including vitamin E, calcium, iron and zinc. They also help to maintain a healthy heart and digestive system.

STORAGE Keep in an airtight container in the fridge for up to 4 days. Alternatively, freeze on a lined tray until frozen, then place in a freezer bag and freeze for up to 3 months.

ALLERGIES/INTOLERANCES ***Gluten/wheat:*** use gluten-free puffed rice or substitute puffed quinoa. ***Almond:*** use an alternative nut or seed butter, such as hulled tahini.

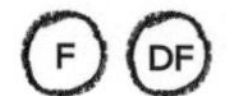

COCONUT MUFFINS WITH A TWIST

MAKES 24 MINI MUFFINS OR 12 REGULAR MUFFINS
PREP TIME 10 minutes
COOKING TIME 20 minutes

½ cup (125 ml) melted coconut oil (or macadamia or olive oil), plus extra for greasing
2 cups (300 g) plain flour
1 tablespoon baking powder
pinch of salt
¼ cup (60 ml) pure maple syrup
1 egg
1 cup (250 ml) coconut milk (or your preferred milk)
1 cup (75 g) shredded coconut
½ cup (80 g) finely chopped dried fruit (such as apricots, figs, apple or raisins) or choc chips

These coconut muffins are great for preschool or school lunchboxes, as they are nut free. The 'twist' is the addition of dried fruit or chocolate chips, which you can vary according to whatever you have on hand.

1. Preheat the oven to 180°C (160°C fan-forced). Grease two 12-hole mini muffin tins or a 12-hole regular muffin tin with oil.
2. Sift the flour, baking powder and salt together into a bowl. Place the coconut oil, maple syrup, egg and coconut milk in a jug and whisk to combine. Add to the dry ingredients and stir until just combined – take care not to overmix or the muffins will be tough. Gently fold through the coconut, then the dried fruit or choc chips (or ½ cup of your chosen 'twist' ingredient).
3. Spoon the mixture into the greased muffin holes. Bake for 13–15 minutes for mini muffins, or 17–20 minutes for regular muffins, or until light golden and a skewer inserted into the centre of a muffin comes out clean. Remove from the oven and set aside for 5 minutes before turning out onto a wire rack to cool.

NUTRITION NOTE Choose sulphite- and preservative-free dried fruit, particularly for children who may be sensitive to their unwanted side effects.

STORAGE The muffins will keep in an airtight container for up to 3 days. Alternatively, wrap individually in plastic film, place in a freezer bag and freeze for up to 2 months.

✱ALLERGIES/INTOLERANCES ***Gluten/wheat:*** use gluten- or wheat-free flour. ***Egg:*** use a 'chia egg' (see page 5) or ½ ripe mashed banana to replace the egg.

CHOC-HAZELNUT SPREAD

MAKES ¾ CUP (150 G)
PREP TIME 10 minutes
COOKING TIME Nil

1 cup (140 g) roasted and skinned hazelnuts
2 tablespoons cacao or cocoa powder
¼ cup (60 ml) pure maple syrup
4 medjool dates, pitted
1 teaspoon pure vanilla extract
2 tablespoons macadamia oil
pinch of salt
fruit or wholegrain toast, to serve

Chocolate hazelnut spreads are cleverly marketed to kids and their love of sweet tastes. Making your own with quality ingredients is a cinch, and allows you to control the level of sweetness.

1. Place the hazelnuts in a high-powered blender or food processor and blitz for 30 seconds to 2 minutes (the time will vary, depending on your processor), until a sticky, dough-like consistency.
2. Add the remaining ingredients and process until smooth and combined, adding more oil if needed to achieve your desired consistency. Transfer to a sterilised glass jar (see tip).
3. Serve with sliced or chopped fruit for dipping, or simply spread over wholegrain toast.

TIP To sterilise a glass jar, preheat the oven to 180°C (160°C fan-forced). Wash jars and lids in hot soapy water, then rinse well. Place the jars, right-side up, on a baking tray. Place in the oven for 10 minutes. Meanwhile, bring a saucepan of water to the boil. Boil the lids for 2–3 minutes. As a general rule, put cold mixtures into cooled jars and hot mixtures into hot jars.

STORAGE Keep in the fridge for up to 2 weeks.

✱ALLERGIES/INTOLERANCES ***Hazelnuts:*** use almonds or peanuts instead.

BANANA AND STRAWBERRY ICE CREAM

SERVES 2
PREP TIME 5 minutes
COOKING TIME Nil

1 frozen chopped banana (ideally, the pieces should be about 1 cm thick)
100 g frozen chopped strawberries

Keep frozen ripe bananas and strawberries, chopped into small pieces (large pieces can damage your food processor), on hand during summer to ensure you have a constant supply of this delicious ice cream. Once you have mastered this combination you can try replacing the strawberries with other fruit, such as raspberries, pear, dates, passionfruit, mango and more.

1 Place the fruit in a blender or food processor and blend until smooth and creamy, stopping to scrape down the side of the blender or bowl as required. Serve immediately.

NUTRITION NOTE Free of added sugars or preservatives and full of flavour, the kids will have no idea this ice cream is made entirely from fruit.

STORAGE If making ahead of time, spoon into popsicle moulds, cover and place in the freezer until required. Use within 1 month.

CHAPTER 8

MAKE FOOD ENJOYABLE

If you make sourcing, preparing and eating food a relaxed, fun, interactive and varied experience for your child, you'll reap the benefits. Involve them in the grocery shopping, meal preparation and cooking, so they feel ownership over the end result. Set up a picnic rug in the garden and have lunch outside every now and then, keep their lunchbox varied and interesting, and let them choose a theme for dinner on the weekend, such as Mexican, Indian or pizza. If they're having fun (and you are, too), they'll look forward to every meal.

Providing children with lots of positive food experiences, from growing to cooking and eating, goes a long way towards raising a healthy eater. The more opportunities they have to interact with different foods, the more familiar with them they'll become and the more likely they may enjoy them. If they eat lunch away from home, avoid the trap of packing the same foods every day by making nutrition, variety and enjoyment your priorities.

GROCERY SHOPPING

Taking your child with you when you shop for groceries is a realistic way to include them in the weekly meal planning and expose them to different types of food. Knowing in advance what foods they'll be eating during the week will also make them feel they're in control. Go at a time when your child is well rested and not hungry, talk to them about behaving well and take a list of what you need. When you reach the shops, encourage your child to help you choose the fruit and vegetables. Suggest they touch and smell them, and point out which fruits are ripe and how you can tell. If they're old enough, send them on a mission to find a certain item that you need. All these small interactions will help them form lots of positive feelings about food.

GARDENING

Children who learn to appreciate plants and whole foods will grow up with a respect for nature and understand where food comes from. Planting some herbs and veggies in your garden or on the balcony is a great way to teach them about ingredients. They will love digging a hole, planting some seeds and watering the seedlings that spring up. Watching fruit and vegetables develop, then picking them and helping you prepare them for dinner is a wonderful hands-on learning experience. Needless to say, they'll be much more interested in trying a new food if they have been watching it grow. If you can't do it at home, ask a relative or friend if you can plant some things in their garden, or get involved with your local community garden.

If gardening really isn't your thing, visit your closest farmers' market or take a day trip to go fruit picking at an orchard. Even a weekend drive through the countryside to look at farm animals and field crops helps a child's understanding of where food comes from.

COOKING

Cooking with kids is a fun, educational and bonding experience. While they practise stirring, rolling and whisking, and watch ingredients transform, they're learning life skills and developing an interest in food. It can be particularly beneficial for fussy eaters, as it engages their curiosity and inspires them to try new foods.

Before you start cooking, work out which tasks your child can do. Young children can get out ingredients and utensils, then stir, whisk and roll, while older children can also measure out the ingredients, cut up soft foods with a round-bladed knife and read out the recipe for you. Work with them at first, then when you're confident they are old enough to understand the rules of the kitchen (cooking with heat and using sharp knives and appliances such as a food processor must be supervised), give them the freedom to create their own masterpieces.

PACKING A HEALTHY LUNCHBOX

When kids eat their snacks and midday meal away from home, it's important to ensure you give them a balanced selection of foods that will provide enough energy to get them through the day. Ideally, a lunchbox should deliver key nutrients such as iron, zinc, protein, quality carbohydrates and omega-3 fatty acids, so they have the energy to grow, the concentration to listen and learn, and a strong immune system to minimise sick days.

Don't feel deflated when your lunchbox comes home largely untouched. Talk to your child about why they didn't eat it, ask them what sort of (healthy) things they would like instead and make some adjustments. Avoid pre-packaged snacks, such as sweet and savoury biscuits, because they are low in nutrients and your child will be lacking in energy and find it hard to concentrate during the day, then come home tired, irritable and over-hungry.

Beat the repetition

Kids love routine and will often go through phases of wanting the same food in their lunchbox, day in, day out. This can occur when they have had the same food prepared in the same way over two or more consecutive days, so try to avoid doing this. If they insist on having a cheese sandwich, cut it into different shapes, such as triangles one day and squares the next. Gradually build on this by suggesting additions like cucumber, lettuce, ham or avocado. When making changes to your child's lunchbox, do it gradually to encourage acceptance. And if your child consistently comes home with their lunch uneaten, offering a nutritious breakfast, afternoon tea and dinner will help.

Nutrition know-how

- Choose wholegrain breads, wraps or rolls, as they give longer-lasting energy than white varieties
- Don't forget the protein to satisfy hungry appetites and promote growth and development. Lean meat, leftover meatballs, chicken, tinned fish, eggs and cheese are great on sandwiches, while yoghurt, milk, cheese slices, nuts and wholegrain muesli bars are good for snacks
- Include veggies to help them meet their requirements. Try cherry tomatoes, carrot, capsicum (pepper), celery and snow peas (mangetout) as snacks and include salad fillings on sandwiches, such as lettuce and grated carrot
- Avoid fruit juice, fruit drinks, cordials and processed fruit snacks – fresh fruit is always best. Chopped fruit is usually more appealing to children than whole pieces, and brushing the cut side of the fruit with a little lemon juice will prevent browning
- Include a bottle of water to ensure they stay hydrated.

Food safety tips

It's natural to worry about food poisoning when packing your child's lunchbox, especially when the weather is hot. As a general rule, keep cold food cold and hot food hot to prevent the growth of harmful bacteria. Here's how to ensure your lunchbox passes the food safety test:

- Wash your hands before handling food
- Buy a good-quality insulated lunchbox or cooler bag
- Thaw frozen food in the fridge overnight
- Only include leftovers that were cooked no more than 24 hours prior and were refrigerated immediately
- Place a frozen bottle of water or ice pack in your child's lunchbox next to the food that needs to be kept cold
- If you are packing your child's lunchbox in advance, keep it in the fridge until you're ready to leave
- Encourage your child to keep their lunchbox out of direct sunlight if possible, and place it in a fridge if there is one available
- Throw out any perishable food that isn't eaten.

LUNCHBOX TIPS

Packaging

The way lunch is prepared and presented is important to some children. Make sure the food is inviting, colourful and fresh. Purchase food containers in different sizes to inspire you to mix things up. Choosing the right lunchbox can be the difference between food being eaten or not. Allow your child to choose their own lunchbox, so they aren't embarrassed to bring it out.

Variety

Keep things interesting by packing a different selection of foods each day. Even if one or two items are the same, make sure the rest is different to the day before. Vary the presentation of the food, too. Try serving it like a bento box, use cookie cutters to cut cheese or fruit into shapes, or give the ingredients for a sandwich and let them put it together themselves.

Do some batch cooking on the weekend and make lots of healthy snacks you can individually freeze, so you have a variety to choose from.

If you'd like to include a new food, introduce it at home to encourage acceptance before putting it in their lunchbox. When you include it, offer a small amount to begin with and ensure there are at least two other items they will accept and enjoy.

Freshness

Pack child-friendly ice packs to keep food fresh and cool. Also, choose foods that stay fresh and appetising all day – soggy textures and offensive smells will put children off the food and may cause embarrassment with their friends.

Simplicity

Make sure your child can open containers and any sealed items. Cut their fruit into suitable portions, and choose foods that are easy to eat. If there's something in the lunchbox that's messy to eat, include a serviette or paper towel, so they can clean themselves up.

NO-NUT CRUNCHY MUESLI BARS

MAKES 12 BARS
PREP TIME 15 minutes
COOKING TIME 35 minutes

1½ cups (135 g) rolled oats
¾ cup (60 g) shredded or desiccated coconut
½ cup (175 g) honey
1 tablespoon soft brown sugar
40 g unsalted butter
1 teaspoon pure vanilla extract
pinch of salt
½ cup (80 g) finely chopped dried fruit (such as dates, apricots or sultanas)
½ cup (70 g) sunflower seeds
½ cup (20 g) low-sodium cornflakes

Irresistibly golden and crunchy, our no-nut muesli bars are perfect for school lunchboxes. The oats and sunflower seeds offer essential nutrients that are needed to fuel little bodies through their busy day.

1. Preheat the oven to 180°C (160°C fan-forced). Line a baking tray and a square 22 cm cake tin with baking paper.
2. Spread the oats over the lined tray and bake for 5 minutes. Add the coconut and bake for a further 2 minutes or until it begins to turn golden brown. Remove from the oven and set aside. Reduce the oven temperature to 150°C (130°C fan-forced).
3. Place the honey, brown sugar, butter, vanilla extract and salt in a small heavy-based saucepan over medium heat and stir constantly until the sugar has dissolved and the mixture begins to froth. Remove from the heat.
4. Combine the oat mixture, honey mixture, dried fruit, sunflower seeds and cornflakes in a large bowl. Use a wooden spoon to stir gently until well combined. Spoon the mixture into the pan and spread evenly. Bake for 25 minutes or until golden. Remove from the oven and set aside on a wire rack to cool completely – it will harden as it cools. Turn onto a chopping board and use a sharp knife to carefully cut into 12 bars.

NUTRITION NOTE Be mindful of the quantity and frequency of dried fruit offered in your child's diet, as it may contribute to excess energy intake, dental caries and even fussy eating behaviours.

STORAGE Keep in an airtight container at room temperature for up to 3 days. Alternatively, wrap individually in plastic film, place in a freezer bag and freeze for up to 1 month.

✱ALLERGIES/INTOLERANCES ***Gluten/wheat:*** use quinoa, quinoa flakes, buckwheat, rye or barley flakes, as appropriate, instead of the oats.
Dairy: replace the butter with coconut, olive or macadamia oil.

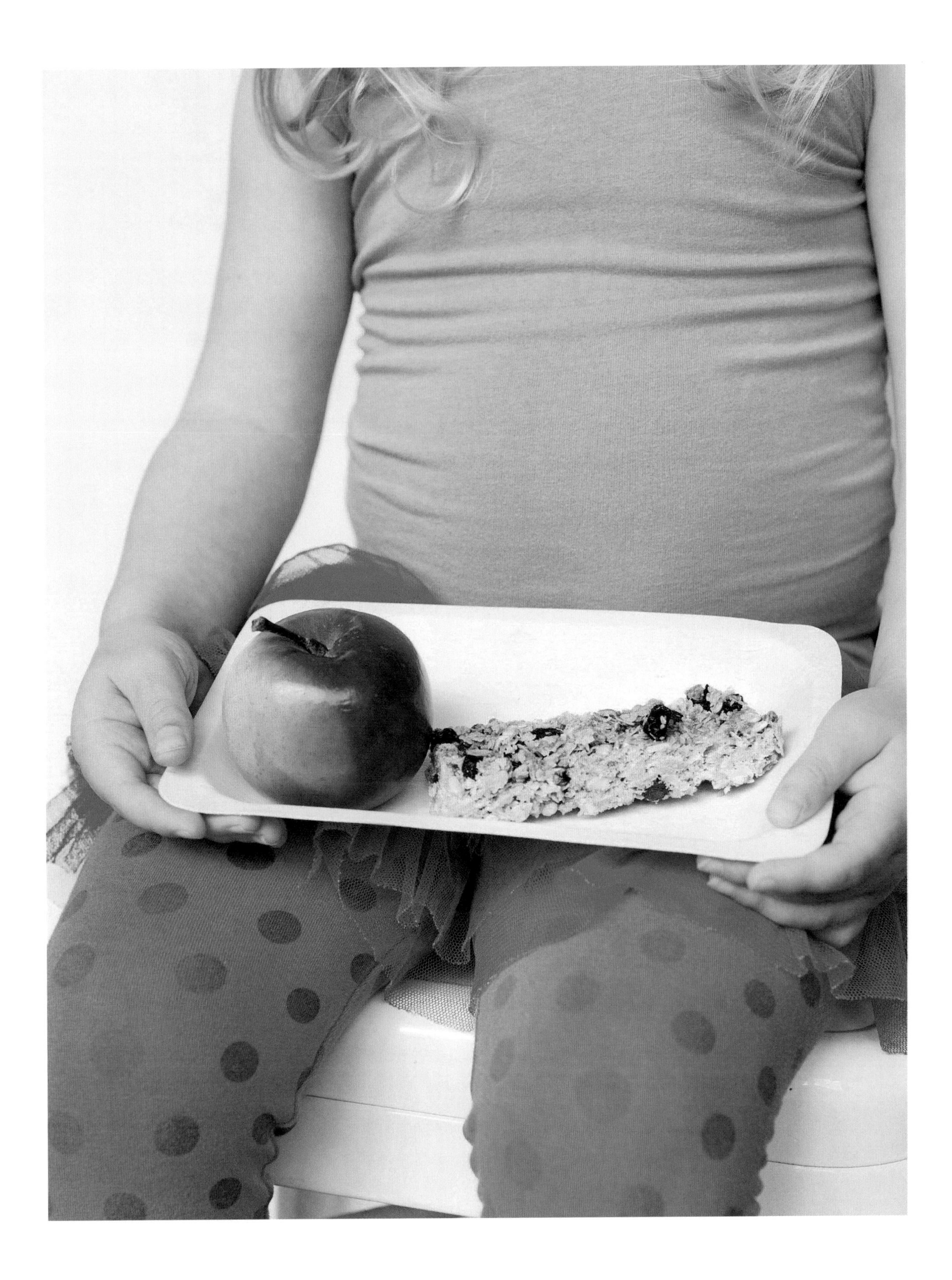

NUTRITION NOTE

Oats are an economical way to add fibre, slow-releasing carbohydrates, protein and B-group vitamins needed for lasting energy.

JOLLY GOOD LUNCHBOX BISCUITS

MAKES ABOUT 24
PREP TIME 10 minutes
COOKING TIME 15 minutes

- 150 g unsalted butter, chopped and softened
- ¾ cup, firmly packed (165 g) soft brown sugar
- 1 egg, lightly whisked
- 1 ripe large banana, mashed
- 1½ cups (240 g) wholemeal plain flour
- ½ teaspoon bicarbonate of soda
- 1 cup (90 g) rolled oats
- ½ cup (75 g) finely chopped pitted dates
- ½ cup (80 g) finely chopped dried apricots

There's an abundance of tempting pre-packaged lunchbox snacks on offer, but their nutritional content is often questionable. It is important to keep offering healthy choices in a variety of ways, and including wholesome home-baked snacks is a great start.

1. Preheat the oven to 180°C (160°C fan-forced) and line a large baking tray with baking paper.
2. Use a wooden spoon to beat the butter, sugar and egg in a medium bowl until pale and creamy. Stir in the banana, then the combined sifted flour and bicarbonate of soda, and the oats, date and apricot.
3. Roll tablespoons of the mixture into balls and place on the lined tray, leaving at least 5 cm between each. Gently push down to flatten the top of each biscuit. Bake for 15 minutes or until golden brown. Remove from the oven and cool on the trays for 5 minutes before transferring to a wire rack to cool completely.

TIP If nuts are allowed, add ¼ cup (25 g) chopped walnuts to the mixture.

STORAGE Keep in an airtight container for up to 5 days. Alternatively, freeze biscuits, wrapped in plastic film or in freezer bags, for up to 2 months.

ALLERGIES/INTOLERANCES ***Gluten/wheat:*** use gluten- or wheat-free flour, and use quinoa flakes instead of the oats. ***Dairy:*** substitute coconut, olive or macadamia oil for the butter. ***Egg:*** replace the egg with a 'chia egg' (see page 5); ½ ripe small banana, mashed; or ¼ cup (75 g) unsweetened apple sauce or apple puree.

CARROT AND BLUEBERRY OATBRAN MUFFINS

MAKES 12
PREP TIME 10 minutes
COOKING TIME 25 minutes

¼ cup (60 ml) macadamia oil or melted coconut oil, plus extra for greasing
1 cup (150 g) plain flour
1 cup (100 g) oatbran
½ cup (110 g) caster sugar
2 teaspoons baking powder
1 teaspoon ground cinnamon
120 g carrots, coarsely grated
2 eggs
¾ cup (180 ml) buttermilk
½ cup (75 g) blueberries (or 1 apple, peeled, cored and grated)

Cooking with your kids not only helps to boost their confidence with food, but also teaches them valuable skills, exposes them to a variety of ingredients and can help improve fussy eating behaviours.

1 Preheat the oven to 180°C (160°C fan-forced). Grease a 12-hole regular muffin tin with oil or line with paper cases.

2 Place the flour, oatbran, sugar, baking powder and cinnamon in a large bowl and stir to combine. Mix in the carrot. Whisk the eggs, buttermilk and oil together in a separate bowl. Add to the flour mixture and stir until just combined – be careful not to over-mix or the muffins will be tough. Add the blueberries or apple and stir until just combined.

3 Spoon the mixture into the prepared muffin holes. Bake for 20–25 minutes or until light golden and a skewer inserted into the centre of a muffin comes out clean. Remove from the oven and leave in the tin for 5 minutes before transferring to a wire rack to cool.

STORAGE Keep in an airtight container for up to 3 days. Alternatively, wrap individually in plastic film, place in a freezer bag and freeze for up to 3 months.

ALLERGIES/INTOLERANCES ***Gluten/wheat:*** use gluten- or wheat-free flour, and replace the oatbran with a nut meal, such as hazelnut or almond. ***Dairy:*** replace the buttermilk with dairy-free milk with 3 teaspoons of lemon juice added. ***Egg:*** replace the eggs with 2 'chia eggs' (see page 5).

LUNCHBOX-FRIENDLY SANDWICHES

FOUR SIMPLE STEPS TO A NUTRITIOUS SANDWICH

Step 1: Choose a base Opt for wholegrain, wholemeal, rye or sourdough. You could use regular bread, pita bread, English muffins, wraps or even crackers.

Step 2: Add a protein Lean roast beef; meatballs or leftover rissoles; chicken; turkey; lean leg ham; boiled eggs; tinned fish – salmon, tuna or sardines; cheese – cheddar, cream cheese, ricotta, cottage cheese, feta or haloumi; hummus; nut butters (if allowed) – look for 100 per cent nuts or reduced-salt varieties; baked beans.

Step 3: Layer at least two vegetables Asparagus, avocado, beetroot, capsicum (pepper), carrot, celery, cucumber, eggplant (aubergine), lettuce, mushrooms, olives, pumpkin (squash), snowpeas (mangetout), spinach, sprouts, sweet potato, tomato.

Step 4 (optional): Add an extra flavour Herbs (parsley, chives, basil, coriander, mint), spring onion, pepper, mayonnaise, mild mustards, chutneys, reduced-salt sauces.

Kids love things that are familiar, especially when it comes to food, and most will have a favourite sandwich filling they will happily eat day in, day out. But considering almost 25 per cent of their weekly food intake occurs at school, it is important to maximise variety to ensure they get a selection of nutrients. Avoid giving them the same sandwich over two consecutive days so you don't get stuck in a rut. Here are our tips to make a nutritious and satisfying sandwich, and some of our favourite fillings.

FUSSY EATING TIP Wholegrain breads are the best choice for nutrition. To ease the transition for fans of white bread, use 1 slice of white and 1 slice of wholemeal, gradually phasing out the white, then progress to wholegrain.

SAFETY NOTE When including leftover meat or hardboiled egg in your child's sandwich for school, only use those cooked the night before, make sure they are refrigerated immediately after cooking and put an ice pack in the lunchbox to prevent the growth of harmful bacteria. You can read more about food safety on page 185.

PUMPKIN, RICOTTA AND SPINACH

MAKES 1
PREP TIME 5 minutes
COOKING TIME Nil

2 slices multigrain bread, buttered if desired
2 tablespoons mashed roasted pumpkin
1 tablespoon fresh ricotta
shredded baby spinach leaves

1 Spread one slice of bread with the pumpkin, then the ricotta. Sprinkle with the baby spinach. Cover with the remaining slice of bread and cut as desired.

CHICKEN, PESTO AND CUCUMBER

MAKES 1
PREP TIME 5 minutes
COOKING TIME Nil

2 slices wholegrain bread, buttered if desired
2 teaspoons Basil pesto (see page 232)
2 tablespoons shredded cooked chicken
thinly sliced cucumber

1 Spread one slice of bread with the basil pesto and top with chicken and cucumber. Cover with the remaining slice of bread and cut as desired.

TIP If your school has a 'nut-free' policy, use sunflower seeds instead of pine nuts in your homemade pesto.

MEATBALL, CHEESE AND LETTUCE

MAKES 1
PREP TIME 5 minutes
COOKING TIME Nil

2 slices multigrain bread, buttered if desired
2–3 leftover Mini meatballs (see page 44), lightly mashed
¼ cup (30 g) grated cheddar cheese
shredded lettuce

1 Layer one slice of bread with the meatballs, sprinkle with cheese and then top with lettuce. Cover with the remaining slice of bread and cut as desired.

TUNA, AVOCADO, MAYO AND CARROT

MAKES 1
PREP TIME 5 minutes
COOKING TIME Nil

2 slices multigrain bread, buttered if desired
2 teaspoons mashed ripe avocado
½ × 95 g tin tuna in springwater or brine, drained
1 teaspoon whole-egg mayonnaise
1 tablespoon coarsely grated carrot

1 Spread one slice of bread with the avocado. Combine the tuna and mayonnaise, then spoon over the avocado and top with grated carrot. Cover with the remaining slice of bread and cut as desired.

WAY-TOO-EASY PIZZA SCROLLS

MAKES ABOUT 15
PREP TIME 15 minutes
(+ 10 minutes resting)
COOKING TIME 25 minutes

- 1⅔ cups (250 g) self-raising flour, plus extra for dusting
- 1 cup (280 g) plain Greek-style yoghurt
- 3 tablespoons no-added-salt tomato paste (puree)
- 100 g shaved ham, chopped or torn into pieces
- 150 g fresh or drained tinned pineapple, chopped
- 1 cup (120 g) grated cheddar cheese

Most kids love pizza scrolls and they are a great addition to lunchboxes. While you can experiment with different fillings, keep it simple and there's no doubt they'll be eaten. We give them an A+ for simplicity and eatability!

1. Preheat the oven to 200°C (180°C fan-forced) and line a baking tray with baking paper.
2. Place the flour and yoghurt in a large bowl and mix until just combined. Gently knead on a floured surface until the mixture forms a dough. If your dough is too sticky, add another tablespoon of flour. Roll into a ball and set aside for 5–10 minutes to rest.
3. Roll out the dough on a lightly floured surface to a rectangle about 1 cm thick. Spread the tomato paste over the dough, leaving a small strip on one long edge. Scatter the ham, pineapple and cheese over the tomato paste.
4. Tightly roll up the dough, starting at the long edge that is covered with topping, to form a log. The edge that is not covered in topping will seal the scrolls. Cut the log into 2–3 cm-thick slices and place on the lined tray, leaving a little space between each.
5. Bake the scrolls for 20–25 minutes or until the dough is light golden and cooked through. Remove from the oven and set aside to cool.

FUSSY EATING TIP Involve your kids by asking them to choose their own fillings from a range of nutritious ingredients. They will love the element of choice and independence, and may even surprise you with their enthusiasm by trying a new vegetable or two.

STORAGE Keep in an airtight container in the fridge for up to 2 days. Alternatively, wrap individually in plastic film, place in a freezer bag and freeze for up to 2 months.

*ALLERGIES/INTOLERANCES ***Gluten/wheat:*** use gluten-free self-raising flour. ***Dairy:*** use our pizza dough on page 74 and omit the cheese.

CHEESE AND SALAD PINWHEELS

SERVES 2
PREP TIME 10 minutes
COOKING TIME Nil

½ ripe small avocado, peeled and mashed
1 tablespoon whole-egg mayonnaise
2 slices mountain bread or lavash bread
½ cup (60 g) grated cheddar cheese
1 small carrot, coarsely grated
½ Lebanese (short) cucumber, sliced lengthways into thin ribbons
2 iceberg lettuce leaves, shredded

If pinwheels are new to your child, try starting with ingredients you know they love and will accept. When they are familiar with them, you can introduce a wider variety of spreads, such as pesto, hummus, mayonnaise; more veggies, such as grilled capsicum (pepper), eggplant (aubergine) and zucchini (courgette); and protein options, such as chicken, turkey, lean meat, fish and hardboiled eggs.

1 Spread half the avocado and then half the mayonnaise over each slice of bread. Divide the cheese, carrot, cucumber and lettuce among them, then roll up tightly to enclose the filling. Slice into small pinwheels and serve.

NUTRITION NOTE Irritability, headaches, stomach upsets and restlessness are just some of the side effects children may experience due to the preservatives added to commercial breads to prolong their shelf life. Check ingredient lists and look out for preservative-free bread, particularly if your child is susceptible to these unwanted reactions.

STORAGE These are best eaten on the day they are made. If you are preparing school lunchboxes the night before, wrap the rolls tightly in plastic film, then slice into pinwheels in the morning and put into airtight containers.

ALLERGIES/INTOLERANCES ***Gluten/wheat:*** use gluten- or wheat-free bread. ***Dairy:*** substitute cooked chicken, turkey, meat, tuna or egg for the cheese. ***Egg:*** omit the mayonnaise or choose an egg-free variety.

PASTA SALAD

SERVES 8
PREP TIME 10 minutes (+ cooling)
COOKING TIME 10 minutes

200 g spiral pasta
1 teaspoon olive oil
⅓ cup (100 g) whole-egg mayonnaise
2 tablespoons plain Greek-style yoghurt
½ teaspoon Dijon mustard
1 small carrot, coarsely grated
1 stalk celery, trimmed and thinly sliced
1 small red capsicum (pepper), finely chopped
1 cup (165 g) cooked corn kernels
1 spring onion, trimmed and thinly sliced
1 cup (120 g) grated cheddar cheese

The secret to satisfying little appetites at school is to mix things up and keep lunchboxes interesting. This simple, creamy pasta salad makes a great change from sandwiches and provides plenty of energy and nutrients.

1. Cook the pasta in a large saucepan of salted boiling water until al dente, following the instructions on the packet. Drain well, then transfer to a large bowl and stir through the olive oil. Set aside to cool.
2. Combine the mayonnaise, yoghurt and mustard in a small bowl.
3. Add the carrot, celery, capsicum, corn and spring onion to the pasta and toss to combine. Mix in the cheese, then add the mayonnaise mixture and toss until well combined.

NUTRITION NOTE Incorporating a variety of vegetables in your child's meals ensures they receive all the health-promoting nutrients they need for their growth and good health.

STORAGE Keep in an airtight container in the fridge for up to 2 days.

ALLERGIES/INTOLERANCES ***Gluten/wheat:*** use gluten-free or wheat-free pasta. ***Dairy:*** omit the yoghurt and cheese, and add some diced avocado. ***Egg:*** use an egg-free mayonnaise or replace with additional yoghurt.

ZUCCHINI AND PEAR BANANA BREAD

MAKES 1 LOAF
PREP TIME 15 minutes
COOKING TIME 1 hour

½ cup (125 ml) macadamia, olive or coconut oil, plus extra for greasing
1 cup (150 g) plain flour
1 cup (160 g) wholemeal plain flour
1½ teaspoons baking powder
½ teaspoon bicarbonate of soda
½ teaspoon ground cinnamon
½ teaspoon salt
½ cup, firmly packed (110 g) brown sugar
¾ cup (180 ml) buttermilk
1 egg, lightly whisked
1 teaspoon pure vanilla extract
2 large overripe bananas, mashed
1 zucchini (courgette), coarsely grated, liquid squeezed out
1 ripe pear, cored, coarsely grated

We've given the ever-popular banana bread a healthy twist by adding extra pear for added sweetness and zucchini to boost your child's veggie intake.

1. Preheat the oven to 180°C (160°C fan-forced). Grease a 22 cm × 12 cm loaf tin with your chosen oil and line with baking paper.
2. Sift the flours, baking powder, bicarbonate of soda, cinnamon and salt together into a large mixing bowl.
3. Place the oil, sugar, buttermilk, egg and vanilla in a separate bowl and mix to combine. Add the mashed banana, zucchini and pear and stir well. Add to the dry ingredients and stir until just combined.
4. Spoon the mixture into the prepared tin and bake for 50–60 minutes or until golden and a skewer inserted into the centre comes out clean. Remove from the oven and allow to cool in the tin for 5 minutes before transferring to a wire rack to cool completely. Slice and serve.

NUTRITION NOTE Keep a variety of nutritious snacks in the freezer so you can put together a healthy lunchbox every day.

STORAGE Keep in an airtight container for up to 5 days. Alternatively, place slices in a freezer bag, separated by freezer paper, and freeze for up to 3 months.

*ALLERGIES/INTOLERANCES ***Gluten/wheat:*** use gluten- or wheat-free flour. ***Dairy:*** replace the buttermilk with the same amount of your preferred dairy-free milk with 3 teaspoons of lemon juice added. ***Egg:*** substitute a 'chia egg' (see page 5) or an additional ½ overripe banana, mashed, for the egg.

CHEESY SEED BISCUITS

MAKES ABOUT 40
PREP TIME 10 minutes
(+ 1 hour chilling)
COOKING TIME 10 minutes

¾ cup (110 g) plain flour, plus extra for dusting
¼ teaspoon baking powder
pinch of salt
60 g unsalted butter, chilled and chopped
1 cup (120 g) grated cheddar cheese
1 tablespoon poppy seeds
1 tablespoon sesame seeds
1 tablespoon pepitas (pumpkin seed kernels)
1 teaspoon chia seeds

Do you often wish you could let your child know you're thinking of them while they're at preschool or school? These more-ish biscuits can be cut into alphabet letters or shapes, so you could send them off with a special word, like 'love' or their name, in their lunchbox. Hearts, stars and hugs and kisses ('o's and 'x's) are cute options for children who can't read yet.

1 Sift the flour, baking powder and salt together into the bowl of an electric mixer. Add the butter and cheese and use the paddle attachment to beat on medium–high speed until the mixture resembles fine breadcrumbs. Scrape down the side of the bowl and continue to beat until the mixture begins to hold together and a soft dough forms. Add the seeds and mix on low speed until they are evenly distributed. (Alternatively, process the mixture in a food processor.)

2 Turn the dough out onto a lightly floured surface and knead until the seeds are well incorporated. If the mixture is sticky, add a little extra flour. Divide into two portions. Roll each portion into a log, about 3 cm in diameter. (If you will be cutting out shapes or letters, roll each portion into a ball.) Wrap in plastic film and place in the fridge for at least 1 hour to firm.

3 Preheat the oven to 170°C (150°C fan-forced) and line 2 baking trays with baking paper.

4 Remove the dough from the fridge. Use a sharp knife to cut each log into 5 mm-thick slices. (If you are cutting out shapes, roll out the dough on a lightly floured surface until 5 mm thick, then use your cutters to cut out shapes or letters.) Place on the lined trays, leaving 3 cm between each.

5 Bake the biscuits for 10 minutes or until golden brown. (Shapes or letters will take less time to cook so keep a close eye on them to prevent burning.)

NUTRITION NOTE These biscuits have no additives or preservatives and with four types of seeds they're a great source of protein, fibre and a variety of health-promoting nutrients. Serve as is or with a homemade dip (such as Cauliflower hummus, see page 170, or Roast beetroot dip, see page 50).

STORAGE Keep in an airtight container for up to 3 days. Uncooked dough can be frozen, wrapped in plastic film, for up to 1 month. Cooked biscuits can be frozen in freezer bags for up to 1 month.

ALLERGIES/INTOLERANCES ***Gluten/wheat:*** use gluten- or wheat-free flour.

CHAPTER 9

INCLUDE 'SOMETIMES' FOODS

It's important to create happy memories around all types of food. Enjoying small amounts of 'sometimes' foods with your children, without feelings of guilt or judgement, is part of a healthy, balanced diet. Make nutritious 'everyday' foods fun and exciting to help them build a positive relationship with all foods.

Offering your child a healthy, balanced diet doesn't mean eliminating sugary or less nutritious foods completely. Enjoy them occasionally as part of normal everyday life, not just on special occasions. Talk about nutrition and discuss the way food tastes and how it makes us feel. Avoid using 'sometimes' foods as a reward or bribe, as this gives children the impression that everyday foods are inferior and the good stuff is yet to come.

A HEALTHY BALANCE

Keeping a healthy balance between 'sometimes' and 'everyday' foods doesn't need to be a battle. Make sure the food you offer every day is nutritious, tasty and varied, keep mealtimes fun and relaxed, and talk to your children about nutrition so they understand that what they eat affects the way they feel. Helping your child build a positive relationship with all foods will enable them to appreciate the value of an event celebrated with food, such as enjoying a birthday party for more than just the sweet treats.

Your child's ability to make healthy food choices independently, stop eating when their tummy tells them they are full and enjoy 'sometimes' foods in moderation begins with trust. Teach them how to recognise and respond to their hunger and fullness cues and trust them to respond to them appropriately. If we interfere too much and force them to eat more than they want to, restrict certain foods, allow them to graze in between scheduled mealtimes or offer food as a reward or to manage feelings of hurt, they can easily lose this wonderful ability.

TOP TIPS

- Explain why 'everyday' foods are important for our bodies. Give examples your child can relate to, such as running fast, growing tall, jumping high, feeling happy and so on, rather than just saying they are good for us. Share your enjoyment and excitement about 'everyday' foods, such as the juiciness of a peach, the sweetness of cherries and the caramelised flavour of roast pumpkin
- Enjoy 'sometimes' foods as appropriate, and talk positively about the way they taste and how they make us feel. Avoid any associations with guilt or judgement
- The expression 'out of sight, out of mind' definitely applies to 'sometimes' foods. If you avoid keeping them in the house, you'll avoid the inevitable (and often interminable!) conversations about why your child can't have them every time they open the cupboard
- Stick to a flexible mealtime schedule (see pages 164–165) so that your child feels satisfied throughout the day
- Don't limit all 'sometimes' foods to special occasions, as this can result in overindulging. Make a batch of chocolate chip cookies on a rainy day or enjoy an ice cream after a day at the beach. Keep portion sizes small and don't let the foods slip into the everyday
- Teach your child to listen to their hunger and fullness cues, so that when 'sometimes' foods are available they are not as likely to overindulge
- Talk to your children about how they feel when eating, especially how they can feel good when enjoying food, but uncomfortable when they've eaten too much.

PARTY PREPPING

Who doesn't love a party? There are games, presents, friends and lots of party food, which kids generally find fun and exciting. This is where it really pays off for children to know how to respond to their hunger and fullness cues, as they will eat their fill and then go off to play, feeling happy and enjoying the occasion. On the way to the party, remind them about how we feel when we eat too much food so it'll be fresh in their mind.

If you're hosting a party, serve some healthy foods, such as fruit, sandwiches and veggie sticks with dip, to balance out the 'sometimes' foods. You could even offer a more substantial meal option, such as crumbed fish bites, savoury slices, sausage sandwiches, burgers or homemade sausage rolls.

Encourage the children to sit down when they are eating, as it's safer and they're more likely to focus on what they're eating (and stop when they feel full). Fill the party bags with small novelty gifts, such as pencils, rubbers, crayons, bouncy balls, stickers and dinosaur toys, and one or two sweet options to enjoy another day. Lastly, consider natural food dye when colouring the icing for the cake, as many children have negative reactions to synthetic food dyes.

HAM, CHEESE AND PINEAPPLE TARTLETS

MAKES 16
PREP TIME 15 minutes
COOKING TIME 20 minutes

- 1 sheet (25 cm × 25 cm) ready-rolled puff pastry, just thawed
- 1 egg white, lightly whisked (optional)
- 1–2 tablespoons no-added-salt tomato paste (puree)
- ½ cup (60 g) grated cheddar cheese
- 80 g thinly sliced ham off the bone, finely chopped
- ½ cup (80 g) finely chopped fresh or tinned pineapple
- 1 tablespoon pure maple syrup (optional)

Please a crowd with this simple savoury food using the traditional flavours of ham and pineapple. You can mix things up by replacing the pineapple with finely chopped mushroom, spinach leaves or grated zucchini (courgette) – a great way to increase the variety for fussy eaters.

1. Preheat the oven to 180°C (160°C fan-forced) and line a large baking tray with baking paper.
2. Cut the pastry into four squares, then cut each square into four again. Brush the egg white over a 5 mm border around each square, if using.
3. Spread a small amount of tomato paste over each square (avoiding the egg-white border) and sprinkle with cheese, ham and pineapple. Use a pastry brush to dab maple syrup over the ham and pineapple, if desired. Bake the tartlets for 15–20 minutes or until the pastry is golden brown. Remove from the oven and serve hot or cold.

NUTRITION NOTE For an everyday option, replace the pastry with pita bread, cut into suitably sized wedges. (Do not brush with egg white.) Bake for 10 minutes or until crisp.

STORAGE Keep in an airtight container in the fridge for up to 3 days.

ALLERGIES/INTOLERANCES ***Gluten/wheat:*** use gluten-free pastry, or gluten- or wheat-free pita bread. ***Dairy:*** omit the cheese. ***Egg:*** substitute milk for the egg white.

CRISPY VEGETABLE SPRING ROLLS

MAKES ABOUT 20
PREP TIME 30 minutes
COOKING TIME 40 minutes

- 100 g dried rice vermicelli noodles
- 1 tablespoon olive oil
- 2 teaspoons finely chopped coriander stalks
- 1 teaspoon finely grated ginger
- 1 clove garlic, finely grated
- 3 Swiss brown mushrooms, chopped
- 3 spring onions, trimmed and finely chopped
- 2½ cups (200 g) finely shredded cabbage
- 1 carrot, coarsely grated
- 1 zucchini (courgette), coarsely grated
- 2 tablespoons salt-reduced soy sauce
- 2 tablespoons chopped coriander leaves
- 20 (20 cm × 20 cm) frozen spring roll wrappers, thawed
- rice bran oil, for frying

DIPPING SAUCE

- 2 tablespoons fresh lime juice
- 1 tablespoon fish sauce
- 1 tablespoon rice vinegar
- 1 tablespoon caster sugar
- 1 small clove garlic, crushed
- coriander sprig, torn (optional)

These crisp and flavourful spring rolls are packed with a variety of nutritious vegetables including mushrooms, cabbage, carrot and zucchini.

1. Soak the noodles in a bowl of warm water for 10–15 minutes or until soft. Drain and rinse, then use kitchen scissors to cut them into shorter lengths.
2. To make the dipping sauce, place all the ingredients in a small bowl and stir until the sugar dissolves.
3. Heat the olive oil in a large heavy-based frying pan over medium–high heat. Add the coriander stalks, ginger and garlic and cook, stirring, for 2 minutes. Add the mushroom and cook for 2–3 minutes or until softened.
4. Add the spring onion, cabbage, carrot and zucchini and sauté for 4–5 minutes or until just softened. Add the soy sauce, coriander leaves and drained noodles and stir to combine. Remove from the heat.
5. Fill a small bowl with water and keep it close at hand. Place a wrapper on the benchtop, with one corner pointing towards you. Place 2–3 tablespoons of the mixture on the corner closest to you (if you prefer smaller, thinner spring rolls, use 1–2 tablespoons of the mixture). Roll the corner over the filling to enclose, then fold in the two sides and continue to roll up firmly, tucking in the sides and brushing the opposite corner with a little water to seal the pastry. Continue with the remaining mixture and wrappers.
6. Fill a large heavy-based saucepan or frying pan with oil to a depth of 2–3 cm. Heat over high heat until a small cube of bread sizzles when added to the oil. Reduce the heat to medium–high and use tongs to place one-quarter of the spring rolls in the hot oil. Cook, turning regularly, for 3–4 minutes or until golden all over. Transfer to paper towel to drain while you cook the remaining spring rolls. (Alternatively, the spring rolls can be baked in an oven preheated to 200°C/180°C fan-forced. Place on a lined baking tray, brush with olive oil and bake for 10–12 minutes or until golden and crisp, turning halfway through cooking.) Serve with the dipping sauce.

STORAGE Keep in an airtight container in the fridge for up to 2 days. Uncooked spring rolls can be kept in the fridge for 1 day or frozen, wrapped individually in plastic film, for 1–2 months. Thaw before frying.

✱ALLERGIES/INTOLERANCES ***Gluten/wheat:*** use gluten-free rice paper spring roll wrappers and gluten-free soy sauce.

FUSSY EATING TIP

If mealtimes are regularly a battle, try making healthier versions of 'sometimes' foods your kids love. It can inject a bit of fun into the meals and relieve some of the anxiety you and the kids might be feeling.

BEEF AND LENTIL SAUSAGE ROLLS

MAKES 36
PREP TIME 20 minutes
COOKING TIME 30 minutes

½ cup (100 g) brown lentils, drained and rinsed
500 g premium lean beef mince
3 spring onions, trimmed and finely chopped
1 carrot, finely grated
1 zucchini (courgette), finely grated, liquid squeezed out
3 Swiss brown mushrooms, finely chopped
2 tablespoons chopped flat-leaf parsley
2 eggs
2 teaspoons Worcestershire sauce
3 sheets (25 cm × 25 cm) ready-rolled puff pastry, just thawed
1 tablespoon poppy seeds (optional)
1 tablespoon sesame seeds (optional)

When sausage rolls are made using quality beef mince, a variety of vegetables and nutrient-rich brown lentils, they're just as suitable for a weeknight meal or lunchbox treat as the party table.

1. Preheat the oven to 200°C (180°C fan-forced) and line 2 baking trays with baking paper.
2. Place the lentils in a large bowl and roughly mash with a back of a fork. Add the beef mince, spring onion, carrot, zucchini, mushroom, parsley, 1 whisked egg and Worcestershire sauce and mix to combine.
3. Cut each sheet of pastry in half. Place one-sixth of the mixture running lengthways down one of the pastry strips, moulding it to form a long sausage. Brush the edges of the pastry with water and fold over to enclose the filling. Cut into 6 pieces (or more, depending on your chosen portion sizes) and place on the lined tray. Repeat with the remaining mixture and pastry strips.
4. Whisk the remaining egg and brush over the tops of the sausage rolls, then sprinkle with the poppy seeds and sesame seeds, if using. Bake for 25–30 minutes or until golden brown and cooked through.

FUSSY EATING TIP Try slicing the sausage rolls thinly for kids who are fussy with meat or find it difficult to chew large mouthfuls of meat. Smaller portions may also encourage those who only want to eat the pastry to enjoy some of the filling, too.

STORAGE Keep in an airtight container in the fridge for up to 2 days. Alternatively, freeze cooked or uncooked sausage rolls in individual portions, wrapped in plastic film, for up to 2 months.

ALLERGIES/INTOLERANCES ***Gluten/wheat:*** use gluten-free pastry. ***Egg:*** replace the egg with ¼ cup (15 g) fresh breadcrumbs and 1 tablespoon tomato sauce, and brush the pastry with your preferred milk instead of egg. ***Sesame:*** use only poppy seeds.

BROWNIES

MAKES 25 PIECES
PREP TIME 15 minutes
COOKING TIME 35 minutes

- 200 g unsalted butter, chopped, plus extra for greasing
- 1⅓ cups (295 g) caster sugar
- ¾ cup (75 g) cacao or cocoa powder
- 1 teaspoon pure vanilla extract
- 3 eggs, lightly whisked
- 1 cup (150 g) plain flour
- ½ cup (95 g) choc chips (optional)
- 1 tablespoon pure icing sugar, to dust (optional)

This simple recipe is ideal for cooking with children and the end result is wonderfully fudgy.

1. Preheat the oven to 160°C (140°C fan-forced). Grease a square 20 cm cake tin with butter and line with baking paper, allowing it to overhang two sides.
2. Place the butter, sugar and cacao or cocoa in a small saucepan over low heat and stir until the butter is melted. Transfer to a large mixing bowl, add the vanilla and egg and stir to combine.
3. Sift the flour over the mixture and stir to combine. Stir through the choc chips, if using, then pour into the prepared tin. Bake for 30–35 minutes or until a skewer inserted in the centre of the brownie comes out with moist crumbs clinging to it. Remove from the oven and cool in the tin for 10 minutes, then use the overhanging paper to lift the brownie onto a wire rack and leave to cool completely. Cut into 4 cm squares and dust with icing sugar to serve, if desired.

NUTRITION NOTE Try to avoid using the words 'good' and 'bad' when talking about food. Even the most nutrient-rich, healthy foods may not be good for us if we eat too much of them and limit variety. Similarly, foods laden with butter and sugar aren't 'bad' for us if we eat small amounts occasionally as part of a balanced diet. Being mindful of the way you talk about food with your kids and enjoying your brownie together is a wonderful lesson in mindful eating (see page 143).

STORAGE Keep in an airtight container for up to 4 days. Alternatively, freeze individual portions, wrapped in plastic film, for up to 3 months.

✱ALLERGIES/INTOLERANCES ***Gluten/wheat:*** use gluten- or wheat-free flour or substitute almond meal. ***Dairy:*** use 200 g coconut oil instead of the butter, use dairy-free cocoa powder (or cacao) and omit the choc chips. ***Egg:*** replace the eggs with 1 cup (250 ml) buttermilk.

JAM DROP BISCUITS

MAKES ABOUT 24
PREP TIME 10 minutes
COOKING TIME 20 minutes

- 1 cup (100 g) wheatgerm (or rolled oats)
- ¼ cup (20 g) shredded coconut
- 80 g unsalted butter, chopped and softened
- ⅓ cup, firmly packed (75 g) brown sugar
- 1¾ cups (260 g) self-raising flour, sifted
- 1 egg
- 1 tablespoon milk
- 1 teaspoon pure vanilla extract
- 3 tablespoons strawberry jam, approximately

Helping your little ones create something delicious and then sharing it with family and friends gives them a sense of pride and achievement. In this recipe, they will enjoy rolling the dough, making the indents and spooning in the jam. Oh, and they won't mind eating the biscuits, too!

1. Preheat the oven to 180°C (160°C fan-forced) and line 2 baking trays with baking paper.
2. Place the wheatgerm and coconut in a food processor. Process for about 20 seconds, until the consistency of fine breadcrumbs. Transfer to a bowl.
3. Use an electric mixer to beat the butter and sugar on low–medium speed for 1–2 minutes or until pale and creamy. Add the flour, wheatgerm mixture, egg, milk and vanilla and beat for 1–2 minutes or until a soft dough forms.
4. Roll tablespoons of the dough into balls, leaving about 5 cm between each, and place on the lined trays. Lightly flatten the top of each ball. Using a clean finger, make a small indent in the centre of each biscuit and spoon ½ teaspoon of jam into each. Bake the biscuits for 15–20 minutes or until light brown and firm to touch. Remove from the oven and set aside on the trays for 10 minutes before transferring to a wire rack to cool completely.

NUTRITION NOTE Wheatgerm offers a delicious nutty flavour while delivering a bunch of protein-packed nutrients, including vitamin E, folate and zinc.

STORAGE Keep in an airtight container for up to 3 days. Alternatively, freeze individual portions in freezer bags for up to 3 months. The uncooked dough can be frozen in logs, wrapped in plastic film, for up to 2 months. Simply slice off biscuits and place on a lined tray, allow to thaw and then bake as required. (You can add the jam before baking if you'd like, or keep them plain.)

ALLERGIES/INTOLERANCES ***Gluten/wheat:*** use quinoa flakes or a nut meal instead of the wheatgerm, and use gluten- or wheat-free flour. Replace the oats with quinoa flakes. ***Dairy:*** use coconut oil or olive oil instead of the butter and use a dairy-free milk. ***Egg:*** substitute an extra tablespoon of milk for the egg.

CHOC OAT BISCUITS

MAKES ABOUT 20
PREP TIME 10 minutes
COOKING TIME 18 minutes

- ½ cup, firmly packed (110 g) brown sugar
- ½ cup (125 ml) olive or macadamia oil
- 1 egg, lightly whisked
- 1 teaspoon pure vanilla extract
- 1 cup (150 g) plain flour
- 1 teaspoon baking powder
- 1¼ cups (110 g) rolled oats
- ½ cup (95 g) choc chips

The kids will never guess these yummy chocolate biscuits are at all good for them. See if they'd like to be your little helpers when you make them – they can crack the eggs, sift the flour, roll the dough and enjoy licking the bowl.

1. Preheat the oven to 180°C (160°C fan-forced) and line a baking tray with baking paper.
2. Whisk the brown sugar and oil in a large bowl until smooth and well combined. Add the egg and vanilla and whisk to combine. Sift in the flour and baking powder, add the oats and choc chips and stir until just combined.
3. Roll tablespoons of the mixture into balls and place on the lined tray, leaving about 5 cm between each, then flatten slightly with the back of a spoon. Bake the biscuits for 15–18 minutes or until light golden and cooked through. Remove from the oven and cool on the tray for a few minutes before transferring to a wire rack to cool completely.

NUTRITION NOTE Including oats in these biscuits gives them a nice nutrient boost. We've also used an oil rich in monounsaturated fatty acids instead of butter and kept the sugar to a minimum.

STORAGE Keep in an airtight container for up to 1 week. Alternatively, wrap individually in plastic film and store in the freezer for up to 3 months. The uncooked dough can be frozen, wrapped in plastic film, for up to 3 months. Thaw before rolling into balls, placing on a lined tray and baking.

ALLERGIES/INTOLERANCES ***Gluten/wheat:*** use gluten- or wheat-free flour, and use quinoa flakes in place of the oats. ***Dairy:*** substitute sultanas for the choc chips. ***Egg:*** replace the egg with ½ overripe mashed banana, ⅓ cup (100 g) unsweetened apple puree, 1 'chia egg' (see page 5) or 1 'linseed egg' (see page 5). ***Nuts:*** use olive oil rather than macadamia oil.

NUTRITION NOTE
Happy food memories are essential for forming positive sensory experiences and associations with food and eating.

OLD-SCHOOL STRAWBERRY MILKSHAKE

MAKES 12 MILKSHAKES AND 15 BISCUIT CRISPS
PREP TIME 20 minutes (+ cooling)
COOKING TIME 35 minutes

- 500 g strawberries, hulled and quartered
- 1 cup (220 g) caster sugar
- ¾ cup (180 ml) milk, per person
- 1 scoop vanilla ice cream, per person

BISCUIT CRISPS

- 2 egg whites
- ⅓ cup (75 g) caster sugar
- ¼ teaspoon pure vanilla extract
- ½ cup (75 g) plain flour
- 40 g unsalted butter, melted and cooled

Strawberry milkshakes evoke wonderful childhood memories – summer holidays by the beach, a day out with Grandma or hanging at the milk bar with friends. Share this old-school treat with your children, using your own 100-per-cent-natural strawberry syrup and served with a sweet biscuit crisp.

1. Place the strawberries and 2 cups (500 ml) water in a saucepan and bring to the boil over medium–high heat. Reduce the heat and simmer for 20 minutes, occasionally skimming any foam from the surface. Strain the liquid in a fine-meshed sieve over a bowl – don't press on the solids to force the liquid through. Discard the solids and then return the liquid to the pan. Add the sugar and bring to the boil over medium–high heat, stirring until it dissolves. Reduce the heat slightly and simmer for a further 5 minutes or until the syrup thickens. Remove from the heat and set aside to cool.
2. To make the biscuits crisps, preheat the oven to 180°C (160°C fan-forced) and line a baking tray and wire rack with baking paper.
3. Whisk the egg whites, sugar and vanilla in a bowl until frothy. Add half of the flour and whisk until combined. Stir in the butter, then the remaining flour; the batter should be smooth and thick. Spoon a teaspoonful onto the baking tray and spread evenly with a palette knife or flexible spatula to make a circle about 6 cm in diameter. Repeat with the remaining mixture.
4. Bake the biscuits for 8–10 minutes or until the edges are golden brown, watching them carefully so they don't burn. Remove from the oven and use a spatula to carefully transfer them to the lined wire rack to cool.
5. Measure out the amount of milk and ice cream you need (depending on how many milkshakes you're making) and place in a blender. Add 2 tablespoons of strawberry syrup per serve. Blend until well combined. Pour into glasses and serve with a biscuit crisp alongside.

TIPS Drizzle the syrup around the inside of the glass, top with grated chocolate or coat the rim of the glass with sprinkles for a café-style look.

STORAGE The biscuits will keep in an airtight container for up to 4 days. Store leftover syrup in a sterilised jar (see page 179) in the fridge for up to 2 weeks.

✱ALLERGIES/INTOLERANCES ***Gluten/wheat:*** use gluten- or wheat-free flour. ***Dairy:*** use dairy-free milk and ice cream. ***Egg:*** omit the biscuit crisps or serve with egg-free biscuits.

SPARKLING FRUIT PUNCH

A popular 'sometimes' drink for older kids, this punch has a touch of sparkling water for fizz and natural sweetness from their favourite fruits. It also adds colour and fun to the party table.

MAKES 2.5 LITRES
PREP TIME 5 minutes (+ 4 hours freezing)
COOKING TIME Nil

- 1 bunch mint
- 1 litre 100-per-cent apple juice
- 1 litre 100-per-cent pineapple juice
- 1 cup (250 ml) sparkling mineral water
- 3 limes, juiced
- 1 cup (130 g) strawberries, hulled and chopped

1. Place 2–3 mint leaves in each hole of an ice cube tray, top up with water and freeze.
2. Combine the apple juice, pineapple juice, mineral water, lime juice and strawberries in a large jug. Place a mint ice cube in a glass, fill with punch and serve.

NUTRITION NOTE Forget the cordial and soft drink – this delicious punch delivers on flavour without any artificial flavours, colours or preservatives.

MINI MERINGUES

Parties and celebrations are a wonderful time for children to relax and enjoy food. Meringues are always a hit and they are simple to make and economical. Look for food colouring and 100s and 1000s with no artificial colours or flavours.

MAKES ABOUT 35
PREP TIME 10 minutes (+ cooling)
COOKING TIME 2 hours

- 2 egg whites, at room temperature
- ½ cup (110 g) caster sugar
- natural food colouring (optional)
- natural 100s and 1000s (optional)

1. Preheat the oven to 90°C (70°C fan-forced) and line a large baking tray with baking paper.
2. Use a clean, dry electric mixer to beat the egg whites until soft peaks form. Gradually add the sugar, a tablespoon at a time, beating until stiff peaks form and the sugar has dissolved (to test, rub a little mixture between your fingers; it should not feel at all grainy). The meringue should be thick and glossy. Add a few drops of food colouring, if using, and gently mix through.
3. Spoon the mixture into a piping bag with a star nozzle attached, and pipe meringues onto the lined tray. (Alternatively, use teaspoons to spoon the mixture onto the tray.) Sprinkle with 100s & 1000s, if using. Bake the meringues for 2 hours or until crisp. Turn off the oven and leave the meringues inside, using a wooden spoon to keep the door slightly ajar, until cooled completely.

NUTRITION NOTE Cooking 'mini' versions of party foods for kids are a great way to control portion sizes and encourage mindful eating and balance at parties.

STORAGE Keep in an airtight container for up to 3 days.

✱ALLERGIES/INTOLERANCES (MINI MERINGUES)

Egg: Drain a 400 g tin of chickpeas, reserving the liquid (keep the chickpeas for another use). Use an electric mixer to beat the liquid until stiff peaks form. Gradually add ¾ cup (165 g) caster sugar, 1 tablespoon at a time, and ½ teaspoon vanilla essence and continue to beat until the mixture is thick and glossy and the sugar has dissolved. Continue with step 3.

VANILLA BIRTHDAY CAKE

MAKES 1 CAKE
PREP TIME 15 minutes
COOKING TIME 45 minutes

175 g unsalted butter, chopped and softened, plus extra for greasing
1½ cups (225 g) self-raising flour, sifted
⅓ cup (50 g) cornflour, sifted
1 cup (220 g) caster sugar
3 eggs, lightly whisked
½ cup (125 ml) milk
1½ teaspoons pure vanilla extract
natural 100s and 1000s, to garnish (optional)

BUTTERCREAM ICING

150 g unsalted butter, chopped and softened
1¾ cups (280 g) icing sugar mixture
¼ teaspoon pure vanilla extract
1 tablespoon milk

Everyone needs a simple, one-bowl cake in their repertoire. This cake can also be made in a 23 cm square tin (it will be slightly thinner so will take a little less time to cook; test it with a skewer) or a 12-hole regular muffin tin to make cupcakes (cook for 15–20 minutes, until a skewer comes out clean). So whether you want delicate fairy cakes or to carve out the number four, Spiderman or a Disney princess, we've got you covered.

1. Preheat the oven to 180°C (160°C fan-forced). Grease a round 20 cm cake tin with butter and line with baking paper.
2. Use an electric mixer to beat the butter, flours, sugar, egg, milk and vanilla on low speed until the mixture starts to come together. Stop and scrape down the side of the bowl, then continue beating on medium speed for 3–4 minutes, until smooth and combined.
3. Spoon the mixture into the prepared tin and bake for 35–45 minutes or until a skewer inserted into the centre of the cake comes out clean. Remove from the oven and cool in the tin for 10 minutes before turning onto a wire rack to cool completely.
4. Meanwhile, to make the buttercream icing, use a clean electric mixture to beat the butter for 1–2 minutes or until pale and creamy. Gradually add the icing sugar, beating well after each addition. Add the vanilla and milk and beat for a further 1–2 minutes or until creamy.
5. Spread the icing over the cooled cake, decorate with 100s and 1000s, if using, and serve.

NUTRITION NOTE When decorating party food, use natural food colourings that are free of artificial colours.

TIP If you don't have time to wait for the butter to come to room temperature, cut it into cubes and microwave on low heat in short bursts until soft.

STORAGE Wrap the uniced cake in baking paper, then plastic film and store in an airtight container in a cool, dry place for up to 2 days or in the freezer for up to 2 months. Thaw in the fridge or at room temperature.

GLUTEN/WHEAT-, EGG- AND DAIRY-FREE VARIATION

MAKES 1 CAKE
PREP TIME 15 minutes
COOKING TIME 45 minutes

- ⅓ cup (80 ml) macadamia or olive oil, plus extra for greasing
- 1½ cups (225 g) gluten-free plain flour
- 1 teaspoon gluten-free baking powder
- 1 teaspoon bicarbonate of soda
- 1 cup (220 g) caster sugar
- 1½ teaspoons pure vanilla extract
- 1½ teaspoons white or apple cider vinegar

1. Preheat the oven to 180°C (160°C fan-forced). Grease a round 20 cm cake tin with extra oil and line with baking paper.
2. Use an electric mixer to beat the oil, flour, baking powder, bicarbonate of soda, sugar, vanilla, vinegar and 1 cup (250 ml) water on low speed until the mixture starts to come together. Stop and scrape down the side of the bowl, then continue beating on medium speed for 3–4 minutes or until smooth and combined.
3. Spoon the mixture into the prepared tin and bake for 35–45 minutes or until a skewer inserted into the centre of the cake comes out clean. Remove from the oven and cool in the tin for 5 minutes before turning onto a wire rack to cool completely.

BE A GOOD ROLE MODEL

Modelling the way you expect your children to behave is an important part of parenting, and it's very beneficial when it comes to their experience of eating. The best way to help them develop a positive relationship with food is by eating together, as often as possible, so they can see you enjoying healthy foods and follow your lead, and you can teach them good table manners. This chapter features meals that can be adapted to feed the whole family – there's no need to sacrifice flavour or cook separate dishes.

Your child's relationship with food is influenced by your own feelings and attitude towards eating. Mealtimes that are relaxed and enjoyable, with no guilt or anxiety about the food itself, are ideal. Let your children know you enjoy a wide range of foods, both 'everyday' and 'sometimes', because they make you feel good and also provide an opportunity to interact with family and friends. When they see you role model this healthy relationship with food they will copy your approach.

THE IMPORTANCE OF FAMILY MEALTIMES

The simple act of sitting at a table and eating as a family has many benefits. It's the perfect time to demonstrate good eating behaviours and teach children how to eat and how to behave at the table, and family discussions can naturally progress to food and nutrition as you praise the meal and talk about how it was cooked. From a child's point of view, seeing their parents eat the same food they have on their own plate can be a great incentive to try new foods. Best of all, enjoying a home-cooked meal creates lasting positive memories around food.

Of course, working parents and families with older children who have late activities may find it difficult to eat together every night. If this is the case, make sure the parent or carer who serves dinner sits with the child while they eat to talk to them and encourage a calm atmosphere. It's helpful if the parent or carer eats a small version of the child's meal, too, especially if there is a new food for them to try or a food they regularly refuse. Children are happier eating with someone else at the table and may be more inspired to eat, or at least interact with, the new food if someone else is eating it too. They will also benefit from the attention – fussy eating behaviours are sometimes simply an attempt to engage an adult's attention. On the weekends, try to eat as a family at least three times (remember, lunch and breakfast count, too!).

HOW TO TALK ABOUT FOOD

The way we talk about and interact around food is an essential part of raising a good eater. Demonstrate positive eating behaviours, eat a variety of nutritious foods and speak positively about food, for example, 'I love carrots, they're one of my favourite vegetables. Do you know why? They are crunchy and a pretty orange colour.' Describe foods in lots of different ways, rather than by taste alone. Are they crunchy, sweet or salty, smooth or chewy, etc?

When things aren't going well, label the behaviour rather than the child. For instance, 'Stop being fussy and just eat your dinner' may discourage your child from exploring new foods and make them believe they are fussy. Try building on interaction, instead. 'Do the peas make a squishy sound when you squash them with the spoon? Do you think you can pick one up with your fork? Very clever! I wonder if you can balance it on the tip of your tongue?' What a success, all of a sudden they have a pea in their mouth. Don't worry if they resist at a certain point, just stop the sequence, and try again at another meal.

THE LANGUAGE OF FOOD

Whenever you eat with your child – at home or out and about – talk a little about the food and the experience on the whole. If you're having an ice cream during a family outing, chat about how nice it is to be out together, how the ice cream tastes, how cool it feels in your mouth, and how it makes your body feel, including hunger and fullness. This helps your child process the sensory experiences that food provides and encourages mindful eating.

SEND CLEAR MESSAGES

When a parent's words don't match their actions, children can become confused. If you tell them how important it is to eat vegetables but don't eat them yourself, for instance, you're sending mixed messages. It's important to take a look at the example that you are setting.

Ask yourself the following:

- Are you on a diet that involves restricting whole food groups from your diet?
- Do you feel guilty or ashamed after eating particular foods or overindulging?
- Do you skip meals?
- Do you eat meals in front of the TV, while looking at your phone or laptop, or even 'on the run'?

Consider your responses to these questions and think about how they may influence the little people in your life.

Everyone wants their children to grow up with a positive relationship with food and eating, because feelings of anxiety or negativity around food and mealtimes can affect their ability to socialise, celebrate, enjoy a meal and, of course, their health and wellbeing. If you have any concerns about your own relationship with food and eating, or your child's, consult your doctor or an Accredited Practising Dietitian (APD).

EFFECTIVE ROLE MODELLING

As for the role modelling itself, interact with the food the way you would like your child to, especially if it's something they haven't tried before. For example, if they are using their fork to squash a broccoli floret on their plate, copy this behaviour. They will think it's a funny game and feel relaxed and happy – and you will have their attention. Now, stick your fork into the broccoli so you can pick it up. They will probably copy you. Sniff or even lick the floret and describe to your child what it smells and tastes like. If they are ready, they may also try smelling and licking the broccoli. Ask them what they think of it. Then, take a little nibble or a big bite and encourage them to do the same and chew it. They will probably spit it out at first, which is fine, but continue to encourage them to interact with it at future meals and before you know it they will love it. In this instance, if you had told your child to stop squashing the broccoli they may have felt discouraged from exploring it further and the next time you offer it they could feel anxious and reluctant to play with it, let alone eat it. Instead, they will be happy and excited to explore food with you again.

ONE MEAL, THREE WAYS

Children who eat with their parents are more likely to perform better at school, have a healthy approach to food, display less fussy eating behaviours, enjoy a varied diet and make healthier food choices. If you can't eat together every night, just grab the opportunity whenever possible. This chapter features five meals that can be adapted slightly to cater for the whole family. You can apply the same strategies to other meals you love, too. In addition to saving time, cooking one meal for all the family reduces mealtime stress, introduces a range of tastes and flavours to younger children, helps their transition to family foods, prevents fussy eating behaviours and promotes nutritious eating.

TIPS AND TRICKS FOR FAMILY MEALS

- Offer fussy eaters a tasting plate (see pages 120–121) of a deconstructed family meal
- When cooking, add vegetables or 'fussy foods' to the dish last, so you can cater for individual preferences. Someone hates peas, but loves carrots? No problem, just dish up their portion and stir through some carrot, then add the peas to the rest of the meal
- Swap pre-packaged ingredients for homemade or fresh foods. For example, if a recipe calls for chicken stock, use homemade stock which has a much lower salt content, and replace a tin of corn kernels with fresh corn to avoid any additives
- Use herbs and spices to add flavour, not salt
- Include grated or pureed veggies in your meals whenever possible
- Incorporate healthy ingredients whenever possible, such as quinoa in a salad and lentils in bolognese, and choose whole grains
- Use lean cuts of meat or trim your favourite cuts
- Reserve some of the family meal (before anything inappropriate is added to it) and blend or mash for your baby. Offering your baby a wide variety of flavours right from the start is a great way to avoid selective eating patterns
- Prepare elements of meals in advance when you get the opportunity, such as chopping vegetables
- Double the quantities of some meals to stock up your freezer – these can be thawed and served with fresh ingredients during busy times
- Planning your weekly meals is a great way to ensure you are offering your family a variety of nutritious foods. It is also more economical and takes away the 'what's for dinner' stress.

LAMB RACK WITH PARSLEY AND PINE NUTS

SERVES 2 ADULTS, 1 TODDLER, 2 BABIES
PREP TIME 10 minutes
COOKING TIME 40 minutes

¼ cup (60 ml) olive oil, plus extra for greasing
3 large (900 g) floury potatoes, peeled and cut into finger-sized chips
½ cup (80 g) pine nuts
large handful of flat-leaf parsley leaves, chopped
½ cup (100 g) Danish feta, crumbled
1 × 8-cutlet lamb rack (about 800 g), fat trimmed
¼ sweet potato, peeled and quartered (for baby puree)
1½ cups (180 g) frozen baby peas

There's no need to sacrifice flavour when cooking one meal for the whole family. Introducing a range of tastes, such as parsley and pine nuts, to your children early will help discourage fussy eating behaviours later in life.

1. Preheat the oven to 220°C (200°C fan-forced). Line a large baking tray with baking paper and grease a roasting pan with olive oil.
2. Use paper towel to pat dry the potato chips. Place in a bowl, add 2 tablespoons of the olive oil and toss to coat. Arrange in a single layer on the lined tray and bake for 35–40 minutes or until golden and crisp.
3. Meanwhile, combine the pine nuts, parsley, feta and remaining 1 tablespoon of olive oil in a small bowl. Place the lamb and sweet potato, if using, in the greased pan. Spread the pine nut mixture over the lamb rack and press down so it sticks to the meat. Roast the lamb and sweet potato for 30 minutes or until the lamb is cooked to your liking and the sweet potato is tender. Remove from the oven and set aside for 5 minutes to rest.
4. While the meat is resting, cook the peas in a saucepan of boiling water for 2 minutes or until tender. Drain well.

FUSSY EATING TIP Give your baby strips of tender cooked meat or a whole lamb cutlet alongside their puree or mashed portion. It will help develop and strengthen their oral motor skills and teaches them how to eat and enjoy meats that require more chewing than minced meals or purees.

STORAGE Keep any leftovers in an airtight container in the fridge for up to 2 days.

ALLERGIES/INTOLERANCES ***Dairy:*** omit the feta. ***Nuts:*** replace the pine nuts with pepitas (pumpkin seed kernels).

BABY SERVE Place the meat from 1 lamb cutlet, the baked sweet potato, ¼ cup (30 g) peas and a teaspoon of the pine nut and parsley mixture (remove any larger pieces of feta) in a food processor. Process until it reaches your desired consistency, adding a few tablespoons of your baby's usual milk if required. Always be very careful to serve a consistent mixture, checking for whole nuts or large chunks of meat within the puree. Depending on the age of your baby you can also offer the cooked cutlet bone to chew on and some whole peas and a few chips as finger food.

TODDLER SERVE Serve 1 lamb cutlet with chips and peas, plus fruit, if desired.

ADULT SERVE Serve 3 lamb cutlets with potato chips and peas alongside.

CHICKEN CURRY

SERVES 3 ADULTS, 2 TODDLERS, 1 BABY
PREP TIME 15 minutes
COOKING TIME 1 hour 15 minutes

- 2 tablespoons olive oil
- 1 teaspoon cumin seeds
- 3 cloves garlic, finely chopped
- 2 cm piece ginger, finely chopped
- 1 large onion, finely chopped
- 2–3 heaped teaspoons garam masala, to taste
- 1 teaspoon ground turmeric
- 1 teaspoon sweet paprika
- 1 bay leaf
- 1 teaspoon salt
- ¼ teaspoon chilli flakes or 1 fresh long red or green chilli, finely chopped
- 1 large tomato, diced
- 1 kg chicken thigh fillets, fat trimmed, cut into 2–3 cm pieces
- 1 cup (250 ml) coconut milk (optional)
- ¼ sweet potato, peeled and diced (optional, for baby puree)
- coriander leaves, to garnish
- steamed basmati rice, plain Greek-style yoghurt and roti or mountain bread, to serve

Our good friend Sonia is an expert on curries – her first food as a baby was dhal – so we asked her for a basic chicken curry recipe that can be adapted for lamb, beef and vegetables. This is mild enough for kids and makes a great introduction to the fragrant spices commonly used in Indian cooking.

1. Heat the olive oil in a large heavy-based saucepan over low heat. Add the cumin seeds, garlic and ginger and sauté for 5 minutes or until fragrant. Add the onion and sauté for a further 5 minutes or until the onion is translucent.
2. Add the garam masala, turmeric, paprika, bay leaf, salt and chilli to the pan, along with ¼ cup (60 ml) water. Increase the heat to medium and cook, stirring, to form a paste. When the water evaporates, add ¼ cup (60 ml) water and continue cooking, adding water as needed, for at least 15 minutes or until the spices release their natural oils and the paste is deep brown in colour. Add the tomato and cook, stirring, for another 2 minutes.
3. Increase the heat to medium–high and add the chicken to the pan. Cook, stirring often, for 10 minutes. Add enough coconut milk or water (or a mixture of the two) to just cover the chicken. Add the sweet potato if you will be making a puree portion for your baby. Cover and simmer over low heat for 20–30 minutes or until the chicken is cooked through and the sweet potato is tender. Remove the lid and cook for a further 10 minutes to thicken the sauce. You can serve the curry immediately, but it benefits from resting so if you have time, let it sit on the stovetop for a little while before serving.

NUTRITION NOTE Introducing spices to children early in their starting solids journey can help develop acceptance for a wider variety of foods later in life.

TIPS Frying off the spices and cooking the paste until the oils are released are essential for a good depth of flavour, so don't be tempted to cut the initial cooking time short. This curry would usually have more salt in the paste, but as this meal is suitable for children we have reduced it. Increase the salt if cooking for adults only, or season adult portions after serving.

STORAGE Keep in an airtight container in the fridge for up to 3 days. Alternatively, freeze individual portions of curry for up to 2 months.

✱ALLERGIES/INTOLERANCES ***Gluten/wheat:*** use gluten- or wheat-free roti or mountain bread for the toddler portion. ***Dairy:*** omit the yoghurt.

BABY SERVE Scoop 4 pieces of chicken and sweet potato out of the curry and mash, finely chop or puree, adding a tablespoon of water or coconut milk at a time to thin the sauce until you reach your desired consistency. Stir through 1 tablespoon of cooked rice for texture, if you like.

TODDLER SERVE Serve your toddler's meal as a tasting plate. Spoon some rice and chicken curry separately onto the plate, add some roti or torn mountain bread, halved cherry tomatoes and some yoghurt. They can dip and mix as much, or as little, of the curry as they like.

ADULT SERVE Spoon the rice into serving bowls, top with the chicken curry and sprinkle with coriander. Serve with yoghurt alongside.

BABY MEATBALLS WITH TOMATO SAUCE

SERVES 1 BABY, 2 TODDLERS, 3 ADULTS
PREP TIME 15 minutes (+ 30 minutes chilling)
COOKING TIME 30 minutes

500 g premium lean beef mince
1 small onion, finely diced
1 egg, lightly whisked
½ cup (35 g) fresh breadcrumbs (or 50 g packaged breadcrumbs)
2 tablespoons finely chopped flat-leaf parsley
½ teaspoon ground cumin
½ teaspoon mild paprika
freshly ground black pepper, to taste
1–2 tablespoons olive oil
2 × 400 g tins no-added-salt chopped tomatoes
½ teaspoon sugar
400 g spiral pasta
grated parmesan, to serve
salad or steamed vegetables, to serve (optional)

Deconstructing family meals for babies and toddlers is a great way to encourage them to accept and enjoy the foods you love, particularly if they tend to refuse mixed-texture meals. Pasta with meatballs is a great example of a recipe you can adapt for different stages of eating, whether spoon-feeding, baby-led weaning or self-feeding.

1. Place the beef, onion, egg, breadcrumbs, parsley, cumin, paprika and pepper in a large bowl and use your hands to mix until well combined.
2. Shape teaspoons of the mixture into small balls and place on a tray lined with baking paper. Chill in the fridge for 30 minutes.
3. Heat 1 tablespoon of oil in a large heavy-based frying pan over medium–high heat. Cook the meatballs, in 2 batches if necessary to avoid overcrowding the pan, for 5–6 minutes or until browned all over. Add a little more oil to the pan if they start to stick during cooking.
4. Pour the tomatoes over the meatballs and sprinkle with the sugar, then carefully stir the meatballs to coat in the sauce. Simmer gently over low–medium heat for 20 minutes.
5. Meanwhile, cook the pasta in a saucepan of boiling salted water until al dente, according to the instructions on the packet. Drain well.

NUTRITION NOTE These mini meatballs are rich in iron, which is essential for growth and development, and low in salt, helping to maintain healthy kidneys and general wellbeing.

STORAGE Keep in an airtight container in the fridge for up to 2 days or freeze individual portions of meatballs (without the pasta) in airtight containers for up to 2 months.

ALLERGIES/INTOLERANCES ***Gluten/wheat:*** substitute quinoa flakes or cooked quinoa for the breadcrumbs, and serve with gluten- or wheat-free pasta. ***Dairy:*** omit the parmesan. ***Egg:*** replace the egg with a 'chia egg' (see page 5).

BABY SERVE Mash or puree some meatballs, sauce and pasta until you reach your desired consistency, adding a little water if you require a thinner puree. Offer a few cooked pasta spirals and 1–2 meatballs alongside the puree as finger food.

TODDLER SERVE Serve a small bowl of pasta topped with a few meatballs and sauce, with a side of steamed vegetables and fruit. Or, serve the pasta and meatballs separately on a tasting plate with some steamed and/or roasted vegetables and fruit.

ADULT SERVE Serve the meatballs and sauce spooned over the pasta. Sprinkle with parmesan and serve accompanied by a salad or steamed vegetables.

BAKED TOMATO AND TUNA RISOTTO

SERVES 2 ADULTS,
2 TODDLERS, 2 BABIES
PREP TIME 15 minutes
COOKING TIME 40 minutes

1 tablespoon olive oil
1 onion, finely diced
¼ leek, white part only, thinly sliced
1 clove garlic, crushed
1½ cups (300 g) arborio rice, rinsed
1 tablespoon salt-reduced tomato paste (puree)
2 cups (500 ml) salt-reduced vegetable stock or homemade vegetable stock (see page 240)
400 g tin no-added salt chopped tomatoes
1 carrot, coarsely grated
1 zucchini (courgette), coarsely grated
185 g tin tuna in springwater, drained
½ cup (40 g) finely grated parmesan (optional)
small handful of flat-leaf parsley, finely chopped

Nothing beats a traditional risotto, but spending 20 minutes at the stovetop, stirring, just isn't always possible. This baked version is still wonderfully creamy, but gives you time to relax and put your feet up, or more realistically help with homework or building that Lego masterpiece.

1. Preheat the oven to 200°C (180°C fan-forced).
2. Heat the oil in a large, heavy-based ovenproof saucepan over medium heat. Add the onion, leek and garlic and cook, stirring, for 5 minutes or until softened. Add the rice and cook, stirring, for 1 minute. Add the tomato paste and stir to coat the rice.
3. Add the stock, 2 cups (500 ml) water and the tomatoes to the pan and bring to the boil. Stir through the carrot, zucchini and tuna. Cover with the lid or two tight layers of foil. Bake for 30 minutes or until the liquid is absorbed and the rice is cooked through.

FUSSY EATING TIP If your baby is refusing to be spoon-fed, adapt the meal so you can offer it as finger food. This risotto, for instance, can be rolled into little balls that are easy to pick up and munch on.

STORAGE Keep in an airtight container in the fridge for up to 2 days. Alternatively, freeze individual portions in freezer bags or airtight containers for up to 2 months.

ALLERGIES/INTOLERANCES ***Gluten:*** use gluten-free stock.
Dairy: omit the parmesan.

BABY SERVE Mash a few tablespoons of your baby's preferred milk and 1 teaspoon parmesan, if desired, into some risotto.

TODDLER SERVE For toddlers and self-feeding babies, stir 1 tablespoon parmesan into ½ cup (100 g) of the risotto mixture, then roll into small balls.

ADULT SERVE Spoon the risotto into serving bowls, season with salt and cracked pepper, to taste, and sprinkle with parmesan and parsley.

CHICKEN AND PESTO SPAGHETTI

SERVES 2 ADULTS, 2–4 TODDLERS, 1–2 BABIES
PREP TIME 20 minutes
COOKING TIME 30 minutes

½ butternut pumpkin (squash), peeled, seeded and cut into 1 cm pieces
2 teaspoons olive oil
1 chicken breast fillet (about 300 g), fat trimmed
300 g wholemeal spaghetti
1½ cups (125 g) chopped broccoli florets
¼ cup (40 g) pine nuts, toasted, to serve (optional)
basil leaves, to serve (optional)

BASIL PESTO

1 cup, firmly packed (45 g) basil leaves
½ cup (125 ml) extra virgin olive oil
⅓ cup (50 g) pine nuts
½–1 clove garlic, crushed
¾ cup (60 g) finely grated parmesan

Pesto is generally a winner with kids, and can be varied using different herbs and nuts or seeds. Combined with chicken, pumpkin and broccoli it makes a meal sure to please the whole family.

1. To make the basil pesto, place the basil, olive oil, pine nuts and garlic in a food processor or blender and process until combined to a smooth paste. Transfer to a bowl, stir in the parmesan and set aside.
2. Preheat the oven to 200°C (180°C fan-forced) and line a baking tray with baking paper.
3. Place the pumpkin on the lined tray, drizzle with the olive oil and toss to coat. Bake for 30 minutes or until golden and tender.
4. Meanwhile, place 3 cups (750 ml) water in a heavy-based saucepan and bring to the boil over high heat. Add the chicken fillet, reduce the heat to low and simmer gently, covered, for 15 minutes or until cooked through. Turn off the heat and set aside for 5 minutes. Remove the chicken from the liquid and leave to cool slightly, then shred and set aside.
5. Cook the spaghetti in a saucepan of salted boiling water until al dente, following the instructions on the packet. Add the broccoli for the final 2 minutes of cooking. Drain. Return the pasta to the pan and toss with ⅓ cup (90 g) of the basil pesto. Mix in the pumpkin, chicken and broccoli.

NUTRITION NOTE Wholegrain pasta is higher in fibre and provides more nutrients, such as B vitamins, iron and selenium, than regular white varieties.

STORAGE Keep leftover pesto in a small jar or airtight container, with a thin layer of olive oil poured over the surface to prevent browning, for up to 1 week in the fridge. To freeze, spoon into an ice cube tray, pour a thin layer of olive oil over each, cover with a lid or plastic film and freeze until frozen. Transfer to a freezer bag and freeze for up to 3 months. Any leftover baby, toddler or adult spaghetti will keep in an airtight container in the fridge for up to 2 days. Leftover baby puree or toddler muffins (see tip) can be frozen in individual portions, in airtight containers or freezer bags, for up to 2 months.

ALLERGIES/INTOLERANCES ***Gluten/wheat:*** use gluten- or wheat-free pasta. ***Dairy:*** omit the parmesan from the pesto or replace with 1 teaspoon fresh lemon juice and omit the cheese from the toddler muffins (if making). ***Nuts:*** substitute sunflower seeds for the pine nuts in the pesto, then omit the optional pine nuts.

TIP

To make pasta muffins, preheat the oven to 180°C (160°C fan-forced). Grease 4 holes of a 12-hole regular muffin tin and line with paper cases. Place 1 cup (150 g) of pasta mixture in a bowl and snip the spaghetti into short lengths. Mix in 1 egg and ½ cup (60 g) grated tasty cheese, then spoon into the lined holes. Bake for 20–25 minutes or until golden.

BABY For younger babies, place ½ cup (100 g) of the spaghetti and broccoli, 2 tablespoons of shredded chicken and 2 tablespoons of pumpkin in a bowl and puree, mash or finely chop to your desired consistency, adding a little water if required. For older babies, include a small amount of pesto if dairy and nuts are tolerated, and serve a few of the elements as finger food alongside the spoon-fed meal.

TODDLER Use kitchen scissors to cut the spaghetti into short lengths to assist with self-feeding, if required. Spoon the finished pasta into a bowl and serve. Or, make into pasta muffins (see tip).

ADULT Spoon the finished pasta into serving bowls. Season with cracked pepper and sprinkle with the toasted pine nuts and basil leaves, if desired.

CHAPTER 11

BASICS

We are big believers in making your own versions of commercial foods whenever possible, so you can avoid unwanted additives, preservatives and 'filler' ingredients, as well as high levels of sugar and/or salt. It also gives you the opportunity to bump up the nutrition content (of sauces in particular), by adding some grated veggies.

HIDDEN VEGGIE SAUCE

MAKES 1 CUP (240 G)
PREP TIME 10 minutes
COOKING TIME 20 minutes

1 tablespoon olive oil
1 small onion, thinly sliced
1 clove garlic, finely chopped
½ red capsicum (pepper), seeded and diced
1 tablespoon no-added-salt tomato paste (puree)
400 g tin no-added-salt chopped tomatoes
½ cup (125 ml) salt-reduced vegetable stock or water
1 cob of corn, husk and silk removed
½ sweet potato, peeled and diced
1 small zucchini (courgette), diced
2 tablespoons chopped herbs (such as basil, parsley; optional)

1. Heat the oil in a heavy-based saucepan over medium heat. Add the onion and garlic and sauté for 2–3 minutes or until softened. Add the capsicum and tomato paste and cook, stirring, for a further minute. Add the tomato and stock or water and bring to the boil, then reduce the heat to hold at a simmer.
2. Cut the corn kernels from the cob and add to the pan with the sweet potato and zucchini. Cover and cook for 10 minutes or until the vegetables are tender. Stir in the herbs, if using, and remove from the heat.
3. Use a blender, stick blender or food processor to process the mixture to a smooth sauce. If you require a smoother consistency, press it through a fine-meshed sieve. Use as a dipping sauce, stir through cooked rice or pasta, or spread over a pizza base instead of a tomato-based sauce.

STORAGE Keep in an airtight container in the fridge for up to 3 days. Alternatively, freeze individual portions in an ice cube tray, then transfer to a freezer bag.

ALLERGIES/INTOLERANCES ***Gluten:*** use gluten-free stock or water.

F GF WF EF V

SPINACH, BROCCOLI AND CASHEW PESTO

MAKES 1 CUP (250 G)
PREP TIME 10 minutes
COOKING TIME Nil

2 cups (80 g) baby spinach leaves
¾ cup (60 g) chopped broccoli florets
¼ cup (40 g) unsalted cashews
2 cloves garlic
⅔ cup, loosely packed (50 g) grated parmesan
⅓ cup (80 ml) extra virgin olive oil

1. Place all the ingredients in a food processor or blender and process until smooth and combined.
2. Spread over pizza bases (you can spread the bases with a thin layer of no-added-salt tomato paste first if you like), toss through cooked pasta or use as a spread on sandwiches.

STORAGE Keep in an airtight container, covered with a thin layer of extra virgin olive oil to prevent browning, in the fridge for up to 5 days. Alternatively, freeze individual portions in covered ice cube trays, topped with a layer of oil, for up to 3 months.

ALLERGIES/INTOLERANCES ***Dairy:*** omit the cheese. ***Nuts:*** use sesame seeds instead of cashews.

TOMATO AND BASIL PASTA SAUCE

MAKES 1½ CUPS (375 G)
PREP TIME 10 minutes
COOKING TIME 15 minutes

⅓ cup (80 ml) extra virgin olive oil
1 onion, finely chopped
500 g ripe tomatoes
2 cloves garlic, finely chopped
10 basil leaves
ground black pepper, to taste

1. Heat the oil in a large, non-stick, heavy-based saucepan or frying pan over medium heat. Add the onion, cover and cook for 5 minutes or until soft, but not browned.
2. Meanwhile, use a small sharp knife to make a cross in the base of each tomato. Place in a heatproof bowl, cover with boiling water and set aside for 1 minute. Drain the tomatoes, return to the bowl and cover with cold water. Working with one tomato at a time, remove from the bowl, peel away the skin and then roughly chop, discarding the core.
3. Add the tomato, garlic and basil to the pan and cook, stirring often, for 10 minutes or until the tomato has collapsed. Season with pepper, to taste. Use a stick blender or food processor to process the sauce until smooth. Use instead of tinned chopped tomatoes, jars of pasta sauce or bottled passata.

STORAGE Keep in an airtight container in the fridge for up to 3 days or freeze in an airtight container for up to 3 months.

F WF DF EF

BASIC BOLOGNESE

MAKES 4½ CUPS (1.2 KG)
PREP TIME 10 minutes
COOKING TIME 35 minutes

1 tablespoon extra virgin olive oil
1 onion, finely chopped
1 clove garlic, crushed
70 g Swiss brown mushrooms, chopped
500 g premium lean beef mince
1 carrot, finely chopped or coarsely grated
1 zucchini (courgette), finely chopped or coarsely grated
2 tablespoons no-added-salt tomato paste (puree)
400 g tin no-added-salt chopped tomatoes
½ cup (125 ml) water or salt-reduced beef stock
½ cup (100 g) tinned brown lentils, drained and rinsed (optional)
small handful of flat-leaf parsley leaves, chopped

1. Heat the oil in a large heavy-based saucepan or frying pan over medium heat and sauté the onion and garlic for 2–3 minutes or until just softened. Add the mushroom and cook, stirring, for 2–3 minutes or until softened.
2. Add the beef to the pan and cook until browned, breaking it up with a wooden spoon. Add the carrot and zucchini and cook for 3 minutes, until softened. Add the tomato paste, tomato and water or stock. Bring to the boil, reduce the heat and simmer, stirring occasionally, for 15 minutes. Add the lentils and parsley and cook for a further 5 minutes.
3. Serve spooned over cooked pasta or use to make our Baby lasagne fingers (see page 85) or Bolognese filo triangles (see page 131).

STORAGE Keep in an airtight container in the fridge for up to 2 days or in the freezer for up to 2 months.

✱ALLERGIES/INTOLERANCES ***Gluten:*** use gluten-free stock or water.

TOMATO SAUCE (KETCHUP)

MAKES 1 CUP (320 G)
PREP TIME 10 minutes
COOKING TIME 35 minutes

1 tablespoon extra virgin olive oil
½ small onion, finely chopped
400 g tin no-added-salt chopped tomatoes
¼ cup (60 ml) apple cider vinegar
2–3 tablespoons pure maple syrup, to taste
2 teaspoons sweet paprika
½ teaspoon ground coriander
½ teaspoon salt
½ teaspoon ground black or white pepper
1 tablespoon no-added-salt tomato paste (puree)
1 tablespoon mild American-style mustard (optional)

1. Heat the olive oil in a heavy-based saucepan over medium heat. Add the onion and sauté for 5 minutes or until softened. Stir in the tomato, reduce the heat and simmer for 7 minutes. Add the vinegar and cook for a further 7 minutes or until the mixture has reduced by half.
2. Add the remaining ingredients to the pan and stir to combine. Simmer, stirring occasionally, for 15 minutes or until a thick and tasty sauce forms. Transfer to a food processor and process until smooth. If you want a smoother consistency, press the sauce through a fine-meshed sieve.

STORAGE Store in a sterilised glass jar (see page 179) in the fridge for up to 1 month. Alternatively, freeze smaller portions in airtight containers for up to 2 months.

*ALLERGIES/INTOLERANCES ***Gluten/wheat:*** omit the mustard.

(GF) (WF) (DF) (EF) (V)

MEXICAN SEASONING MIX

MAKES ½ CUP (50 G)
PREP TIME 5 minutes
COOKING TIME Nil

¼ cup (30 g) ground cumin
1 tablespoon garlic powder
1 tablespoon onion powder
1 teaspoon dried oregano
1 teaspoon smoked paprika
1 teaspoon ground coriander
½ teaspoon chilli powder (optional)
pinch of salt
pinch of ground black pepper

1. Combine all the ingredients in a food processor or snap-lock bag. Process or shake for a few seconds or until well combined.

NUTRITION NOTE Unfortunately, most pre-packaged Mexican spice mixes have synthetic colours, additives and preservatives. Making your own is as simple as shaking some herbs and spices together.

STORAGE Store in a clean, dry airtight jar for up to 3 months.

F EF V

TORTILLAS

MAKES 8
PREP TIME 20 minutes (+ 30 minutes resting)
COOKING TIME 25 minutes

- 2 cups (300 g) ‘00’ plain flour, plus extra for dusting
- 1 teaspoon salt
- ¼ teaspoon baking powder
- 60 g unsalted butter, chilled and chopped
- ⅔ cup (160 ml) warm water

1. Sift the combined flour, salt and baking powder into a food processor, add the butter and process until the mixture resembles fine breadcrumbs. Tip the mixture back into the bowl. Add the water and stir with a fork until the mixture comes together. Turn onto a lightly floured surface and knead until the dough is smooth and elastic (about 4–5 minutes).
2. Divide into eight portions and roll into balls. Cover with plastic film and set aside for 30 minutes to rest.
3. Heat a large, heavy-based non-stick frying pan or saucepan over medium heat until hot. Roll out a ball of dough on a lightly floured surface into a thin round. The dough should be so thin that you can almost see through it. If you’re having problems, roll the dough between two sheets of baking paper. Place in the hot pan and cook until it bubbles and puffs and there are browned patches underneath. Turn and cook the other side until it also has brown patches. Transfer to a plate and cover with foil to keep warm while you roll and cook the remaining tortillas. Reduce the heat if your tortillas are starting to burn.
4. Top the tortillas burrito-style or use to make our chicken burritos (see page 61).

STORAGE Keep in an airtight container for up to 2 days. Alternatively, place in a freezer bag, separated with freezer paper, and freeze for up to 3 months.

✱ALLERGIES/INTOLERANCES ***Gluten/wheat:*** use bought gluten- or wheat-free tortillas or wraps instead.

GUACAMOLE

MAKES 1 CUP (240 G)
PREP TIME 5 minutes
COOKING TIME Nil

- 2 ripe avocados, peeled, seeded and diced
- juice of ½ a lime
- pinch of salt
- ¼ red onion, finely diced
- 1 tomato, seeds removed and diced
- 1 tablespoon chopped coriander leaves

1. Place the avocado, lime juice and salt in a bowl and roughly mash together. Stir in the onion, tomato and coriander until just combined, and serve. (Alternatively, use a blender if you prefer a silky smooth consistency.)

STORAGE Place the avocado seed in the centre of the guacamole, cover with plastic film and keep in the fridge for up to 2 hours.

CHICKEN STOCK

MAKES 1.5 LITRES
PREP TIME 10 minutes
COOKING TIME 3–4 hours

1 tablespoon olive oil
1 onion, roughly chopped
2 small cloves garlic, crushed
1 cm piece ginger, finely chopped
1 carrot, roughly chopped
2 stalks celery, trimmed and roughly chopped
4 large chicken drumsticks
1 bay leaf
handful of mixed herbs (such as parsley, thyme; optional)
salt and ground black pepper

1 Heat the oil in a large heavy-based saucepan over medium heat. Add the onion, garlic and ginger and sauté for 3 minutes or until softened. Add the carrot and celery and sauté for a further 3 minutes.
2 Add the chicken to the pan and cook, stirring, for 2 minutes or until browned all over. Add 1.5–2 litres water, the bay leaf and herbs, if using. The water should completely cover the chicken and vegetables. Season with a pinch of salt and some pepper.
3 Bring to a simmer and cook, partially covered, for 3–4 hours, skimming any foam from the surface every 30 minutes. The longer you cook the stock, the fuller the flavour will be. (If you are short on time, you can cook it for 2 hours and will still get a good result.) Pour the stock through a fine-meshed sieve over a heatproof bowl and discard the solids.

STORAGE Keep in an airtight container in the fridge for up to 3 days. Alternatively, freeze 1 cup (250 ml) portions in airtight containers for up to 2 months.

VEGETABLE STOCK

MAKES 1.5 LITRES
PREP TIME 10 minutes
COOKING TIME 3–4 hours

1 tablespoon olive oil
1 onion, roughly chopped
2 small cloves garlic, crushed
1 cm piece ginger, finely chopped
50 g button mushrooms, sliced
1 carrot, roughly chopped
2 stalks celery, trimmed and roughly chopped
1 bay leaf
handful of mixed herbs (such as parsley, thyme; optional)
salt and ground black pepper

1 Heat the oil in a large heavy-based saucepan over medium heat. Add the onion, garlic and ginger and sauté for 5 minutes or until softened. Add the mushroom, carrot and celery and sauté for another 3 minutes.
2 Add 1.5–2 litres of water, the bay leaf and herbs, if using. The water should completely cover the vegetables. Season with a pinch of salt and some pepper.
3 Bring to a simmer and cook, partially covered, for 3–4 hours, skimming any foam from the surface every 30 minutes. The longer you cook the stock, the fuller the flavour will be. (If you are short on time, you can cook it for 2 hours and will still get a good result.) Pour the stock through a fine-meshed sieve over a heatproof bowl and discard the solids.

STORAGE Keep in an airtight container in the fridge for up to 3 days. Alternatively, freeze 1 cup (250 ml) portions in airtight containers for up to 2 months.

CARROT, APPLE AND FENNEL COLESLAW

SERVES 4–6
PREP TIME 10 minutes
COOKING TIME Nil

2 carrots
1 apple, cored
½ fennel bulb, trimmed
1 small red onion
juice of 1 lemon
2 tablespoons whole-egg mayonnaise
1 heaped teaspoon Dijon mustard
ground black pepper, to taste
small handful of flat-leaf parsley, finely chopped

1. Thinly slice the carrots, apple, fennel and onion, or use a food processor to slice the fennel and onion and julienne the carrots and apple. Combine in a large bowl.
2. Place the lemon juice, mayonnaise and mustard in a small bowl and mix to combine. Season with pepper. Add to the coleslaw along with the parsley and toss to combine. Serve.

STORAGE Keep in the fridge, covered with plastic film, for up to 24 hours.

✱ALLERGIES/INTOLERANCES ***Gluten/wheat:*** use gluten-free mustard and mayonnaise. ***Egg:*** use egg-free mayonnaise.

SIMPLE CUSTARD

MAKES 2 CUPS (520 G)
PREP TIME 2 minutes
COOKING TIME 15 minutes

2 cups (500 ml) milk
1 teaspoon pure vanilla extract
4 egg yolks
1 tablespoon gluten-free cornflour
1½ tablespoons caster sugar (optional)

1. Warm the milk and vanilla extract in a small heavy-based saucepan over medium heat until the milk is just below boiling point.
2. Place the egg yolks, cornflour and sugar, if using, in a large heatproof bowl and whisk until well combined. While whisking constantly, slowly pour the milk mixture over the egg mixture.
3. Transfer to the pan and cook over low–medium heat, stirring constantly to ensure the custard doesn't stick to the base of the pan, until the custard has thickened enough to coat the back of a spoon. Serve.

STORAGE Keep, covered with plastic film, in the fridge for up to 2 days.

✱ALLERGIES/INTOLERANCES ***Egg:*** omit the egg yolks and increase the cornflour to 2 tablespoons.

ACKNOWLEDGEMENTS

We are incredibly grateful to everyone who has helped make this book happen. Firstly, Pippa Masson, our agent at Curtis Brown, who helped us realise our long-held dream of publishing a cookbook. You have been a wonderful source of guidance, confidence and knowledge, and we appreciate all you have done for us.

Our sincere thanks to the team at Lantern. To Julie Gibbs: we've loved your enthusiasm, energy and support from day one and it has been an absolute pleasure to work with you and your team. Anna Scobie, our editor: your hard work and attention to detail have transformed our collection of words into something so meaningful. Hannah Schubert: for designing the book we dreamed of. Alissa Dinallo and Evi O.: for additional design work and illustrations. Cass Stokes, our stylist: for immersing yourself in the world of children's food and making it shine. And Katrina O'Brien: for always keeping us at ease and offering encouragement when we needed it.

A huge thanks to our sponsors – Naked Foods, Brookfarm Macadamia Oil, The Butcher & The Chef, EcoEggs, Barilla pasta, RACO Cookware, Nikon and Lettuce Deliver Organics – who provided produce and products for recipe testing and photography. We love what you do and are grateful for your generosity and support.

To our friends: for being a source of inspiration and motivation, and for giving it to us straight. Thanks, too, to all our recipe testers and little taste-testers for ensuring our food appeals to a wide range of children. A special thanks to Matilda, Chloé and Sophie for featuring in this book.

And finally, to our families. To our parents David, Cathy, Neil, Margie, Peter, Sarah, Jan and Rob: for your love, support and encouragement for all that we do. To 'The Buckles': for giving up their kitchen so we could photograph the food for this book.

To our gorgeous children, Harry, Amelia, George and Hamish: you teach and inspire us every day, and this book wouldn't exist without you. And to our patient and dedicated husbands, Henry and Charlie: your love, support and encouragement is more than we could dream of.

Allie, Jess and Sarah xxx

BIBLIOGRAPHY

Infant Feeding Advice, Australasian Society of Clinical Immunology and Allergy (ASCIA), allergy.org.au

Infant Feeding Guidelines and Australian Dietary Guidelines, National Health & Medical Research Council (NHMRC), nhmrc.gov.au

SENSE-ational Mealtimes by G. Griffiths & D. Stapleton, sense-ationalmealtimes.com.au

'Early Oral-Motor Interventions for Pediatric Feeding Problems: What, When and How' by C.J. Manno, C. Fox, P.S. Eicher and M.E. Kerwin, Journal of Early & Intensive Behavior Intervention, Vol 2, 2005

'The Importance of Postural Control for Feeding' by F. Redstone and J.F. West, Pediatric Nursing journal, March–April 2004

'The Feeding Relationship' by E.M. Satter, Journal of the American Dietetic Association, March 1986

'Feeding Strategies for Older Infants and Toddlers' by K. Toomey, Journal of Paediatric Nutrition and Development, Autumn 2002

Sequential Oral Sensory (SOS) Approach to Feeding, sosapproach-conferences.com.

INDEX

A
agar agar 5
almonds 5
  Almond power balls 176
  Apple and almond biscuits 36
  Super-start toasted muesli 142, 144
anaphylaxis 4
apple 5
  Apple and almond biscuits 36
  Apple and pear crumble 77
  Breakfast muffins 153
  Carrot, apple and fennel coleslaw 87, 241
  Chicken and apple fingers 41
  Creamy banana and apple porridge 142, 150
  Green veg and apple puree 12
  Hazelnut and oat baby bars 45, 142
  Red lentil and veggie puree 15
  Sparkling fruit punch 216
  Sweet lamb couscous 29
Arrowroot biscuits 116
avocado 4
  Avocado dippers 56
  Avocado salsa 142, 157
  Bananavo egg mash 31
  Cheese and salad pinwheels 197
  Cucumber salsa 61
  Guacamole 239
  Tuna, avocado, mayo and carrot sandwich 193

B
babies 1
  foods to avoid 3
  fruit 2, 143
  mealtime ritual 48
  selective eating 223
  vegetarian diet 2
Baby lasagne fingers 85
Baby meatballs with tomato sauce 228–9
Baby's first carrot cake 37
Baked falafels 93
Baked tomato and tuna risotto 230–1
banana 5
  Baby's first carrot cake 37
  Banana cinnamon toast fingers 34
  Banana and strawberry ice cream 180
  Bananavo egg mash 31
  'Choose your own' smoothie 94
  Creamy banana and apple porridge 142, 150
  Hazelnut and oat baby bars 45
  Jolly good lunchbox biscuits 189
  Smoothie bowl 149
  Zucchini and pear banana bread 200
Basic bolognese 237
basil
  Basil pesto 232
  Tomato and basil pasta sauce 237
batter, tempura 64, 65
beans, tinned
  Beef and bean rice 26
  Cheesy baked beans on toast 142, 159
  Vegetable ratatouille lasagne 71
beef
  Baby lasagne fingers 85
  Baby meatballs with tomato sauce 228–9
  Basic bolognese 237
  Beef and bean rice 26
  Beef, lentil and mushroom pie 66
  Beef and lentil sausage rolls 208
  Beef, veggie and quinoa mash 25
  Beef burgers with hidden veggies 133
  Mini meatballs 44
  Simple beef puree 11
beetroot
  Roast beetroot dip 50
berries
  Carrot and blueberry oatbran muffins 142, 190
  Smoothie bowl 149
  see also raspberries; strawberries
biscuits
  Apple and almond biscuits 36
  Arrowroot biscuits 116
  Biscuit crisps 215
  Cheesy seed biscuits 201
  Choc oat biscuits 213
  Jam drop biscuits 212
  Jolly good lunchbox biscuits 189
  Teeny teddies 172
'bliss balls' 176
bok choy
  Sticky honey chicken with rice and bok choy 72
Bolognese filo triangles 131
bread
  Cheese and salad pinwheels 197
  Chicken, pumpkin and spinach bread pies 130
  Salmon and ricotta cakes 53
  Zucchini and pear banana bread 200
breadcrumbs 112
  Chicken and zucchini nuggets 82
  Crumbed fish bites 88
breakfast 142, 164
  Breakfast muffins 153
  finger food 153–60
breastmilk 2, 4, 8, 10
Broad bean and pea dip 110
broccoli
  Chicken and hokkien noodle stir-fry 58
  Chicken and pesto spaghetti 232–3
  Eat-your-greens frittata 38
  Green veg and apple puree 12
  Little quinoa bites 105
  Pumpkin-spiced quinoa balls 43
  Rainbow vegetable shreddies 88
  Roast vegetable couscous salad 138
  Salmon and veggie mash 20
  Spinach, broccoli and cashew pesto 236
Brownies 210
Buttercream icing 218

C
cakes
  Baby's first carrot cake 37
  'one-bowl' 218
  Vanilla birthday cake 218, 219
calcium 2, 142
carbohydrates 2
carrots 3
  Baby's first carrot cake 37
  Carrot, apple and fennel coleslaw 87, 241
  Carrot and blueberry oatbran muffins 142, 190
  Carrot, parsnip and cashew puree 14
  Cheese and salad pinwheels 197
  Cheesy veggie pasta with thyme 57
  Crispy vegetable spring rolls 206
  Lentil and quinoa dhal 30
  Pasta salad 198
  Red lentil and veggie puree 15
  Savoury veggie slice 167
  Tuna, avocado, mayo and carrot sandwich 193
cashews
  Carrot, parsnip and cashew puree 14
  nut cream 5
  Spinach, broccoli and cashew pesto 236
cauliflower
  Cauliflower hummus 170
  Creamy chicken and cauliflower crepes 84
  Fish, cauliflower and leek puree 14
  Irresistible lamb puree 24
  Turkey and cauliflower tots 124
  Winner winner chicken dinner 19
cereals 2, 5, 144
cheese 2, 5
  Beef burgers with hidden veggies 133
  Bolognese filo triangles 131
  Cheese and salad pinwheels 197
  Cheesy baked beans on toast 142, 159
  Cheesy polenta chippies with roast beetroot dip 50
  Cheesy seed biscuits 201
  Cheesy veggie pasta with thyme 57
  Cucumber salsa 61
  Eat-your-greens frittata 38
  Ham, cheese and pineapple tartlets 205
  Kale and mushroom omelette 160
  Little quinoa bites 105
  Meatball, cheese and lettuce sandwich 193
  Mini quiches 90
  Pasta salad 198
  Pea and ham couscous squares 109
  Prawn and pesto pizza 75
  Savoury scones 171

Savoury veggie slice 167
Spinach, ham and cheese pizza 75
Sweet potato, mushroom and cheese pizza 75
Way-too-easy pizza scrolls 194
see also ricotta
chewing 9, 10, 24, 165
chia seeds 5
Almond power balls 176
Creamy chia bircher muesli 146
Peach and raspberry oats with chia and LSA 32
Super-start toasted muesli 142, 144
chicken
Chicken and apple fingers 41
Chicken burritos with cucumber salsa 61
Chicken and chive sausages 54
Chicken curry 226–7
Chicken and hokkien noodle stir-fry 58
Chicken and mushroom bolognese 23
Chicken and pesto spaghetti 232–3
Chicken, pesto and cucumber sandwich 193
Chicken, pumpkin and spinach bread pies 130
Chicken and sweetcorn puree 11
Chicken and zucchini nuggets 82
Chicken stock 240
Creamy chicken and cauliflower crepes 84
Satay chicken skewers 129
Sesame-crumbed chicken fingers 112
Sticky honey chicken with rice and bok choy 72
Winner winner chicken dinner 19
chickpeas
Baked falafels 93
Cauliflower hummus 170
Vegetable ratatouille lasagne 71
Veggie, tomato and quinoa soup 68
chips
Cheesy polenta chippies with roast beetroot dip 50
Sweet potato fries 65
chocolate
Brownies 210
Choc oat biscuits 213
Choc popcorn balls 175
Choc-hazelnut spread 179
Coconut muffins with a twist 178
choking 3, 9, 81, 164
'Choose your own' smoothie 94
coconut, desiccated
Almond power balls 176
Coconut muffins with a twist 178
No-nut crunchy muesli bars 186
Smoothie bowl 149
Super-start toasted muesli 142, 144
coconut cream/milk 5
Chicken curry 226–7
Satay chicken skewers 129
constipation 8, 16, 100–101
cooking with kids 184, 190, 210
Jam drop biscuits 212
coriander
Crispy vegetable spring rolls 206
Cucumber salsa 61
Guacamole 239
corn
Beef, veggie and quinoa mash 25
Chicken and sweetcorn puree 11
Corn fritters with avocado salsa 142, 157
Hidden veggie sauce 66, 236
Pasta salad 198
couscous 146
Pea and ham couscous squares 109
Roast vegetable couscous salad 138
Sweet lamb couscous 29
Creamy banana and apple porridge 142, 150
Creamy chia bircher muesli 146
Creamy chicken and cauliflower crepes 84
crepes
Creamy chicken and cauliflower crepes 84
Crispy polenta pork fingers 87
Crispy vegetable spring rolls 206
Crumbed fish bites 88
cucumber
Cheese and salad pinwheels 197
Chicken, pesto and cucumber sandwich 193
Cucumber salsa 61
curry
Chicken curry 226–7
custard
Simple custard 241
cutlery, starting to use 10

D
dairy and dairy alternatives 2–3, 4–5, 100
dates
Almond power balls 176
Choc-hazelnut spread 179
Jolly good lunchbox biscuits 189
dental checks 165
dhal
Lentil and quinoa dhal 30
dips
Broad bean and pea dip 110
Dipping sauce 206
Roast beetroot dip 50
Yoghurt dipping sauce 93
dried fruit 2, 4
Coconut muffins with a twist 178
Jolly good lunchbox biscuits 189
No-nut crunchy muesli bars 186
Scones three ways 171
Super-start toasted muesli 142, 144
drinks 3, 81
Sparkling fruit punch 216
Old-school strawberry milkshake 215
see also smoothies

E
Eat-your-greens frittata 38
eating 81
'everything on your plate' 164, 165
mindful 143, 172, 210, 216, 217, 222
overstuffing mouth 136
parental role models 61, 138
spoon technique 8–9
supervising 110
at the table 141–3
see also family meals, deconstructing; oral motor skills
eggs
allergy to 4, 31
Bananavo egg mash 31
introducing 31
Mini meringues 216, 217
nutrients 5, 90, 160
raw, undercooked 3
sandwich 192
substitutes 5
emotional eating 164, 165

F
falafel
Baked falafels 93
family meals, deconstructing 224–33
fats 3
feeding milestones 10
fibre 66, 100–1, 142
fine motor skills 120
finger foods 81, 100, 101
breakfast 153–60
starting 10, 41
see also tasting plate
finger foods, hard
Arrowroot biscuits 116
Broad bean and pea dip 110
Herby lamb cutlets 115
Homemade teething rusks 101, 117
Sesame-crumbed chicken fingers 112
finger foods, soft
Apple and almond biscuits 36
Banana cinnamon toast fingers 34
Beef burgers with hidden veggies 133
Chicken and apple fingers 41
Chicken and hokkien noodle stir-fry 58
Corn fritters with avocado salsa 142, 157
Creamy chicken and cauliflower crepes 84
Crispy polenta pork fingers 87
Eat-your-greens frittata 38
Hazelnut and oat baby bars 45, 142
Little quinoa bites 105
Maple pumpkin tempters 34
Mini meatballs 44
Pea and ham couscous squares 109
Pumpkin-spiced quinoa balls 43
Pumpkin, pear and spelt baby bars 108
Raspberry pikelets 154

Salmon and leek potato croquettes 102
Sesame-crumbed chicken fingers 112
Spinach and ricotta nudies 136
Turkey and cauliflower tots 124
Veggie and ricotta fritters 106, 142
fish 5
allergy to 4
Crumbed fish bites 88
Fish, cauliflower and leek puree 14
fussy eaters 64
health benefits 88
starting 14
storing 14, 88
Tempura fish and sweet potato fries 65
see also salmon; tuna
folate 2, 5, 23, 160, 212
food allergies/intolerances 4, 77, 170, 217
see also eggs; nuts
food colourings 1, 4, 216
food groups 1–3
food refusal 3, 8, 40, 48, 80, 99, 100, 101, 121, 142, 165
food safety 185, 192
food substitutes 4–5
formula feeding 2, 4, 10, 101
frittata
Eat-your-greens frittata 38
fritters
Corn fritters with avocado salsa 142, 157
Rainbow vegetable shreddies 88
Veggie and ricotta fritters 106, 142
fruit
for babies 2, 143
for breakfast 142
daily serves 2, 143
dried 2
frozen 101, 180
skin on 100
stool-softening 101
see also specific fruits; smoothies
fruit juice 2, 3, 143
fullness cues 9, 80, 165
fussy eaters 40, 184, 190
causes 2–3, 101, 121, 164, 165, 186, 222
coping with 48–9, 65, 80–1, 84, 134, 167
snacks 164
'sometimes foods' 207, 208
tips 223, 224
see also lunchboxes; tasting plate

G
gagging 9, 10, 117, 120
gluten 4, 5
gluten-free 5
Vanilla birthday cake 218, 219
grains and cereals 2, 5, 146
whole grains 142, 150, 223
see also bread; couscous; noodles; oats; pasta; quinoa; rice
grazing 80, 204
green, leafy vegetables 149
Eat-your-greens frittata 38
Green veg and apple puree 12
see also broccoli; kale; spinach
Guacamole 239

H
ham
Ham, cheese and pineapple tartlets 205
Mini quiches 90
Pea and ham couscous squares 109
Spinach, ham and cheese pizza 75
Way-too-easy pizza scrolls 194
'happy chuckers' 100
hard munchables 9, 10, 24, 100, 110
see also finger foods, hard
hazelnuts
allergies 179
Choc-hazelnut spread 179
Hazelnut and oat baby bars 45, 142
Raspberry pikelets 154
herbs 121, 184
Cheesy polenta chippies with roast beetroot dip 50
Cheesy veggie pasta with thyme 57
Chicken and chive sausages 54
Chicken and hokkien noodle stir-fry 58
Herby lamb cutlets 115
Hidden veggie sauce 66, 236
Mexican seasoning mix 238
Mini meatballs 44
Rainbow vegetable shreddies 88
Savoury scones 171
Savoury veggie slice 167
Vegetable ratatouille lasagne 71
see also parsley
Hidden veggie sauce 66, 236
Homemade teething rusks 101, 117
honey 3, 94
Breakfast muffins 153
Choc popcorn balls 175
No-nut crunchy muesli bars 186
Sticky honey chicken with rice and bok choy 72
Super-start toasted muesli 142, 144
hummus
Cauliflower hummus 170
hunger signs 9, 49, 204

I
ice cream
Banana and strawberry ice cream 180
Old-school strawberry milkshake 215
immune system 19, 29
iron 2–3, 5, 11, 29, 66, 85, 100, 229
Irresistible lamb puree 24

J
Jam drop biscuits 212
jars, sterilising 179
Jolly good lunchbox biscuits 189

K
kale
Kale and mushroom omelette 160
Smoothie bowl 149
kids cooking *see* cooking with kids
kiwifruit
Kiwi-go yoghurt 12, 142
Tri-fruit icy pops 96

L
lamb 29
Herby lamb cutlets 115
Irresistible lamb puree 24
Lamb and pesto sausages 134
Lamb and risoni bake 62
Lamb rack with parsley and pine nuts 224–5
Sweet lamb couscous 29
lasagne
Baby lasagne fingers 85
'learning plate' 48
leeks
Fish, cauliflower and leek puree 14
Salmon and leek potato croquettes 102
Winner winner chicken dinner 19
leftovers 84, 131, 142, 224
legumes 5, 158
lentils 5
Basic bolognese 237
Beef and lentil sausage rolls 208
Beef, lentil and mushroom pie 66
Lentil and quinoa dhal 30
Red lentil and veggie puree 15
Vegetable ratatouille lasagne 71
linseed 5
Breakfast muffins 153
Super-start toasted muesli 142, 144
see also LSA (linseed, sunflower, almonds)
Little quinoa bites 105
LSA (linseed, sunflower, almonds)
Peach and raspberry oats with chia and LSA 32
Smoothie bowl 149
lunchbox 143, 183, 184, 185, 189, 192
see also sandwiches

M
macadamia oil 4, 77, 144
Choc-hazelnut spread 179
mangoes
Kiwi-go yoghurt 12
seed 'teether' 16
Taste the tropics puree 16
maple syrup
Almond power balls 176

Choc popcorn balls 175
Maple pumpkin tempters 34
Super-start toasted muesli 142, 144
Tomato sauce (ketchup) 238
mash 10
Beef, veggie and quinoa mash 25
Salmon and veggie mash 20
mealtimes
babies 48
as a family 61, 164, 222–3
fussy behaviour 49, 164, 222
rules 81
schedule 164, 165, 204, 223
school-age children 49
weekends 222
meat 2, 111, 112, 192
meat-free meals 93
see also beef; ham; lamb; pork
Meatball, cheese and lettuce sandwich 193
meringues
Mini meringues 216, 217
Mexican seasoning mix 238
milk 3, 4
'Choose your own' smoothie 94
Hazelnut and oat baby bars 45, 142
Old-school strawberry milkshake 215
mindful eating 143, 172, 210, 216, 217, 222
Mini meatballs 44
Mini meringues 216, 217
Mini quiches 90
Mini sushi rolls 126
MSG (monosodium glutamate) 4
muesli
Breakfast muffins 153
Creamy chia bircher muesli 146
No-nut crunchy muesli bars 186
No-soak quinoa bircher 142, 146
Smoothie bowl 149
Super-start toasted muesli 142, 144
muffins
Breakfast muffins 153
Carrot and blueberry oatbran muffins 142, 190
Coconut muffins with a twist 178
Pasta muffins 232, 233
Seeded pesto muffins 168
mushrooms 23
Basic bolognese 237
Beef and lentil sausage rolls 208
Beef, lentil and mushroom pie 66
Beef burgers with hidden veggies 133
Chicken and hokkien noodle stir-fry 58
Chicken and mushroom bolognese 23
Crispy vegetable spring rolls 206
Kale and mushroom omelette 160
Sweet potato, mushroom and cheese pizza 75

N
new foods, trying 81
non-hungry eating 164, 165
No-nut crunchy muesli bars 186
noodles
Chicken and hokkien noodle stir-fry 58
Crispy vegetable spring rolls 206
No-soak quinoa bircher 142, 146
'nudies'
Spinach and ricotta nudies 136
nuts 3, 176
allergies 4, 168
Creamy chia bircher muesli 146
see also almonds; cashews; hazelnuts; peanuts
nut alternatives 3, 5, 36, 176
No-nut crunchy muesli bars 186
Seeded pesto muffins 168
nut butter 5, 176
nut cream 5
nut meal 5, 212

O
oats 5, 42, 100, 151, 188
Apple and pear crumble 77
Choc oat biscuits 213
Creamy banana and apple porridge 142, 150
Creamy chia bircher muesli 146
Hazelnut and oat baby bars 45, 142
Jam drop biscuits 212
Jolly good lunchbox biscuits 189
No-nut crunchy muesli bars 186
Peach and raspberry oats with chia and LSA 32
Super-start toasted muesli 142, 144
oils 3, 65
extra virgin olive oil 3, 4
macadamia oil 4, 77, 144, 179
Old-school strawberry milkshake 215
omega-3 fatty acids 20, 5, 53, 88, 102, 154
omelette
Kale and mushroom omelette 160
oral motor skills 8, 10, 117, 120, 121, 224
orange
Breakfast muffins 153
Tri-fruit icy pops 96
overeating 143, 164, 165, 204
overtiredness 164

P
parsley
Baked falafels 93
Lamb rack with parsley and pine nuts 224–5
Salmon and ricotta cakes 53
Turkey and cauliflower tots 124
parsnip
Carrot, parsnip and cashew puree 14
party food 1, 204, 216
see also 'sometimes foods'

pasta 2
Baby lasagne fingers 85
Cheesy veggie pasta with thyme 57
Chicken and mushroom bolognese 23
Chicken and pesto spaghetti 232–3
Lamb and risoni bake 62
Pasta muffins 232, 233
Pasta salad 198
Spinach and ricotta nudies 136
Tomato and basil pasta sauce 237
Vegetable ratatouille lasagne 71
pastries
Beef and lentil sausage rolls 208
Bolognese filo triangles 131
Mini quiches 90
see also pies
Peach and raspberry oats with chia and LSA 32
peanut allergy 4
peanut butter 5
Satay chicken skewers 129
pears 101
Apple and pear crumble 77
Hazelnut and oat baby bars 45, 142
Pumpkin, pear and spelt baby bars 108
Stewed rhubarb and pear puree 16, 142
Taste the tropics puree 16
Zucchini and pear banana bread 200
peas
Beef, veggie and quinoa mash 25
Broad bean and pea dip 110
Green veg and apple puree 12
Hazelnut and oat baby bars 45, 142
Lentil and quinoa dhal 30
Pea and ham couscous squares 109
Salmon and veggie mash 20
pesto
Basil pesto 232
Chicken and pesto spaghetti 232–3
Chicken, pesto and cucumber sandwich 193
Lamb and pesto sausages 134
nut-free 193
Prawn and pesto pizza 75
Seeded pesto muffins 168
Spinach, broccoli and cashew pesto 236
phytochemicals 1, 38, 89
pies and tarts 67
Beef, lentil and mushroom pie 66
Chicken, pumpkin and spinach bread pies 130
Ham, cheese and pineapple tartlets 205
pikelets
Raspberry pikelets 154
pineapple
Ham, cheese and pineapple tartlets 205
Sparkling fruit punch 216
Way-too-easy pizza scrolls 194

pizza
Pizza with three toppings 74
Prawn and pesto 75
Spinach, broccoli and cashew pesto 236
Spinach, ham and cheese 75
Sweet potato, mushroom and cheese pizza 75
Way-too-easy pizza scrolls 194
playing with food 34, 80, 121
polenta
Cheesy polenta chippies with roast beetroot dip 50
Crispy polenta pork fingers 87
popcorn
Choc popcorn balls 175
pork
Crispy polenta pork fingers 87
Pork puree 15
porridge
Creamy banana and apple porridge 142, 150
potatoes
Irresistible lamb puree 24
Salmon and leek potato croquettes 102
Prawn and pesto pizza 75
preservatives 4, 197
probiotics 12
pumpkin
Chicken and pesto spaghetti 232–3
Chicken and sweetcorn puree 11
Chicken, pumpkin and spinach bread pies 130
Lentil and quinoa dhal 30
Maple pumpkin tempters 34
Pumpkin, pear and spelt baby bars 108
Pumpkin, ricotta and spinach sandwich 193
Pumpkin-spiced quinoa balls 43
Pumpkin scones 171
Roast vegetable couscous salad 138
Roast pumpkin soup with avocado dippers 56
purees 1, 9, 10
Carrot, parsnip and cashew 14
Chicken and sweetcorn 11
Fish, cauliflower and leek 14
Green veg and apple 12
Irresistible lamb 24
Pork 15
Red lentil and veggie 15
Simple beef 11
Stewed rhubarb and pear 16, 142
Taste the tropics 16

Q
quinoa 5, 77, 100, 142, 212
Beef, veggie and quinoa mash 25
Crumbed fish bites 88
Lentil and quinoa dhal 30
Little quinoa bites 105
No-soak quinoa bircher 146
Pumpkin-spiced quinoa balls 43
Veggie, tomato and quinoa soup 68

R
Rainbow vegetable shreddies 88
raspberries
Peach and raspberry oats with chia and LSA 32
Raspberry pikelets 154
recipe symbols 5
Red lentil and veggie puree 15
reflux 100
rhubarb
Stewed rhubarb and pear puree 16, 142
rice 146
Baked tomato and tuna risotto 230
Beef and bean rice 26
brown 5, 26, 100
Mini sushi rolls 126
Sticky honey chicken with rice and bok choy 72
Yakitori salmon skewers 122
ricotta
Creamy chicken and cauliflower crepes 84
Pumpkin, ricotta and spinach sandwich 193
Roast vegetable couscous salad 138
Salmon and ricotta cakes 53
Salmon and veggie mash 20
Spinach and ricotta nudies 136
Vegetable ratatouille lasagne 71
Veggie and ricotta fritters 106, 142
risotto
Baked tomato and tuna risotto 230
Roast beetroot dip 50
Roast pumpkin soup with avocado dippers 56
Roast vegetable couscous salad 138
rusks
Homemade teething rusks 101, 117

S
salads
Carrot, apple and fennel coleslaw 87, 241
Pasta salad 198
Roast vegetable couscous salad 138
salmon
Salmon and leek potato croquettes 102
Salmon and ricotta cakes 53
Salmon and veggie mash 20
Yakitori salmon skewers 122
salsa
Avocado salsa 142, 157
Cucumber salsa 61
sandwiches, lunchbox 185, 192
Chicken, pesto and cucumber 193
Meatball, cheese and lettuce 193
Pumpkin, ricotta and spinach 193
Spinach, broccoli and cashew pesto 236
Tuna, avocado, mayo and carrot 193
Satay chicken skewers 129
sauces
Asian 58, 72
Basic bolognese 237
Chicken and mushroom bolognese 23
Dipping 206
Hidden veggie 66, 236
salt content 72, 129
thickening 5
Tomato and basil pasta 237
Tomato sauce (ketchup) 238
Yoghurt dipping sauce 93
sausages
Chicken and chive sausages 54
Lamb and pesto sausages 134
Savoury scones 171
Savoury veggie slice 167
Scones three ways 171
seafood allergy 4
seeds 3, 5
Cheesy seed biscuits 201
Creamy chia bircher muesli 146
Seeded pesto muffins 168
see also sesame seeds
selective eating 34, 100–101, 165, 223
self-feeding 8, 100, 120
sesame allergy 4
sesame oil 5
sesame seeds
Sesame-crumbed chicken fingers 112
Super-start toasted muesli 142, 144
shellfish allergy 4
Simple beef puree 11
Simple custard 241
sippy cup 81
skewers
Satay chicken skewers 129
Yakitori salmon skewers 122
skim milk 3
Smoothie bowl 149
smoothies 94, 142, 149
snack foods 143
dairy 100, 164, 165
portion size 164
recipes 108, 167–201
supermarket 108
soft drinks 81
solid foods, starting 8–10, 100, 121
'sometimes foods' 172, 203, 204
Beef and lentil sausage rolls 208
Choc oat biscuits 213
Crispy vegetable spring rolls 206
fussy eaters 207, 208
Ham, cheese and pineapple tartlets 205
Jam drop biscuits 212
Old-school strawberry milkshake 215

Sparkling fruit punch 216
Vanilla birthday cake 218, 219
soup 5
Roast pumpkin soup with avocado dippers 56
Veggie, tomato and quinoa soup 68
soy sauce 129, 206
soybean allergy 4
Sparkling fruit punch 216
spices 26, 30, 57, 121, 223
spinach
Bolognese filo triangles 131
Chicken, pumpkin and spinach bread pies 130
Eat-your-greens frittata 38
Pumpkin, ricotta and spinach sandwich 193
Roast vegetable couscous salad 138
Smoothie bowl 149
Spinach, broccoli and cashew pesto 236
Spinach, ham and cheese pizza 75
Spinach and ricotta nudies 136
Vegetable ratatouille lasagne 71
spitting out food 80
spoon refusal 8–9, 100, 120
spring rolls
Crispy vegetable spring rolls 206
sterilising jars 179
Stewed rhubarb and pear puree 16, 142
Sticky honey chicken with rice and bok choy 72
stock
Chicken stock 240
Vegetable stock 240
stool-softeners 16, 101
strawberries
Banana and strawberry ice cream 180
Old-school strawberry milkshake 215
Sparkling fruit punch 216
sunflower seeds 5, 144
No-nut crunchy muesli bars 186
Super-start toasted muesli 142, 144
sushi
Mini sushi rolls 126
Sweet lamb couscous 29
sweet potato
Beef, veggie and quinoa mash 25
Eat-your-greens frittata 38
Hidden veggie sauce 66, 236
Mini meatballs 44
Rainbow vegetable shreddies 88
Red lentil and veggie puree 15
Salmon and veggie mash 20
Sweet lamb couscous 29
Sweet potato fries 65
Sweet potato, mushroom and cheese pizza 75
Sweet potato and tuna cakes 40
Tempura fish and sweet potato fries 65
Winner winner chicken dinner 19
sweeteners, artificial 3

T
tahini
Cauliflower hummus 170
Yoghurt dipping sauce 93
tartrazine 4
tarts *see* pies and tarts
Taste the tropics puree 16
tasting plate 101, 120–1, 121, 125, 142, 152, 223
Teeny teddies 172
teeth 3, 81, 165, 186
Homemade teething rusks 101, 117
teething 101
Tempura fish and sweet potato fries 65
texture of food 11, 12, 24, 29
thickeners 5
throwing food 80
toast
Avocado dippers 56
Banana cinnamon toast fingers 34
tomatoes
Avocado salsa 142, 157
Baked tomato and tuna risotto 230
Basic bolognese 237
Beef and bean rice 26
Cheesy baked beans on toast 142, 159
Cheesy veggie pasta with thyme 57
Chicken and mushroom bolognese 23
Chicken curry 226–7
Cucumber salsa 61
Guacamole 239
Hidden veggie sauce 66, 236
Lamb and risoni bake 62
peeling 237
Roast vegetable couscous salad 138
Tomato and basil pasta sauce 237
Vegetable ratatouille lasagne 71
Veggie, tomato and quinoa soup 68
Way-too-easy pizza scrolls 194
Tomato sauce (ketchup) 238
tongue-thrust reflex 8
Tortillas 239
Chicken burritos with cucumber salsa 61
Tri-fruit icy pops 96
tuna
Baked tomato and tuna risotto 230
Sweet potato and tuna cakes 40
Tuna, avocado, mayo and carrot sandwich 193
Turkey and cauliflower tots 124

V
Vanilla birthday cake 218, 219
vegetables 100, 184
Beef burgers with hidden veggies 133
Cheesy veggie pasta with thyme 57
Crispy vegetable spring rolls 206
green vegetable smoothies 149
Hidden veggie sauce 66, 236
introducing 1, 106
Rainbow vegetable shreddies 88
Red lentil and veggie puree 15
Roast vegetable couscous salad 138
Savoury veggie slice 167
Vegetable ratatouille lasagne 71
Vegetable stock 240
Veggie and ricotta fritters 106, 142
Veggie, tomato and quinoa soup 68
see also green, leafy vegetables; mash; specific vegetables
vegetarian 2
Spinach and ricotta nudies 136
vitamins 2, 5, 100, 124, 142, 154, 155, 188

W
watermelon
Tri-fruit icy pops 96
Way-too-easy pizza scrolls 194
wheat allergy 4, 5
whole grains 100–101, 150, 223
bread 2, 142, 192
Winner winner chicken dinner 19

Y
Yakitori salmon skewers 122
yoghurt
'Choose your own' smoothie 94
Creamy chia bircher muesli 146
Cucumber salsa 61
Kiwi-go yoghurt 12, 142
No-soak quinoa bircher 142, 146
Way-too-easy pizza scrolls 194
Yoghurt dipping sauce 93

Z
zinc 2, 29, 100
zucchini
Beef and lentil sausage rolls 208
Beef burgers with hidden veggies 133
Beef, veggie and quinoa mash 25
Cheesy veggie pasta with thyme 57
Chicken and zucchini nuggets 82
Corn fritters with avocado salsa 142, 157
Crispy vegetable spring rolls 206
Green veg and apple puree 12
Hidden veggie sauce 66, 236
Mini quiches 90
Rainbow vegetable shreddies 88
Savoury scones 171
Savoury veggie slice 167
Vegetable ratatouille lasagne 71
Veggie and ricotta fritters 106, 142
Zucchini and pear banana bread 200

VIKING

UK | USA | Canada | Ireland | Australia
India | New Zealand | South Africa | China

Penguin Books is part of the Penguin Random House group of companies whose addresses can be found at global.penguinrandomhouse.com.

First published by Penguin Random House Australia Pty Ltd, 2016

Text copyright © Allie Gaunt and Jessica Beaton 2016
Photographs copyright © Sarah Buckle 2016

The moral right of the author has been asserted.

All rights reserved. Without limiting the rights under copyright reserved above, no part of this publication may be reproduced, stored in or introduced into a retrieval system, or transmitted, in any form or by any means (electronic, mechanical, photocopying, recording or otherwise), without the prior written permission of both the copyright owner and the above publisher of this book.

Cover and text design by Hannah Schubert © Penguin Random House Australia Pty Ltd
Illustrations by Alissa Dinallo © Penguin Random House Australia Pty Ltd
Styling by Cass Stokes
Typeset in Minion by Post Pre-press Group, Brisbane, Queensland
Colour separation by Splitting Image Colour Studio, Clayton, Victoria
Printed and bound in China by RR Donnelley Asia Printing Solutions Ltd

National Library of Australia Cataloguing-in-Publication entry

Gaunt, Allie, author.
One handed cooks: raising a healthy, happy eater – from baby to school age / Allie Gaunt, Jessica Beaton and Sarah Buckle.
ISBN: 9780670079018 (paperback)
Notes: Includes index.
Subjects: Children--Nutrition.
Cooking.
Other Creators/Contributors: Beaton, Jessica, author.
Buckle, Sarah, author, photographer.

641.5622

penguin.com.au

Many thanks to:
Mud Australia for generously loaning colourful props.
Exquira for the Stokke Tripp Trapp highchair, which proved to be invaluable for photography.

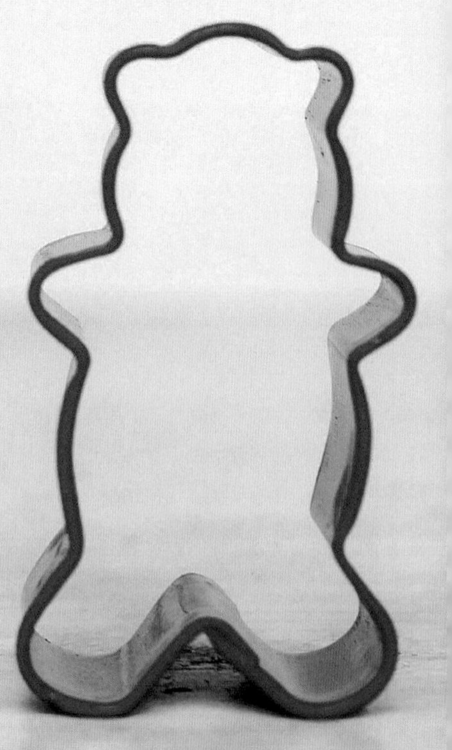